Egon Schiele

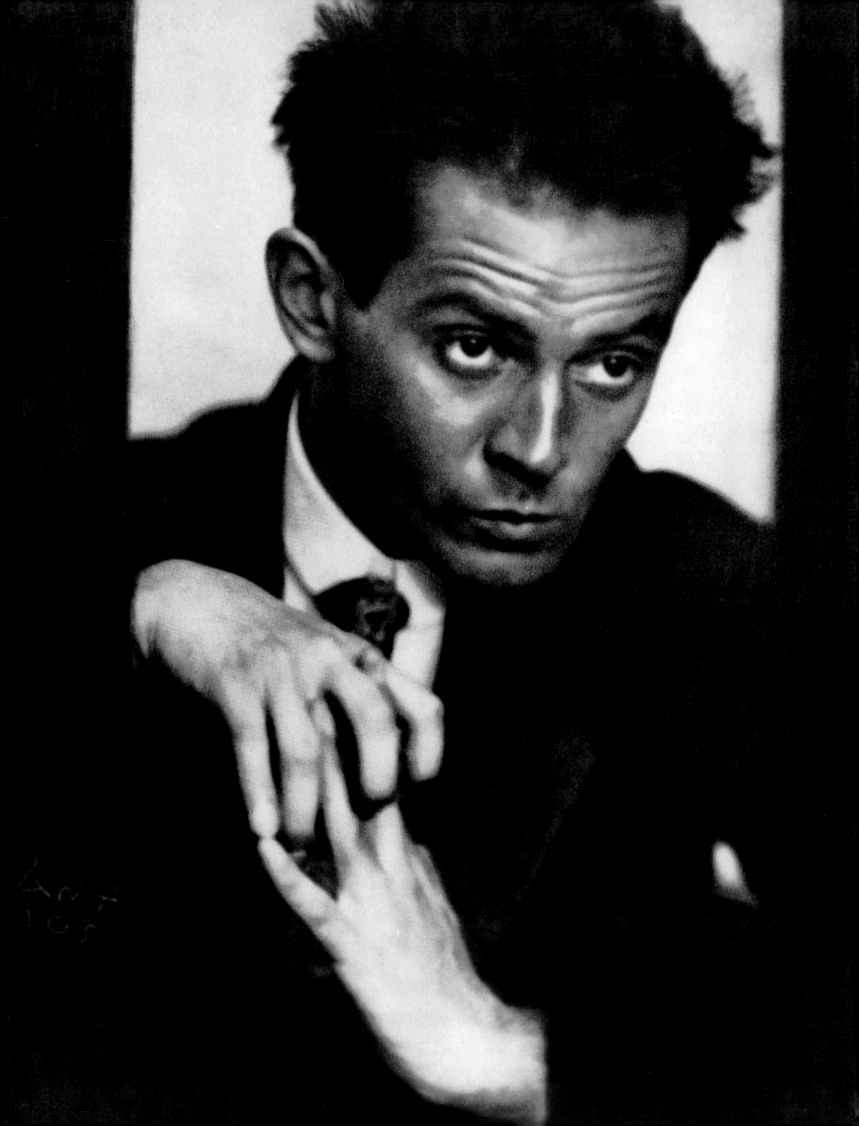

Wolfgang Georg Fischer

EGON SCHIELE
1890–1918

Desire and Decay

TASCHEN

HONG KONG KÖLN LONDON LOS ANGELES MADRID PARIS TOKYO

To stay informed about upcoming TASCHEN titles, please request our magazine at www.taschen.com/magazine or write to TASCHEN America, 6671 Sunset Boulevard, Suite 1508, USA–Los Angeles, CA 90028, contact-us@taschen.com, Fax: +1-323-463.4442. We will be happy to send you a free copy of our magazine which is filled with information about all of our books.

Contents

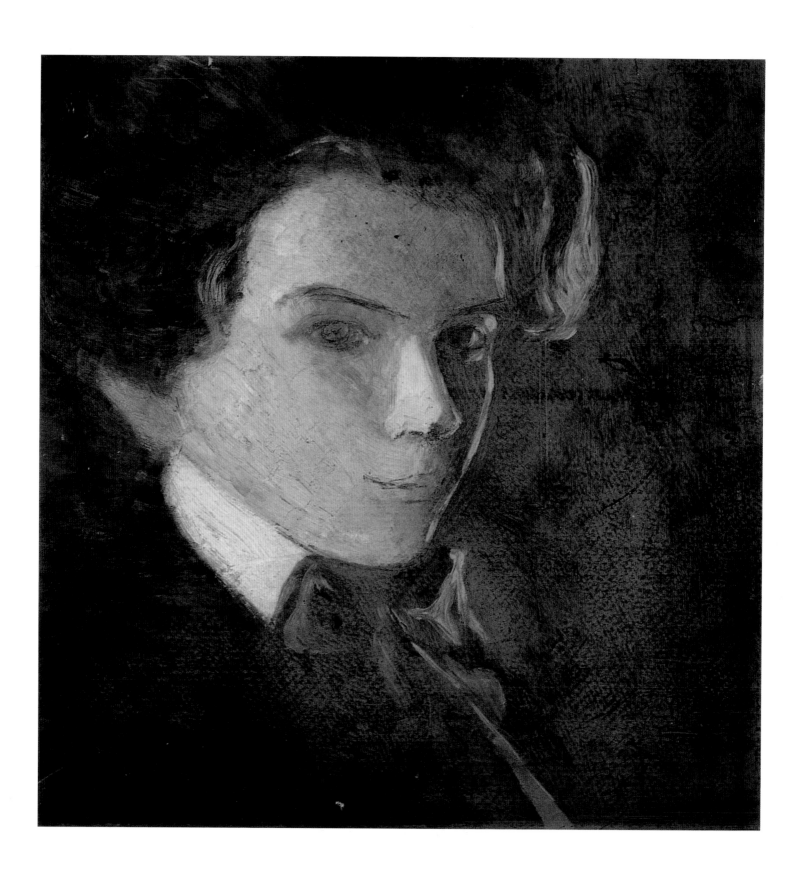

Fighting Teachers and Society: A Brief Life

"I love antitheses", wrote Egon Schiele on 24 April 1912, on one of the drawings he had done in his prison cell. On another, on 23 April, he noted emphatically: "Hindering the artist is a crime, it is murdering life in the bud!" Deeply hurt and humiliated by the charges brought against him, the artist was sounding the note that we hear throughout his early work, a note of defiance, rebellion and provocation. Much of this stance can be understood if we consider the experience that life had by then brought Schiele – at the age of twenty-two.

Time and time again in his letters, Schiele bemoaned the incomprehension of the world about him. "My uncultivated teachers were always my worst enemies"[1], he once wrote. Yet it would be mistaken to see Schiele – as has often been the case – as a misunderstood and embittered artist. He was in fact of a passionate nature, and no defeatist.

Moreover, from the outset he had both friends and patrons who, each in his own way, took his part. Schiele's greatest distress was caused by the rejection of those who were closest to him – his mother, with her eternal reproaches; his uncle and guardian, irreconcilably disposed; and the teachers who spurned his work. Against all of them, however, Schiele stood his ground.

Schiele, born on 12 June 1890, was of a middle-class background. He was the third child of Adolf Eugen Schiele and his wife Marie (née Soukoup). Adolf Schiele was then stationmaster at Tulln, a small town on the Danube some 30 kilometres upriver from Vienna, in a fertile if scenically unprepossessing part of the country. More interesting, however, were the neighbouring towns with Gothic churches and fortifications, set amidst vineyards sloping down to the Danube, which provided the backdrop to Schiele's youth: Krems, where he went to first year of grammar school; Klosterneuburg, where he continued his schooling; and Stein, renderings of which appear in his later work.

The Schiele family, which had produced generations of ministers, civil servants, officers and doctors, originally came from northern Germany. On the maternal side, the Soukoups came from Krumau in southern Bohemia, where they moved in agricultural and provincial circles. The Schieles had made their move south when Egon's grandfather, Ludwig Schiele (1817–1862), an architect and railway engineer, builder and first inspector general of the Austrian Imperial Privileged Bohemian Western Railway, settled in Prague. It was probably from this grandfather that the artist inherited his gift for drawing. With a railway father and grandfather,

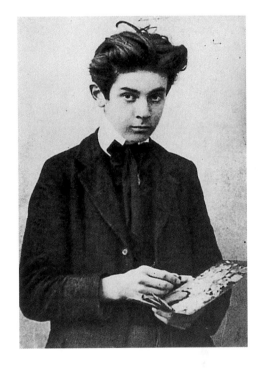

Egon Schiele with palette, 1906
Photograph
Vienna, Graphische Sammlung Albertina

Photographer Adolf Bernhard took this portrait shot of the Klosterneuburg schoolboy with the tools of his hoped-for trade. The young Schiele's teachers had been quick to recognise his gifts and had advised him to study art.

PAGE 6:
Self-Portrait, Facing Right, 1907
Selbstbildnis nach rechts
Oil on card, 32.4 x 31.2cm
Kallir P 26; private collection, courtesy Galerie St. Etienne, New York

Egon Schiele began his visual soliloquy of self-portraiture early in life. This self-assured picture shows him at seventeen, dressed for the role of the artist, a year after passing the Vienna Academy entrance exam.

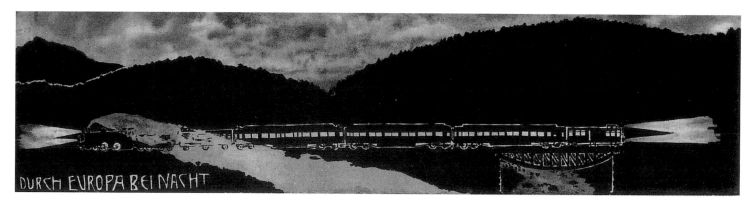

Through Europe by Night, 1906
Durch Europa bei Nacht
Watercolour and Indian ink, 9.4 x 39.2cm
Kallir D 76; Vienna, Niederösterreichisches
Landesmuseum

The world of railways was in Schiele's blood, so
to speak, and he never lost his enthusiasm for
trains. He did this almost Expressionist drawing
of a brightly-lit train speeding through the night
when he was sixteen.

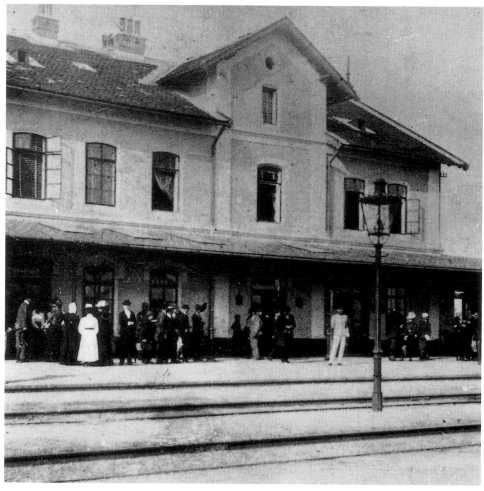

The station at Tulln, Schiele's birthplace,
about 1900
Photograph
Vienna, Graphische Sammlung Albertina

Egon's father, Adolf Eugen Schiele, was the stationmaster in Tulln, and the boy grew up with
trains on his doorstep. His grandfather Ludwig
Schiele had been a railway engineer and an inspector on the Bohemian railways.

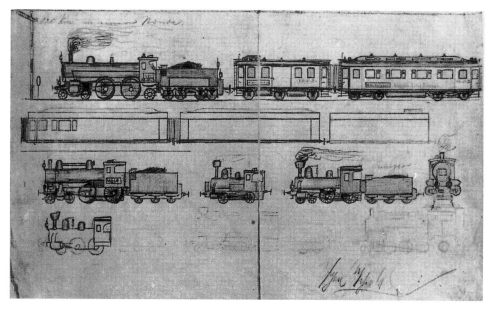

Trains, c. 1900
Züge
Pencil on paper
Kallir D 73; private collection, courtesy
Galerie St. Etienne, New York

Inspired by his father's example, Schiele became
amazingly skilful at drawing locomotives and
rolling stock in his boyhood. His father wanted
him to become an engineer and to work on the
railways too. At the turn of the century, the railways were at their peak, and stood for the allure
of faraway places.

Harbour of Trieste, 1907
Hafen von Triest
Oil and pencil on card, 25 x 18 cm
Kallir P 84; Graz, Neue Galerie am Landesmuseum Joanneum

Egon Schiele was not slow to take advantage of the free rail travel he enjoyed as a railwayman's son. When he was seventeen, he and his sister Gerti, four years his junior, went to Trieste, then part of the Austro-Hungarian Empire. His oil sketch of the harbour features the arabesque decorativeness characteristic of Art Nouveau.

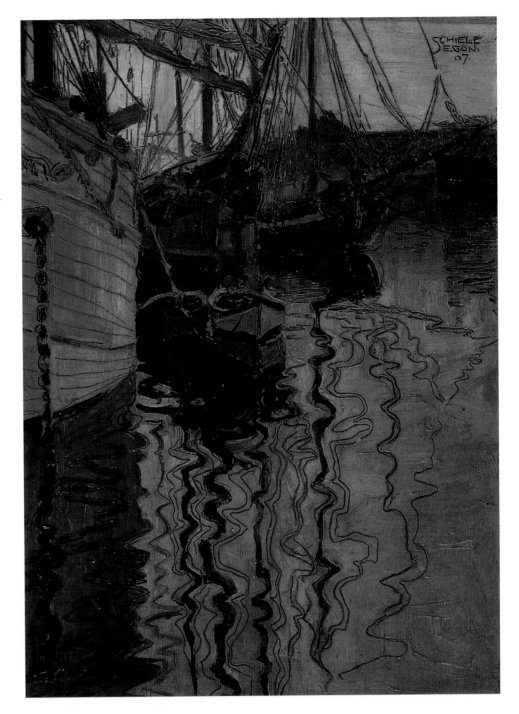

and free rail tickets as a child, Schiele developed a taste for travel. Growing up in rooms provided by the company in the station building at Tulln, with good views of the trains that came and departed, he had railways in his blood, as it were; and at sixteen he was already drawing trains in a manner that married technical precision and a visionary longing for far-away places. In the drawing *Through Europe by Night* (1906, p. 8) a train is roaring across a bridge at night, the very image of steam and speed and light against a landscape backdrop of darkly silhouetted hills. The fascination with foreign parts took Schiele on many a rail journey: at seventeen he was already travelling to Trieste with his sister Gerti (Gertrude), four years his junior. In 1913 he made a number of trips, to the Wachau region near Krems, to Krumau and Munich, to Villach, Tarvis and Altmünster; all of these were recorded in his work. In this travel fever there was of course an element of escape from the parental home. Adolf Eugen

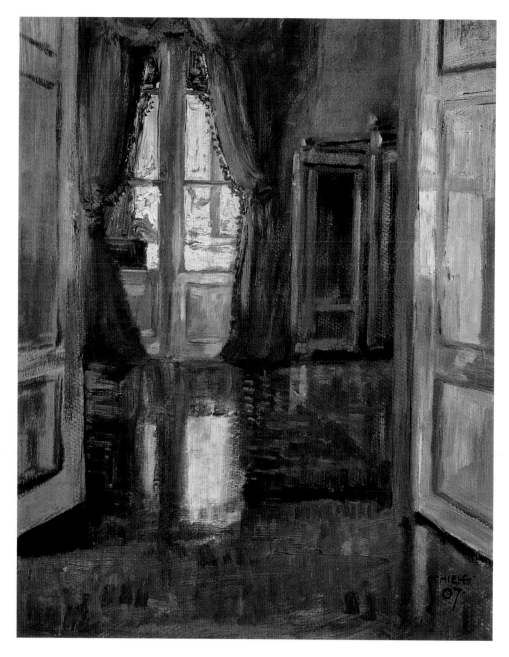

View into the Apartment of Leopold and Marie Czihaczek, 1907
Blick in die Wohnung von Leopold und Marie Czihaczek
Oil on card, 39.1 x 31.2 cm
Kallir P 35; Vienna, Österreichische Galerie.
Belvedere

The middle-class interior of the Czihaczek home, elegant and airy, its parquet floor shining. Egon Schiele lived there with his guardian and aunt when he first arrived in Vienna.

The salon of Leopold (at the piano) und Marie Czihaczek, née Schiele
Photograph
Vienna, Graphische Sammlung Albertina

Leopold Czihaczek, seen here in his salon with his wife Marie, a sister of Egon Schiele's father, was a chief inspector on the Emperor Ferdinand Northern Railways. Himself a music lover, he was nonetheless baffled by the rebellious temperament of his artistic nephew.

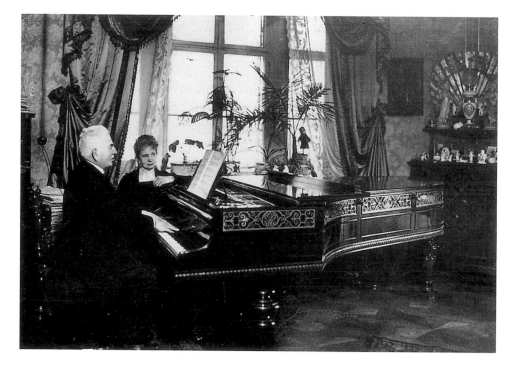

Schiele (1850–1905) did not have a happy life; the inspector general's son failed to rise higher than stationmaster at Tulln, and at fifty-two, seriously ill (possibly the result of syphilis), took early retirement, only to become the evil spirit of the family in the last three years of his life. His mind became unsettled; he burnt the family's stocks and bonds in a fit of insanity; he had visions of invisible visitors for whom a place must be laid at the table. When he died, Egon was fifteen.

Schiele's uncle Leopold Czihaczek (1842–1929; cf. p. 11), chief inspector of the Emperor Ferdinand Northern Railways and married to Adolf Eugen's sister, became the youngster's guardian. Solemn in appearance and demeanour, Leopold was the prosperous middle class personified: an affluent property owner, a man both pedantic and musical, with a season ticket for the undisputed capital of Viennese theatre, the Burgtheater. A photograph (p. 10) shows him white-haired and with a neatly trimmed goatee beard, seated at the grand piano, with his admiring wife at his side. Their salon is furnished with all the typical turn-of-the-century props: potted palms, white figurines, a decorative lidded vase positioned in front of an enormous fan, and heavy curtains gathered up. The irruption of Leopold's unshaven nephew into this stately realm, in his artist's cravat, poverty-stricken yet laying claims to genius, must have been deeply unsettling. Yet Schiele's much-maligned uncle must surely have had his good sides. When the lad had passed his Academy entrance exam, Leopold sent a telegram to Schiele's mother: "Egon passed with flying colours."

This was in 1906. Egon had had the recommendation of three Klosterneuburg supporters who were convinced that he had the talent needed for the Vienna Academy: Dr. Wolfgang Pauker (p. 18), art historian, choirmaster with the Augustinians; Karl Strauch, art teacher at the grammar school; and the painter Max Kahrer. In 1911, however, Leopold Czihaczek relinquished his guardianship, and from that time on remained obdurately deaf to the attempts of well-meaning outsiders (such as Heinrich Benesch, an early collector of Schiele) to pour oil on the troubled waters.

Acceptance into the Vienna Academy marked the end of Schiele's life in a small country town. The change to city life cannot have been easy for him, not least since his means were distinctly modest. In 1910, feeling he had to get out of the city, he wrote to fellow artist Anton Peschka, later his brother-in-law: "Vienna is a city of shadows. It is black..."[2]

When Schiele arrived in its great metropolis, the Austro-Hungarian Empire was in a state of transition. In the latter half of the 19th century, the emergent middle class had taken its place alongside the aristocracy and church as a force in imperial society. Vienna's Ringstrasse, with its neo-Gothic town hall, its neo-Renaissance opera house and Burgtheater, and its Moorish-inspired stock exchange, was a majestic statement of 19th-century confidence; and yet, even so, the first cracks were fissuring the Habsburg world. Rapid industrialization was attracting immigrants, workers who lived in pitiful conditions in outlying suburban districts that subsequently became part of the city. The population of the capital rose from 801,176 in 1890 to over 1,300,000 at the turn of the century. The days of Hans Makart (1848–1884), that prince among artists who had given the affluent middle classes the bombastic art they wanted, were over.

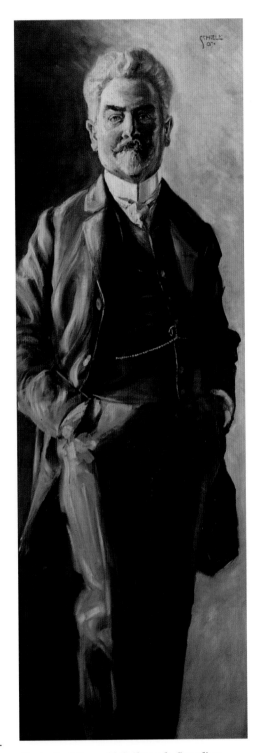

Portrait of Leopold Czihaczek, Standing, 1907
Bildnis Leopold Czihaczek, stehend
Oil on canvas, 149.8 x 49.7 cm
Kallir P 20; private collection

11

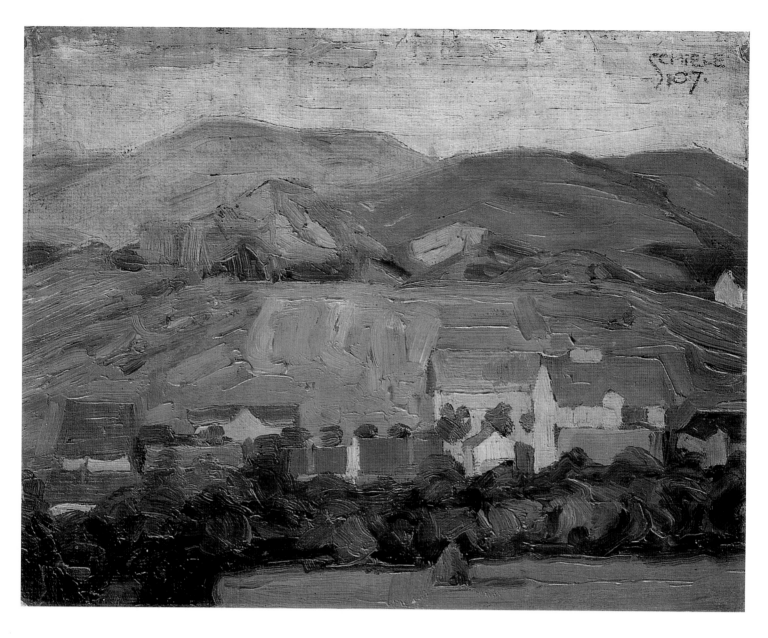

Village with Mountains, 1907
Dorf mit Bergen
Oil on paper, 21.7 x 28 cm
Kallir P 64; private collection

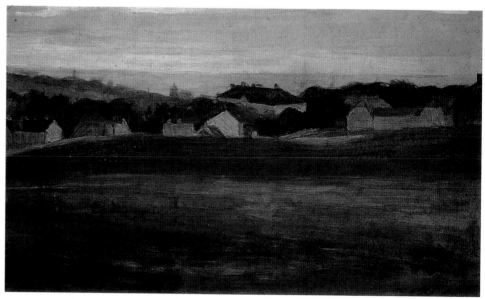

Meadow with Village in Background II, 1907
Wiese mit Dorf im Hintergrund II
Oil on card, 19.8 x 34.4 cm
Kallir P 66; Vienna, Österreichische Galerie.
Belvedere

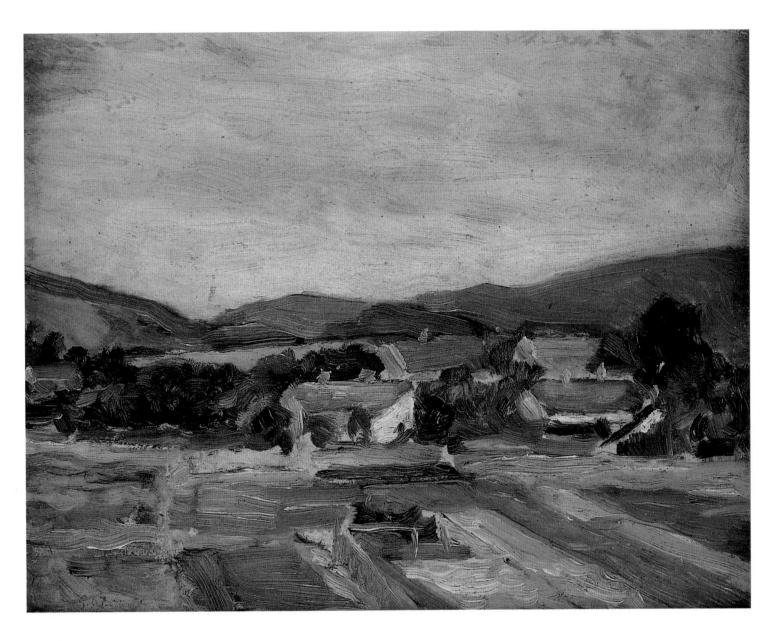

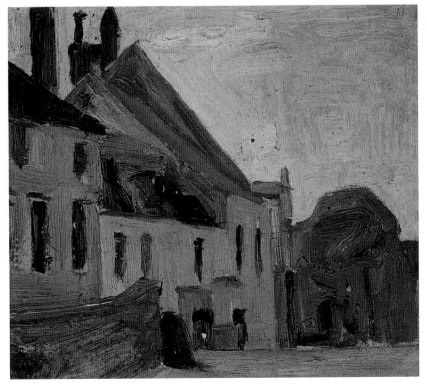

Landscape in Lower Austria, 1907
Landschaft in Niederösterreich
Oil on card, 17.5 x 22.5 cm
Kallir P 67; private collection

The young Schiele's first landscapes were in an academic post-Romantic vein. Clearly the work of a gifted youngster with a grasp of his craft, they nonetheless give no indication of the expressive power he was later to develop.

Houses on the Town Square in Klosterneuburg, 1908
Häuser am Rathaus in Klosterneuburg
Oil on card, 19.4 x 21.9 cm
Kallir P 127; private collection

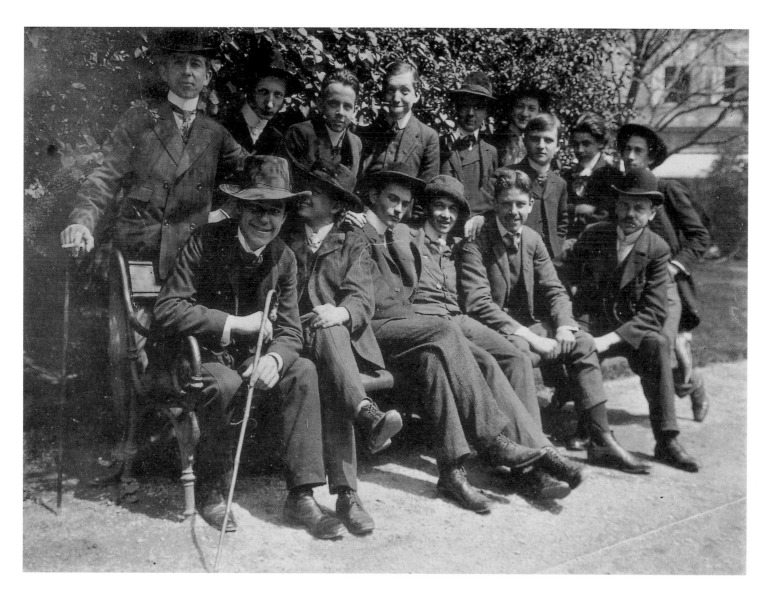

In this photograph of Academy students in June 1907, Egon Schiele is second from right in the back row. Nothing in the picture betrays the anxiety of his Academy years, caused by his conflict with his teacher, Professor Christian Griepenkerl.
Photograph: W.G. Fischer

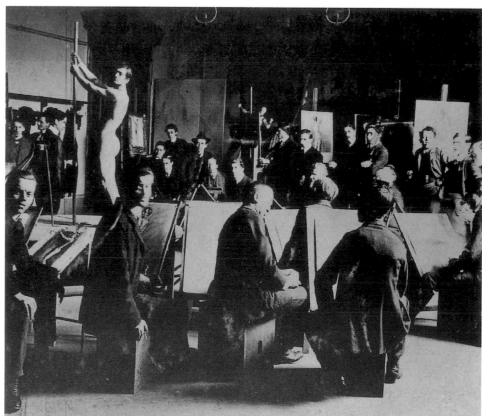

Life drawing was a key component of the curriculum at the Vienna Academy. Schiele, in high white collars, can be seen standing at the back somewhat left of centre.

14

Artists were especially sensitive to the immense societal upheavals. Gustav Klimt (1862–1918; p.18), who may seem on cursory inspection so utterly the decadent in his art, was in fact also one of the first rebels against the Makart era; decried and derided at first, he earned recognition in due course. In 1897, in protest against the Establishment's notions of art, a number of Viennese artists founded the Secession – an association that Klimt and those close to him left in 1905, however. The architects and designers of Vienna – especially Otto Wagner (1841–1918; p.18), his pupil Josef Hoffmann (1870–1956) and the radical Adolf Loos (1870–1933; p.18) – created a new style, decorative yet simple, that contrasted with the pomp of Habsburg triumphalism. They also supported and promoted new departures in art. Joseph Maria Olbrich's Secession building (p.19), built in 1898, proved an extremely busy exhibition venue, and new art from France and Germany was fast to reach Vienna. In 1903, with financial support from industrialists, a number of artists and architects established the Wiener Werkstätte (Vienna Workshops), where artists and craftsmen devoted their skills to collaboration on Viennese Art Nouveau artefacts. One of the Wiener Werkstätte's publications, *The Dreaming Youths* (Die träumenden Knaben; 1908), a highly successful tale by Oskar Kokoschka (1886–1980; p.18), deserves particular mention.

If turn-of-the-century Vienna continued to wear the aesthetic façade of the prosperous middle classes, it also crackled with nervous energies and tensions and doubts, with the hopes that attach to the radically new, and perhaps also with premonitions of imminent disaster. Vienna at that time had its doomfulness, but it also possessed the confidence of new beginnings. Sigmund Freud (1856–1939; p.18) was making his breakthroughs in psychoanalytic theory, while Ludwig Wittgenstein (1889–1951; p.18) was engaged on the logical and philosophical inquiries that were to begin a new chapter in the history of western thought.

The doors of the affluent middle-class world were not quick to open to the young Schiele, though. Klimt and Kokoschka were more fortunate: as early as the 1870s, Klimt had painted large-scale frescoes for the Burgtheater, and at the turn of the century was increasingly in demand as a portrait painter of society ladies, while Kokoschka – through his liaison with Alma Mahler, the young widow of Gustav Mahler, who had been artistic director of the court opera house – was at least able to steal a brief glimpse through the keyhole. Schiele lacked this access; nor was he one of the admiring listeners at the famed coffee-house gatherings of the Viennese writers and intellectuals Hermann Bahr (1863–1934), Egon Friedell (1878–1938) and Peter Altenberg (1859–1919; p.18). Literary circles that met in cafés such as the Central or the Museum would hardly have insisted on grooming and deportment as impeccable as those of an Austro-Hungarian army officer; yet, even so, professional revolutionaries such as Lenin and Trotsky maintained a certain standard of dress when frequenting such "hotbeds" of intellectual megalomania – a standard that the lean sixteen-year-old Schiele, wearing the cast-off clothes of his guardian, could scarcely be said to meet.

Schiele described himself at this time to his friend and supporter Arthur Roessler: "When I made my own independent way, against the wish of my mother and my guardian, in order to be a freelance artist, I was in a

Letter from Egon Schiele to the Munich artist and Academy professor Franz von Stuck, 1908 Estate of Franz von Stuck

"Vienna, 15. II. 1908
Dear Herr Stuck!
On the occasion of the Secession spring exhibition I am bound and tormented by the sweet hope of seeing my three works approved by the assessment panel. Here I stand, alone, as it were, with the grey day behind me, a yawning abyss before me, and happiness beyond, with dazzling lights around it. Here I stand, without a penny, at dizzy heights and with no firm ground beneath my feet. Reach out your hand to me, Herr Stuck. You will know how it feels to want to exhibit for the first time. One word from your divine self would be enough and my first works would be accepted. You could make me happy, could give me the courage afresh to create new work. It is beyond words! How wonderful it would be. I beseech you to say the word, say yes, and heaven will be open to me.
In youthful gratitude, in advance, and without the pleasure of being known to you, I remain, Schiele Egon.
A reply from your esteemed hand would be a sacred relic."

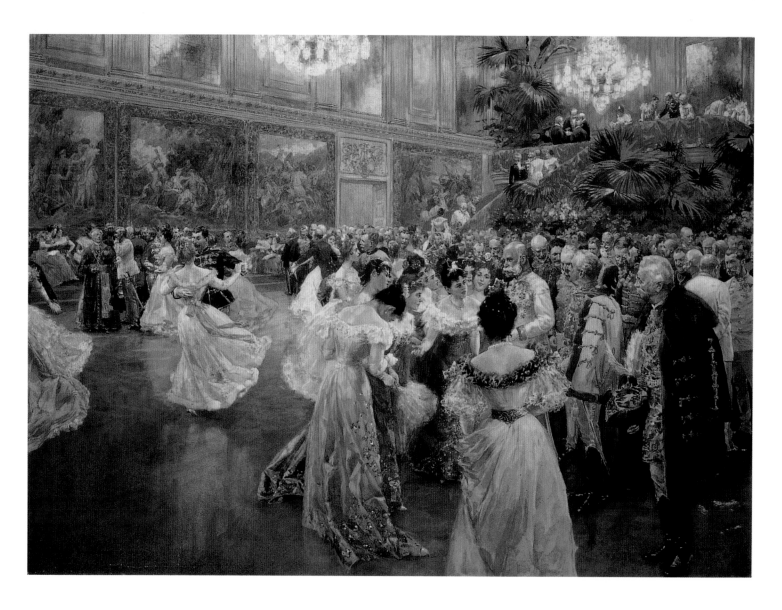

Wilhelm Gause
Court Ball in Vienna, 1900
Hofball in Wien
Watercolour, 49.8 x 69.3 cm
Vienna, Historisches Museum der Stadt Wien

Vienna at the turn of the century loved to waltz:
from stylish court balls to middle-class dances,
everyone loved the triple-time-rhythm of Johann
Strauss.

Josef Engelhart
At the Sophiensaal in Vienna, 1903
Gesellschaft im Sophiensaal Wien
Oil on canvas, 100.5 x 65.5 cm
Vienna, Historisches Museum der Stadt Wien

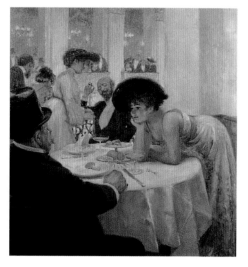

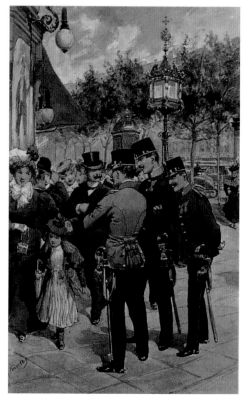

Karl Feiertag
On the Ringstrasse in Vienna, c. 1900
Auf der Ringstraße in Wien
Watercolour, 29.1 x 18.3 cm
Vienna, Historisches Museum der Stadt Wien

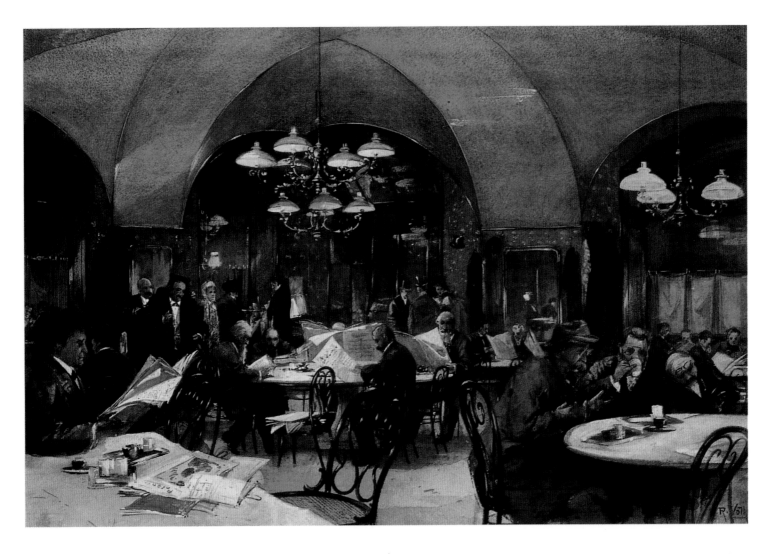

wretched state. I wore clothes, shoes and hats cast off by my guardian, all
too big for me. The coat lining was torn, the material worn, and it was
baggy and loose on my thin frame. The shoes were worn out, with cracks
in the uppers and big holes in the soles, and I had to drag my feet in the
tattered old boats. The felt hat was faded, fingered, and greasy in places,
and I had to stuff whole folded newspapers into it to prevent it from falling over my eyes. Undergarments were a particularly delicate item in my
wardrobe in those days. I do not know whether the fantastic rags I had –
they were like tattered remnants of linen – could really be described as
underwear at all. My shirt collars were inherited from my father, and far
too big for my thin neck, and too high into the bargain. So on Sundays
and other special occasions I wore unusual paper collars that I had cut
out myself; they were very presentable and at least they were clean,
though unfortunately not durable. To crown it all, my hair was long and I
was usually unshaven. In all, I did not remotely strike people as the 'nice
young man from a decent civil servant family' that I in fact essentially
was. My accommodation matched my 'grooming'. It consisted of one
meagre room, where the light that entered by the dirty window was dim
[Schiele's first studio at number 6, Kurzbauergasse]. From the walls,
which sloped in part, the faded wallpaper hung off in tatters. Little by
little I tore off these scraps of wallpaper, which was of a revolting pat-

Reinhold Völkel
In Café Griensteidl in Vienna, 1896
Im Café Griensteidl in Wien
Watercolour, 23 x 34.3 cm
Vienna, Historisches Museum der Stadt Wien

Vienna's famous coffee houses were the seed-
bed of the doom-laden atmosphere of *fin de
siècle* Vienna. Writers and critics, artists and revolutionaries would meet there to talk, work or
read the papers. At the very next table might be
an unknown who would later change the world:
Adolf Hitler, Joseph Stalin or Leon Trotsky.

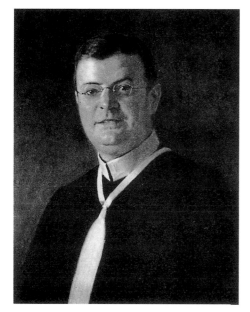

Wolfgang Pauker

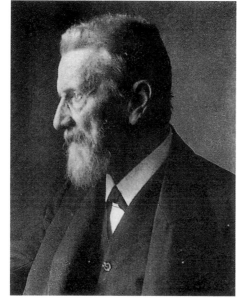

Christian Griepenkerl

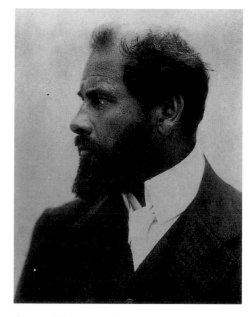

Gustav Klimt

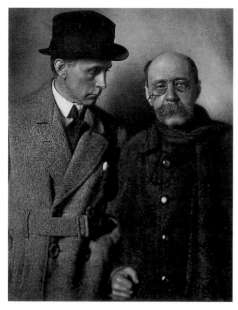

Adolf Loos and Peter Altenberg

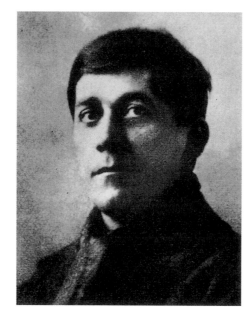

Oskar Kokoschka

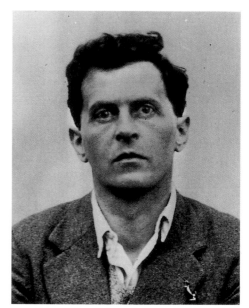

Ludwig Wittgenstein

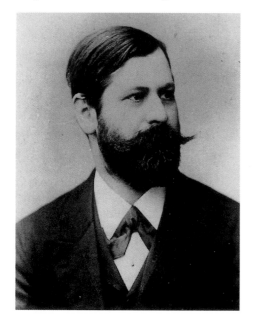

Sigmund Freud

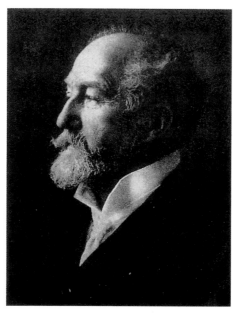

Otto Wagner

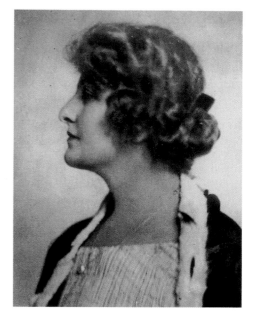

Alma Mahler

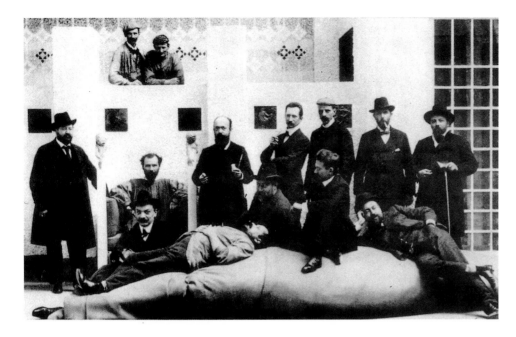

The members of the Vienna Secession at the 14th exhibition in April 1902: (from the left) Anton Staub, Gustav Klimt, Koloman Moser (in front of Klimt, in the hat), Adolf Böhm, Maximilian Lenz (lying on his back), Ernst Stöhr, Wilhelm List, Ernst Orlik (sitting), Maximilian Kurzweil (in the cap), Leopold Stolba, Carl Moll (reclining), Rudolf Bacher

tern, entirely, and every week I would paint one more patch of wall plain white. Whenever I saw my mother I would get reproaches, and that was all; from my guardian I received five crowns every Monday. The money would mainly go on twenty cigarettes, which understandably did not last me seven days, so that, come the weekend, I was obliged to fish the butts out of the rubbish and improvise a new cigarette that way."[3]

The Academy of Fine Arts on the Schillerplatz was not the place where Schiele might sniff the bracing air of a new century or find support for experiments. The classes taught by the extremely conservative Professor Christian Griepenkerl (1839–1916; p. 18) – whose name is remembered now only because he taught Schiele – were academic in the pejorative sense of the word. The curriculum, set down in Schiele's Academy pass, had been unchanged for two hundred years:

"The subjects of tuition in the general painting class are:
1. Drawing and painting from the art of classical antiquity;
2. Figure drawing and painting from the human body;
3. Life drawing (evening);
4. The study of drapes;
5. Composition exercises."

It comes as no surprise to learn that Griepenkerl, the pedantically academic painter of portraits and history scenes, whose decorative work for the immense Ringstrasse buildings had met with approval, once retorted to the young and rebellious Schiele: "The Devil must have shat you into my class."

Schiele rebelled against constraints. He and his friends of a heated, revolutionary turn of mind boldly submitted a petition to Griepenkerl, containing thirteen questions, including: "Do evening and night not count as available light? Are only those things Nature that the Herr Professor concedes to be Nature?"

The capital of the Austro-Hungarian empire, the seat of the Habsburg dynasty, seemed a veritably hostile place to the young artist – as it also did to a contemporary who later made a name for himself distinctly less savoury than Schiele's, Adolf Hitler. Hitler was unable to take up the Acad-

In November 1898, the Secession building designed by Joseph Maria Olbrich, with its golden dome of laurel leaves, was opened. In 1897 a group of young artists led by Gustav Klimt had left the Artists' Association in protest at its policies. Klimt was the first Secession president. The Secession motto was: To the age its art, to art its freedom.

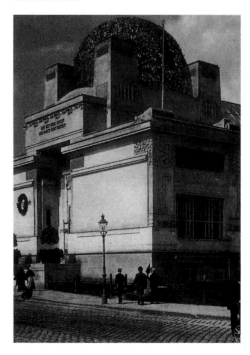

Two Men with Haloes, 1909
Zwei Männer mit Nimben
Indian ink and wash and pencil, 15.4 x 9.9 cm
Kallir D 366; Vienna, Graphische Sammlung
Albertina

Child with Halo in a Field of Flowers, 1909
Kind mit Nimbus auf einer Blumenwiese
Indian ink and wash and pencil, 15.7 x 10.2 cm
Kallir D 369; Vienna, Graphische Sammlung
Albertina

Egon Schiele repeatedly presented himself and
his revered Gustav Klimt as pupil and master, as
in *Two Men with Haloes*. The wash drawing,
like *Child with Halo in a Field of Flowers*,
was a design for a Wiener Werkstätte postcard
but was never in fact used. As in Klimt's portraits, the motif merges with the decorative
ornamental plane which surrounds it.

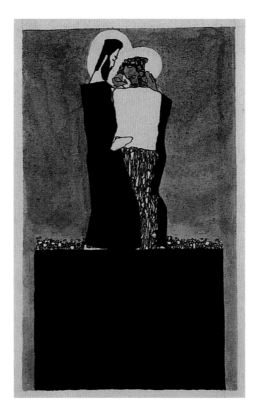
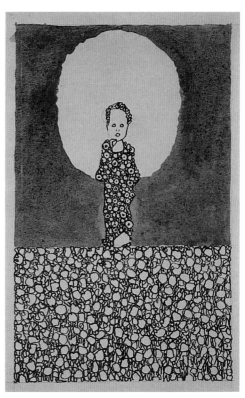

Anton Faistauer
Poster for the New Art Group exhibition at the
Salon Pisko, 1909
Print with watercolour

Egon Schiele left the Academy, probably after
the summer semester of 1909, and founded the
New Art Group with fellow students, including
his close friend Anton Peschka. The group exhibited that December at the Salon Pisko on the
Schwarzenbergplatz. The poster was designed by
another member of the group, Anton Faistauer.

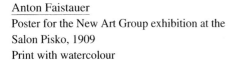
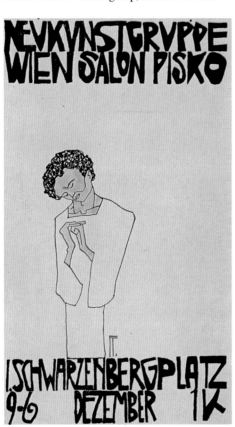

emy studies he hoped to pursue because he failed the entrance exam. As
Kokoschka later joked, "Hitler unfortunately failed the exam. If I had
failed in his place, the world would have been spared a good deal of mis-
ery – Hitler would have become a bad painter, and I should have been a
reasonable, understanding politician."

Professor Griepenkerl was so ashamed of Schiele that he begged him
never to let anyone know he had studied under him. It was in the trust
that Schiele would respect this wish that he was to pass Schiele in his
finals, albeit with the lowest pass grade possible.

With psychological pressure on him from three sides – his mother, all
distrust and reproaches; his teacher, who could see no good at all in his
work; and his implacable uncle – Egon Schiele took the first steps towards
his own freedom as an artist. The main milestones along the path of eman-
cipation can be dated to the years from 1909 to 1913. He had already
moved into a studio of his own, in Kurzbauergasse, in 1907, and in the
same year had met Gustav Klimt, who recognised the seventeen-year-
old's ability and gave him generous, unenvious support. Then in 1909,
most probably in April (though some accounts say not till that summer),
Schiele left the Academy. In June, together with others of like mind, he established the *Neukunstgruppe* (New Art Group), which held its first exhibition at the Salon Pisko on the Schwarzenbergplatz that December. Also in
1909, Schiele had four pictures in the International Art Show in Vienna,
an exhibition of the contemporary avant-garde organized by Josef Hoffmann in a space specially designed for the purpose, also on the Schwarzenbergplatz. There, amongst many other important works, Schiele saw
eleven paintings by Vincent van Gogh, including *The Artist's Bedroom in
Arles* (1889; p. 60), which Carl Reininghaus acquired for his collection.
Through Hoffmann Schiele made contact with the Wiener Werkstätte.

The show at Pisko's decided Schiele's future. There he met Arthur

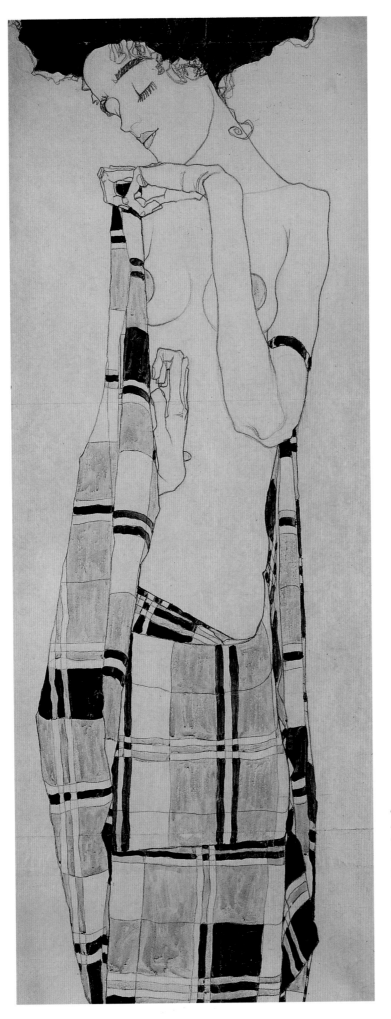

Standing Girl in Plaid Garment, 1908/09
Stehendes Mädchen in kariertem Tuch
Charcoal and body colour, 140 x 52.7 cm
Kallir D 541; Minneapolis (MN), The Minnea-
polis Institute of Arts

Egon Schiele met Gustav Klimt in 1907. Under
his influence he put his impersonal, academic
style behind him. His works of the period 1908
to 1910, such as this, pay homage to the master's
flat, ornamental style. The position of the hands
here already anticipates the expressiveness of
Schiele's later manner.

21

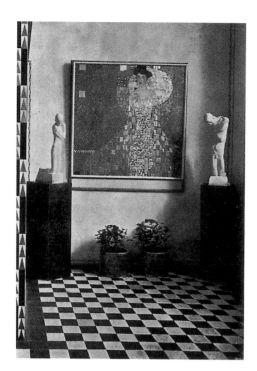

In 1909 Schiele had four pictures in the International Art Show in Vienna, an exhibition of European avant-garde art. It included eleven pictures by Vincent van Gogh and major Klimts, such as his *Portrait of Adele Bloch-Bauer I* shown in this photograph. The architect Josef Hoffmann designed the show.

Roessler, a writer who contributed art criticism to the *Arbeiterzeitung* (Workers' Journal). Henceforth, Roessler was to be a consistent advocate of Schiele's work, and introduced him to important collectors such as Carl Reininghaus and Dr. Oskar Reichel, as well as the art publisher Eduard Kosmack. It would be tempting to imagine that the large-format portraits of Roessler (1910; p. 138), Kosmack (1910; p. 140) and Reichel that Schiele subsequently proceeded to paint helped to mitigate the worst of his financial plight. But in fact Schiele's sitters either refused to take their portrait, as Reichel did, or refused to pay, as Kosmack did. We do not know whether Roessler, at least, paid for his portrait.

In 1910, through Hoffmann's good offices, Schiele was able to show a picture – a nude (1910; p. 24) – at the International Hunting Exhibition in Vienna. He also met Heinrich Benesch (1862–1947; p. 141), a railway official and art collector. Though Benesch's means were extremely limited, he was to become one of Schiele's most loyal devotees. He had already seen work by Schiele at an exhibition in Klosterneuburg in 1908, though it was not till two years later that he made personal contact with the artist.

The following year, through Roessler, Schiele succeeded in crossing the border to Germany: Hans Goltz, a Munich book and art dealer, mounted an exhibition of oils and works on paper at his premises. These first

Portrait of the Painter Anton Peschka, 1909
Bildnis des Malers Anton Peschka
Oil and metallic paint and pencil on canvas,
110.2 x 100cm
Kallir P 150; private collection, courtesy Galerie St. Etienne, New York

Schiele's portrait of his friend and later brother-in-law (Peschka married Gerti Schiele) is in the Klimt style. The silhouette, chair and background all establish flat two-dimensionality rather than the illusion of space. The composition is relieved by Viennese Art Nouveau motifs.

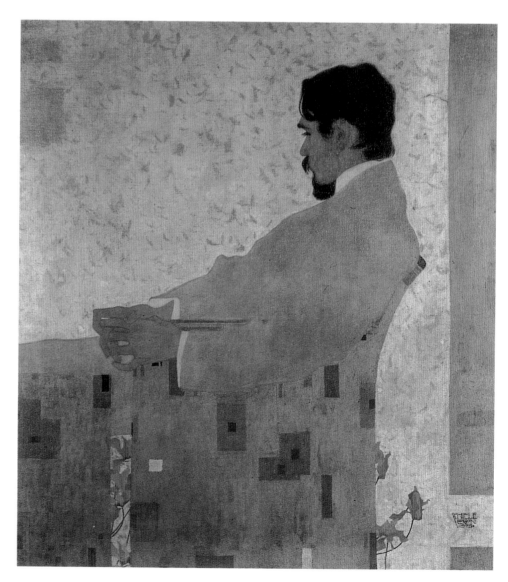

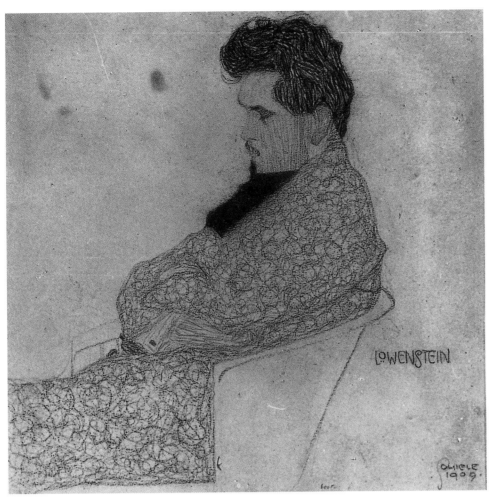

modest successes were doubtless encouraging; yet they did next to nothing to ease Schiele's financial predicament.

In that year of 1911, Schiele took a provocative step: he and his model Wally (Valerie) Neuzil lived together openly in a garden house they had rented at Krumau, his mother's home town. Wally, then under age, also acted as his model. For a small town, where anyone who breached the moral code and failed to make regular appearances at mass was suspected of being a Red and a troublemaker, it was too much to bear: Egon and Wally were driven out of their Krumau idyll, now grown thorny, in early August.

Schiele took refuge in the village of Neulengbach, where the next scandal promptly followed in the spring of 1912. He was arrested on a charge of seducing a minor, kept in custody for two weeks while the matter was investigated, and then (in St. Pölten, where he had been transferred) sentenced to three days' imprisonment for disseminating immoral drawings, the original charge being dropped. The judge who handed down the sentence burnt one of the offending drawings over a candle flame – in the Austria of 1912, images could still be consigned to the fire.

In prison, Schiele did not cease to be active and produced about a dozen drawings and watercolours to which he appended heavily meaningful statements (pp. 29 – 31). Taken together, they have the painful quality of a *de profundis* lament:

"The Single Orange Was the Only Light." (19 April 1912)
"I Feel Not Punished but Cleansed!" (20 April)
"The Door to the Open!" (21 April)

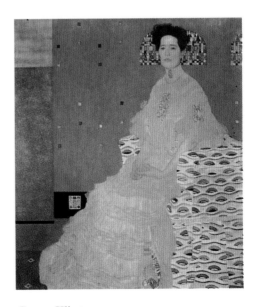

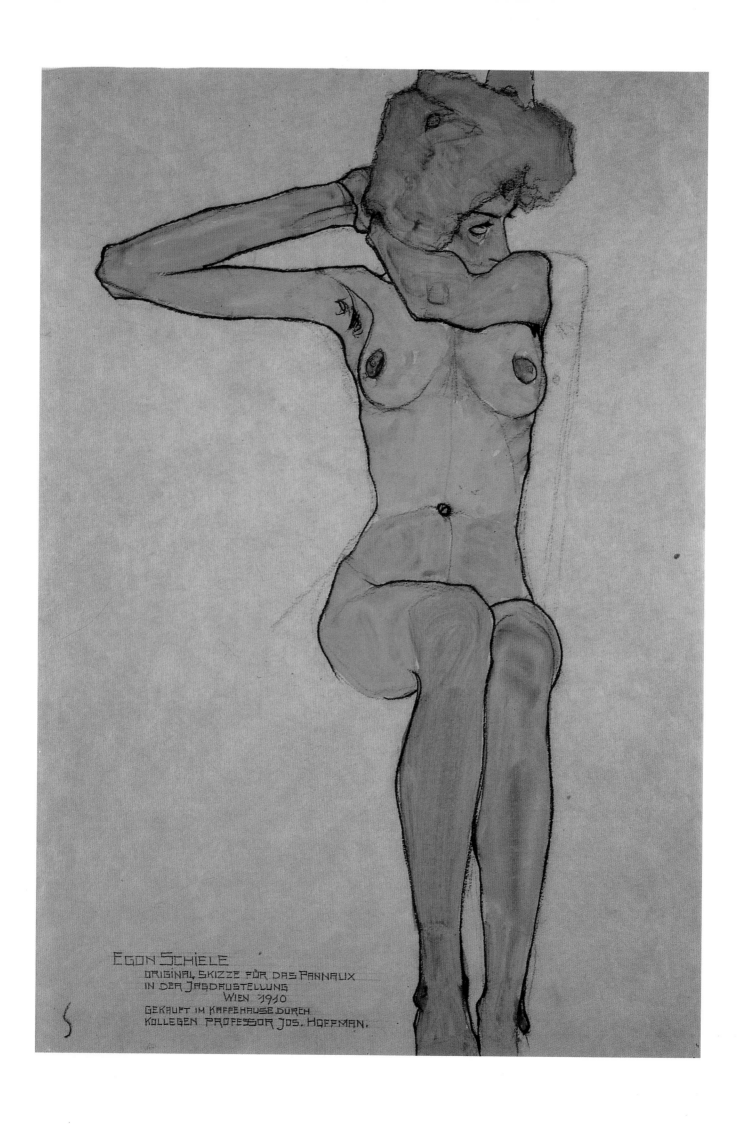

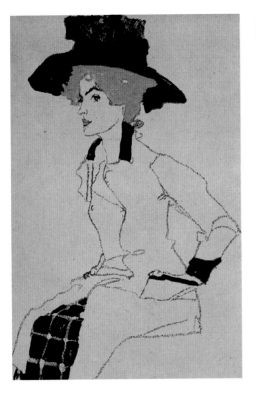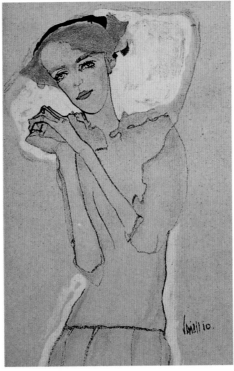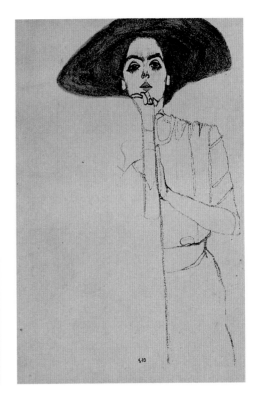

"Organic Movement of Chair and Pitcher." (21 April)

"Two of My Handkerchiefs." (21 April)

"Art Cannot Be Modern; Art Is Primordially Eternal." (22 April)

"Hindering the Artist Is a Crime, It Is Murdering Life in the Bud!" (23 April)

"I Love Antitheses." (24 April)

"Prisoner!" (25 April)

"For Art and for My Loved Ones I Will Gladly Endure to the End!" (25 April)

"All Things Balance out Physically Most Surely." (26 April)

"My Wandering Path Leads over Abysses." (27 April)

The drawings reflect a dramatic vision of woe. *Hindering the Artist Is a Crime, It Is Murdering Life in the Bud!* (p.29) shows Schiele unshaven, eyes wide open, huddled in a coat on the bed in his detention cell.

Even amongst his well-disposed friends there were those who were taken aback by the offences Schiele was charged with: the unproven seduction of a girl under the age of consent, his proven use of children as models, his drawings of lesbian couples embracing, and his blasphemous disrespect for the Catholic church in works such as *Cardinal and Nun (Caress)* (1912; p.164), which shows a nun in her habit locked in a passionate embrace with a cardinal in full regalia. And then there was the watercolour *The Red Host* (1911; p.68), in which a girl is holding the artist's erect, outsize member in her right hand, as if presenting a cultic object to us. And, furthermore, there were countless lascivious semi-nudes with their skirts hauled up to expose their genitals, or models masturbating. Schiele's patron Carl Reininghaus paid for his lawyer at the St. Pölten trial, but was mildly shocked himself and returned to more formal relations with the artist.

Even pioneering and similarly reviled contemporaries such as Oskar

Wiener Werkstätte Postcards (Gertrude and Melanie Schiele), 1910
Postcards
Kallir D 488, D 486, D 468; Vienna, Historisches Museum der Stadt Wien

Schiele's sisters Gerti (left and centre) and Melanie (right) sat for the postcards he designed for the Wiener Werkstätte in 1910.

PAGE 24:
Seated Female Nude with Raised Right Arm, 1910
Sitzender weiblicher Akt mit abgespreiztem rechten Arm
Watercolour and black crayon, 45 x 31.5 cm
Kallir D 518; Vienna, Historisches Museum der Stadt Wien

The stylistic change in Schiele's work occurred in 1910. He abandoned Art Nouveau and began to evolve a distinctive Expressionist style of his own, angular and eloquent.

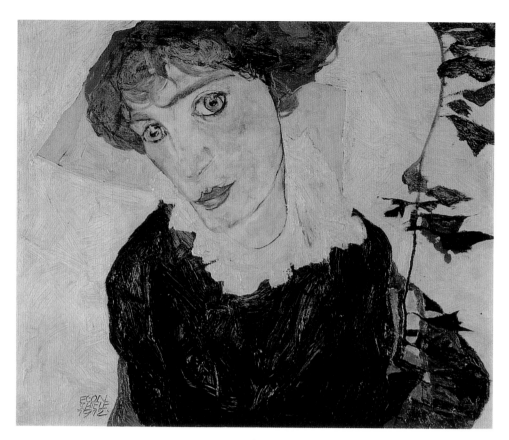

Portrait of Valerie Neuzil, 1912
Bildnis Valerie Neuzil
Oil on wood, 32 x 40cm
Kallir P 234; Vienna, Sammlung Rudolf Leopold

The portrait of Schiele's model and partner Wally is a striking example of his idiosyncratic eloquence. Her face is elongated and her eyes as large as those in icons. The portrait seems framed by jagged shapes, and the dry leaves on the right seem to be blowing in a wind.

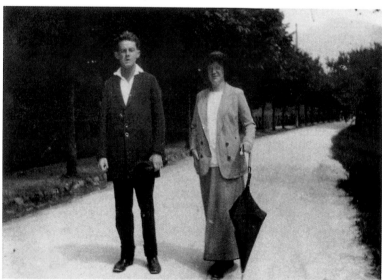

In July 1913, Egon Schiele and Wally went to Altmünster near Salzburg to join the artist's friend, patron and subsequent biographer Arthur Roessler for a summer break. Roessler took a number of photographs of the couple.

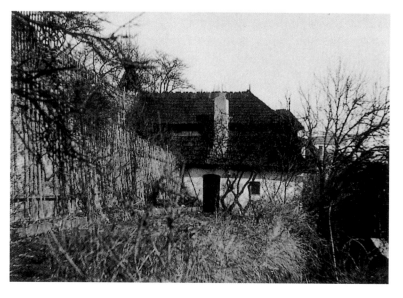

From mid-May to August 1911, Schiele and Wally lived in this garden house at Krumau. Their candid partnership, and Schiele's use of very young girls as models, offended the local people, and on 5 August the couple beat a hasty retreat from the town.

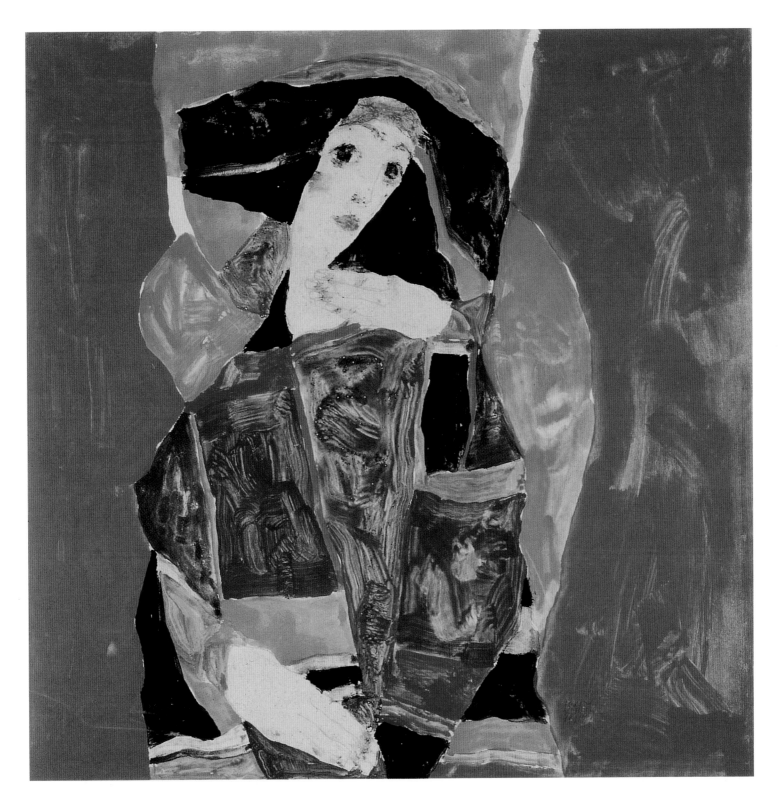

Portrait of a Woman (Valerie Neuzil), 1912
Porträt einer Frau (Valerie Neuzil)
Gouache and pencil, 24.8 x 24.8 cm
Kallir D 1196; whereabouts unknown, courtesy Galerie St. Etienne, New York

Bright colours and patterned materials fascinated Schiele. The clothing and
background in this portrait of Wally are almost completely abstract. Only the
face and hands serve as a reminder that this is a figural composition. Schiele
often bordered on the abstract in his early work.

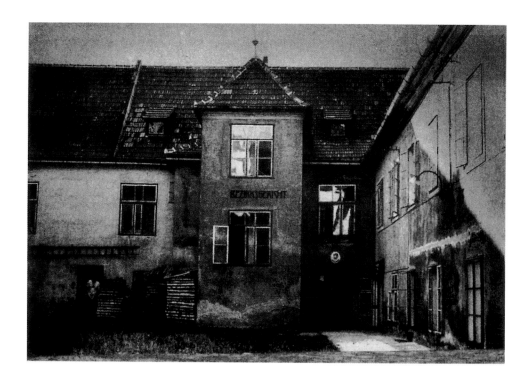

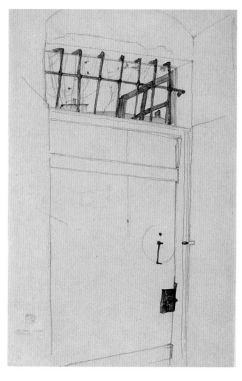

The Door to the Open!, 1912
Die Tür in das Offene!
Watercolour and pencil, 48.2 x 32cm
Kallir D 1181; Vienna, Graphische Sammlung
Albertina

PAGE 29:
***Hindering the Artist Is a Crime, It Is
Murdering Life in the Bud!***, 1912
*Den Künstler hemmen ist ein Verbrechen, es
heißt keimendes Leben morden!*
Watercolour and pencil, 48.6 x 31.8cm
Kallir D 1186; Vienna, Graphische Sammlung
Albertina

Kokoschka had their reservations about this "pornographic" side to Schiele's visual world. Following the first major Schiele exhibition in London in 1964, Kokoschka, then an old man, dismissed his rival as a "pornographer". Kokoschka also belittled Schiele's renowned sureness of line, claiming that while he himself, the valiant Oskar, was fighting at the front during the First World War, Schiele had stolen his line from his (Kokoschka's) Vienna studio.

The painter and mime artist Erwin Dominik Osen (1891–1970) also had a small part to play in establishing Schiele's image as the bogey of the respectable classes. Osen, who painted backdrops for the theatre, intoxicated the credulous Schiele with tales of travel and adventure in the Orient and Far East – every syllable a fabrication. Schiele often drew the lean panjandrum Osen in the nude, posed in the ecstatic attitude of an opium eater. Heinrich Benesch, by contrast, was surely Schiele's guardian angel. He visited him in prison, saw to the hiring of a lawyer, and asked the artist never to throw away any sheet or misfired sketch but to keep even the slightest scrap for the Benesch collection. Modest though his means were, Benesch thus acquired the largest private Schiele collection during the artist's lifetime, subsequently the substantial foundation of the Vienna Albertina's Schiele holdings.

If Schiele faced a conservative front united in their rejection and opposition, he could also count a far larger, motley array of friends, patrons and models who enthusiastically accompanied his career. Foremost among them was Wally Neuzil, the woman who was not only Schiele's faithful lover and favourite model until his marriage to Edith Harms in 1915 but who also acted with consistently selfless friendship towards him. Four years Schiele's junior, Wally looks good-natured, if somewhat bland of feature, in the photographs we have. In the numerous drawings he did of her, and the oil *Portrait of Valerie Neuzil* (1912; p.26), Schiele made her features tauter and leaner, her chin longer, and her eyes, larger than in life, of an iconic beauty. Transformed in this way, Wally's face and features appear

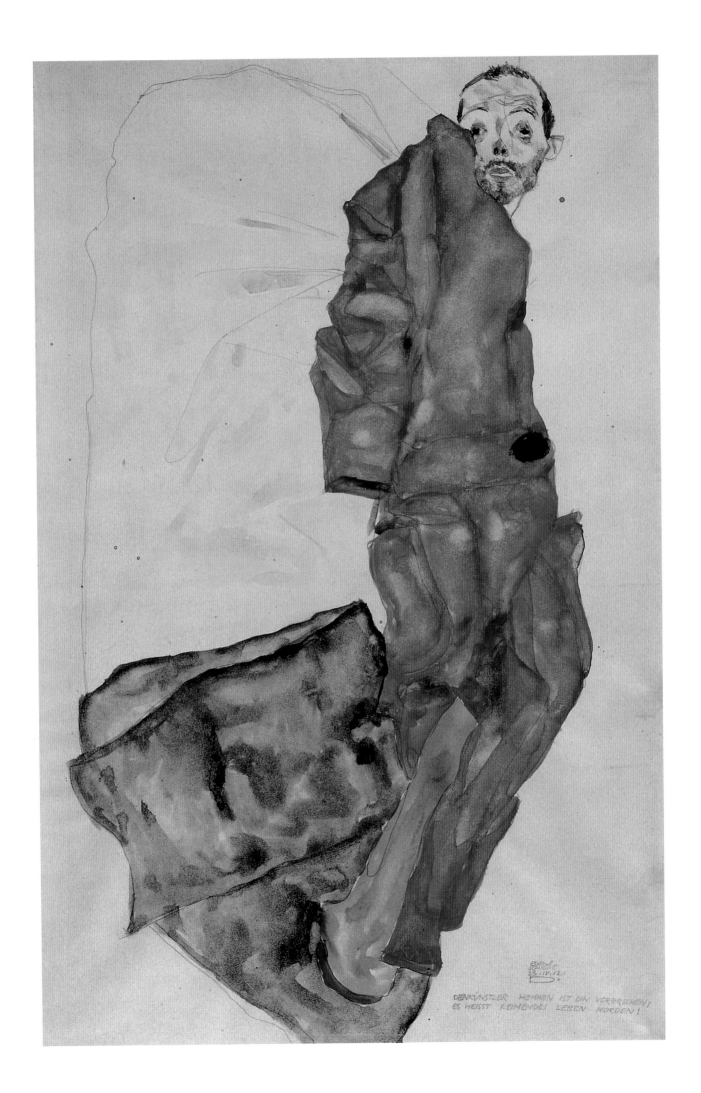

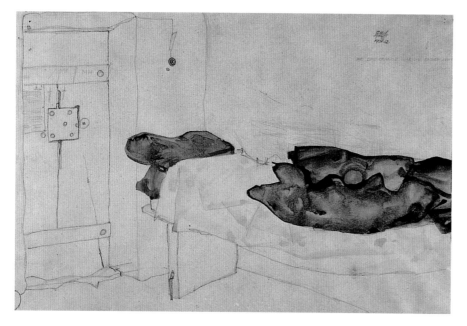

The Single Orange Was the Only Light, 1912
Die eine Orange war das einzige Licht
Gouache, watercolour and pencil, 31.9 x 48cm
Kallir D 1179; Vienna, Graphische Sammlung Albertina

Art Cannot Be Modern; Art Is Primordially Eternal,
1912
Kunst kann nicht modern sein; Kunst ist urewig
Gouache, watercolour and pencil, 32 x 48.3cm
Kallir D 1185; Vienna, Graphische Sammlung Albertina

Organic Movement of Chair and Pitcher, 1912
Organische Bewegung des Sessels und des Kruges
Watercolour and pencil, 31.8 x 48cm
Kallir D 1184; Vienna, Graphische Sammlung Albertina

Schiele's preference for child models caught up with him
in spring 1912. In Neulengbach, where he planned to
spend the summer, he was charged with seducing a minor
and disseminating immoral drawings. The sketches illustrated here, glossed by Schiele with meaningful pro-
nouncements, record his experience of gaol.

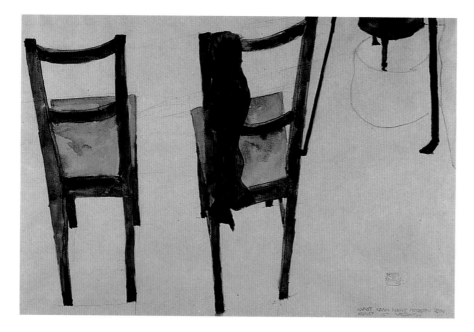

PAGE 31 TOP LEFT:
**For Art and for My Loved Ones I Will Gladly
Endure to the End!**, 1912
*Ich werde für die Kunst und für meine Geliebten gerne
ausharren*
Watercolour and pencil, 48.2 x 31.8cm
Kallir D 1189; Vienna, Graphische Sammlung Albertina

PAGE 31 TOP RIGHT:
Prisoner!, 1912
Gefangener
Watercolour and pencil, 48.2 x 31.7cm
Kallir D 1188; Vienna, Graphische Sammlung Albertina

PAGE 31 BOTTOM LEFT:
I Feel Not Punished but Cleansed!, 1912
Nicht gestraft, sondern gereinigt fühle ich mich!
Gouache, watercolour and pencil, 48.4 x 31.6cm
Kallir D 1180; Vienna, Graphische Sammlung Albertina

PAGE 31 BOTTOM RIGHT:
Two of My Handkerchiefs, 1912
Zwei meiner Taschentücher
Watercolour and pencil, 48.2 x 31.7cm
Kallir D 1182; Vienna, Graphische Sammlung Albertina

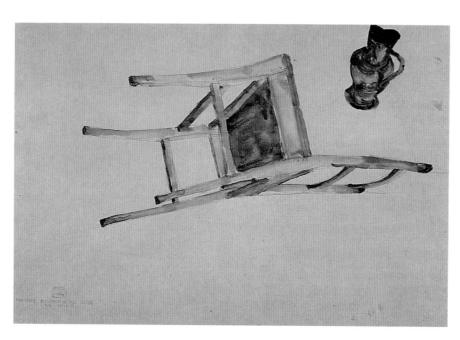

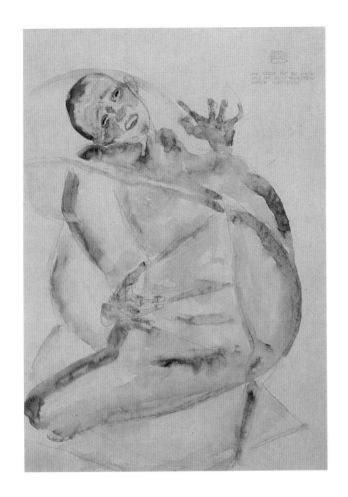

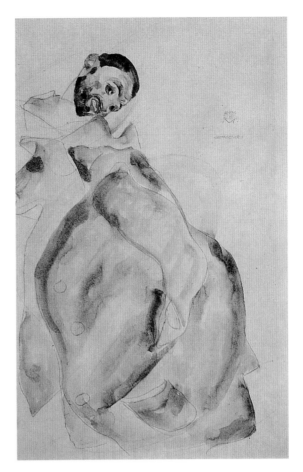

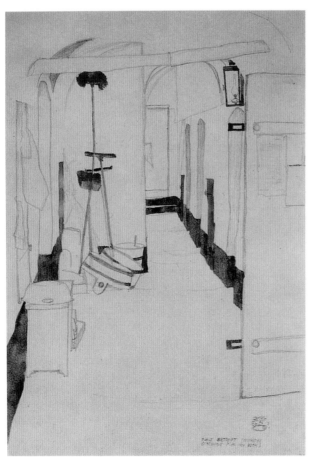

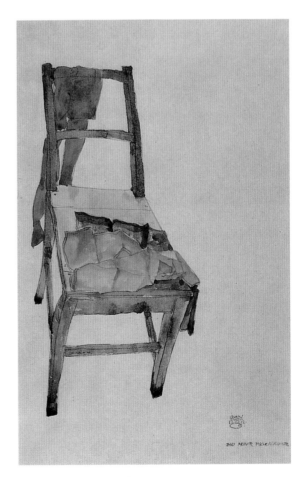

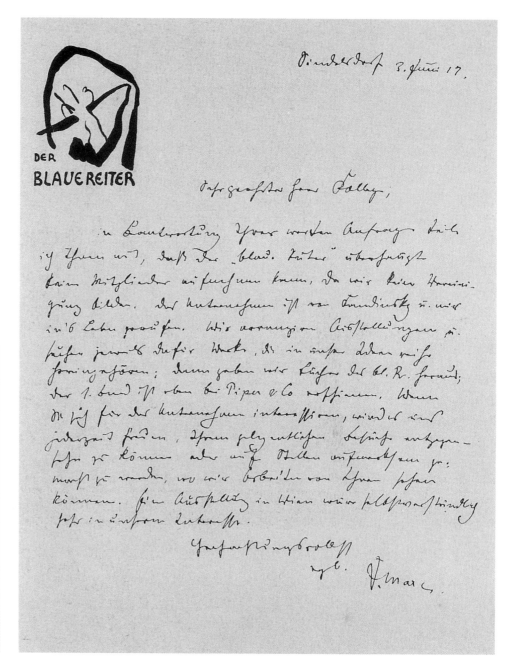

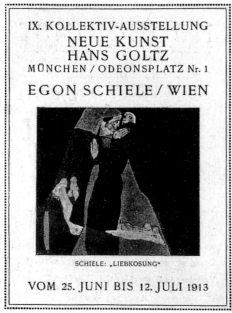

IX. KOLLEKTIV-AUSSTELLUNG
NEUE KUNST
HANS GOLTZ
MÜNCHEN / ODEONSPLATZ Nr. 1

EGON SCHIELE / WIEN

SCHIELE: „LIEBKOSUNG"

VOM 25. JUNI BIS 12. JULI 1913

Egon Schiele enjoyed early recognition. In 1912 he exhibited with the Munich Blaue Reiter group at Hans Goltz's gallery. In 1913 Goltz published a catalogue with Schiele's *Cardinal and Nun (Caress)* on the cover. That same year, Schiele exhibited elsewhere in Germany too.

Schiele assiduously built up contacts and ways of exhibiting. In June 1912, in response to his own feeler, he received a letter from Blaue Reiter artist Franz Marc, informing him that the group was not accepting any new members but was nonetheless most interested in Schiele's work.

Letter from Franz Marc to Schiele:
"Sinderdorf, 3 June 1912
Dear fellow artist,
In reply to your enquiry I must inform you that the Blaue Reiter cannot accept any members at all, since we are not an association. The enterprise was started by Kandinsky and me. We ar-
range exhibitions and seek out work that accords with our own ideas; we also edit the Blaue Reiter books, the first of which has just been published by Piper & Co. If you are interested in this venture, we would be delighted to see you at any time you can visit or to be informed where we can see your work. An exhibition in Vienna would of course be greatly in our interests.
Yours faithfully, F. Marc"

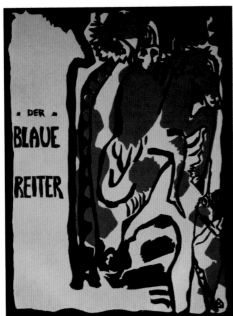

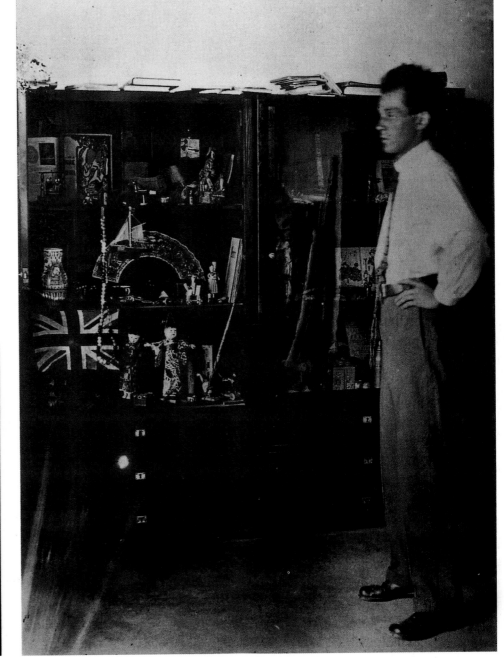

Wassily Kandinsky
Design for the cover of the Blaue Reiter almanac, 1911
Indian ink and watercolour over tracing paper and pencil, 27.9 x 21.9 cm
Munich, Städtische Galerie im Lenbachhaus

Egon Schiele with his collection, 1915
Photograph
Vienna, Graphische Sammlung Albertina

Schiele collected toys and folk artefacts. This picture shows him by his glass cases of curios in his studio at 101, Hietzinger Hauptstrasse. The 1912 Blaue Reiter almanac with Kandinsky's cover can be seen in the case at top left.

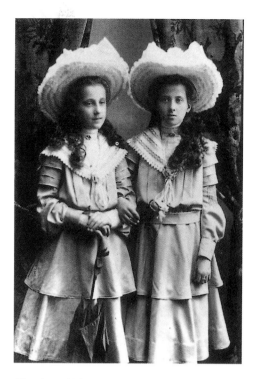

The sisters Edith and Adele Harms, two middle-class girls, in 1903. Twelve years after this picture was taken, Schiele decided to marry Edith, the younger by three years.

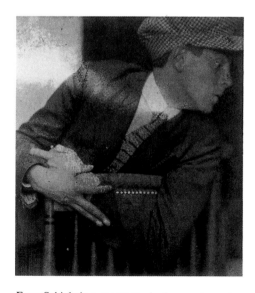

Egon Schiele in a sporty cap in the year he met the Harms girls. His reference in a letter to posing as an "apache" (in the sense of a street ruffian) may relate to this photograph.

PAGE 35:
The letter in which Schiele established contact with the Harms sisters, who lived across the road from his studio. He asked them out to the cinema, which was then considered unsuitable for young ladies. Wally, whom he was soon to throw over, played the part of chaperone.

seductive; Schiele's rendering attests the depth of their relations. Wally is seen as the feeling companion, the woman at the artist's side, with big, earnest eyes. Elsewhere, in paintings such as the aforementioned *Cardinal and Nun (Caress)* (p.164) or the gouache drawing *Holy Family* (1913; p.127), she is presented in an allegorically provocative pose, or as the temptress with her legs raised to reveal her garters and undergarments, as in the watercolour *Wally in Red Blouse with Raised Knees* (1913; p.54).

Girls and women had of course modelled for Schiele before Wally. There had been his two sisters, for instance: Melanie, his elder by four years, and Gertrude (Gerti), four years his junior. His relations with the pretty, younger Gerti in particular seem to have been very close. She went with him on his first visit to Trieste, and acted as model, both clothed and naked. The contrast is striking when we turn to the almost academic dryness with which Schiele recorded his mother's stern, somewhat careworn features in a charcoal drawing. We see her again in the watercolour *The Artist's Mother, Sleeping* (1911) and in the painting entitled *Dead Mother I* (1910; p. 126). Schiele's choice of title was made after talking to Roessler about his mother's utter incomprehension of his art and her lack of sympathy.

In addition to his family, lovers and (later) his wife, Schiele also used professional models, prostitutes and under-age working-class girls. These last he would find on the streets and would talk them into giving their services for a small sum. Like the writer Peter Altenberg, Schiele seems to have had a distinct penchant for young girls in the first flush of pubescence. Long before Vladimir Nabokov taught us the name, Schiele was recording a world of Lolitas, in watercolours and drawings, that beggars comparison in 20th-century art.

Interest in Schiele's work was growing rapidly. In 1912 he exhibited at a number of shows, including the Blaue Reiter exhibition at Galerie Goltz in Munich, with the Munich Secession, and in the acclaimed Sonderbund exhibition in Cologne. In 1913 he had work in the International Black-and-White Exhibition and in the Vienna Secession's 43rd show. He was also exhibiting in Germany: with Goltz in Munich, at the Folkwang Museum in Essen, in Hagen, Hamburg, Dresden and Stuttgart, in Berlin and in Breslau (now Wroclaw). Schiele also began to contribute to the Berlin periodical *Die Aktion* (The Action; cf. pp. 168 and 169), which published both poems and drawings by the Austrian over the next few years. In July 1913, together with Wally, Schiele visited Arthur Roessler in Altmünster near Salzburg (cf. p. 26).

The outbreak of the First World War in 1914 did not initially interrupt Schiele's exhibition activities. That year he showed works in the International Secession exhibition in Rome, the Werkbund exhibition in Cologne, the Munich Secession, and in Brussels, Paris, and (early in 1915) the Zurich Kunsthaus.

In 1915 Schiele decided to marry – not Wally, though, but Edith Harms, who was three years younger. The meeting that was to be Egon's and Wally's last, at Café Eichberger in Hietzing, was notable for its grotesqueness, if Roessler's report can be trusted: Schiele produced from his pocket a bizarre document, couched in the terms of a contract, proposing a mutual obligation upon himself and Wally to spend a recreational vaca-

Donnerstag, den 10. Dezember 1914.

<u>Liebes Fräulein D. & AD. oder AD. & D.</u>

ich glaube, daß Ihre Frau Mutter Ihnen erlauben wird, mit Walli und mir, in's Kino oder in's Theater, oder wohin Sie wollen, zu gehen. Sie können begreifen, daß ich in Wirklichkeit ein ehrsam anderer bin, — als "Argentin", das ist eine bloß momentane Rolle auf Übermut. — Wenn Sie also Lust haben, daß wir und W. uns hier verbringen, so würde ich mich freuen und erwarte Ihrerseits die Antwort an welchem Tag es Ihnen convenirt.

Herzlichste Grüße

[Unterschrift]

666

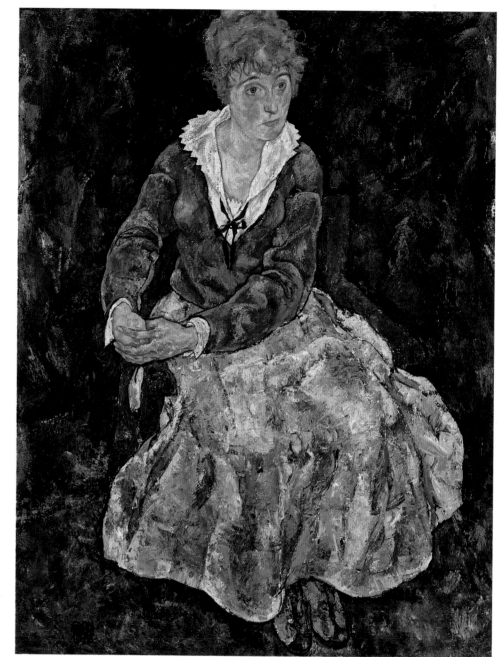

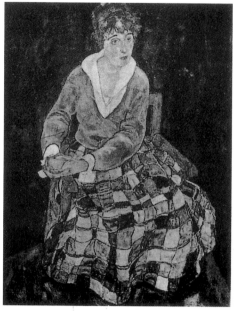

Portrait of the Artist's Wife, Seated
(first state), 1917
Bildnis der Frau des Künstlers, sitzend
Oil on canvas, 139.5 x 109.2 cm
Kallir P 316

Portrait of the Artist's Wife, Seated
(present state), 1918
Bildnis der Frau des Künstlers, sitzend
Oil on canvas, 139.5 x 109.2 cm
Kallir P 316; Vienna, Österreichische Galerie.
Belvedere

Schiele's wife Edith now replaced Wally as his
model; Edith was jealous of other models. Her
portrait was the first Schiele to be acquired by a
national collection, the Moderne Galerie in
Vienna. But Edith's checked skirt in the first version had to be overpainted because it was considered offensively Bohemian.

tion of several weeks every summer together, despite his marriage to
Edith. Roessler seems to have indulged a little journalistic licence in his
account of Wally's understandably outraged response to Schiele's naive
suggestion: "'But Egon', Wally is said to have replied, 'what do you imagine it would really be like? Do you honestly think that Edith would
ever consent – or that I could possibly agree! No doubt you mean well,
I'm certain of that; but it is out of the question, quite out of the question
for me! – I renounce my claims, once and for all, and that's that.' 'Well,
if that's how you see it, there's nothing to be done; we shall have to say
good-bye for ever. A pity! – the idea wouldn't really have been impossible, believe me', said Schiele resignedly, lighting a cigarette and gazing
dreamily at the coils of smoke..."[4]

Schiele, the "perpetual child" (his own phrase), simply blamed other
people whenever any figure in his plaything universe was knocked over.

He had gone strategically about the matter of establishing relations with
his future wife Edith Harms and her sister Adele (cf. p. 34), who lived

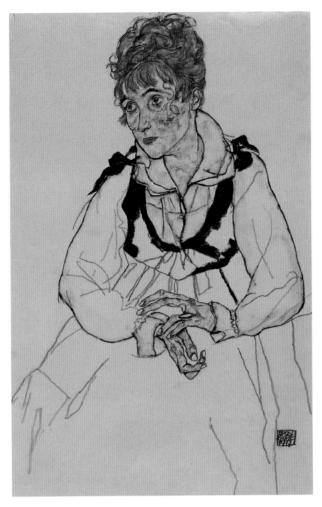

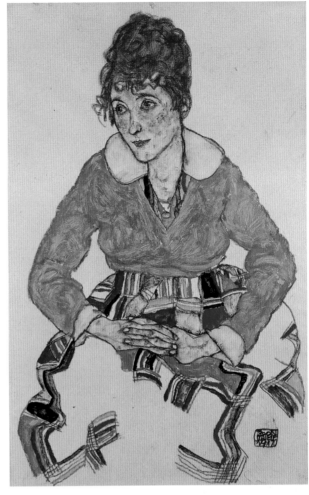

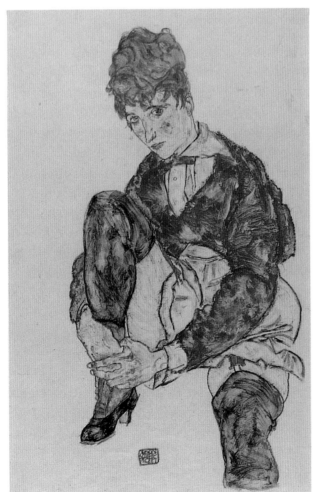

TOP LEFT:
The Artist's Wife, Seated, 1917
Die Frau des Künstlers, sitzend
Gouache and black crayon, 46.1 x 29.7 cm
Kallir D 1907; Vienna, Graphische Sammlung Albertina

TOP RIGHT:
Portrait of the Artist's Wife, 1917
Bildnis der Gattin des Künstlers
Gouache and black crayon, 44 x 28 cm
Kallir D 1908; private collection

BOTTOM LEFT:
Portrait of the Artist's Wife Seated, Holding Her Right Leg,
1917
Bildnis der Gattin des Künstlers, ihr rechtes Bein haltend
Gouache and black crayon, 46.3 x 29.2 cm
Kallir D 1982; New York, The Pierpont Morgan Library

Schiele made many preparatory drawings before embarking on
the large portrait of his wife, and some of them are not only more
relaxed but also more flattering than the final painting. After
1915 his style became clearly and progressively more three-
dimensional and physical and also more tender.

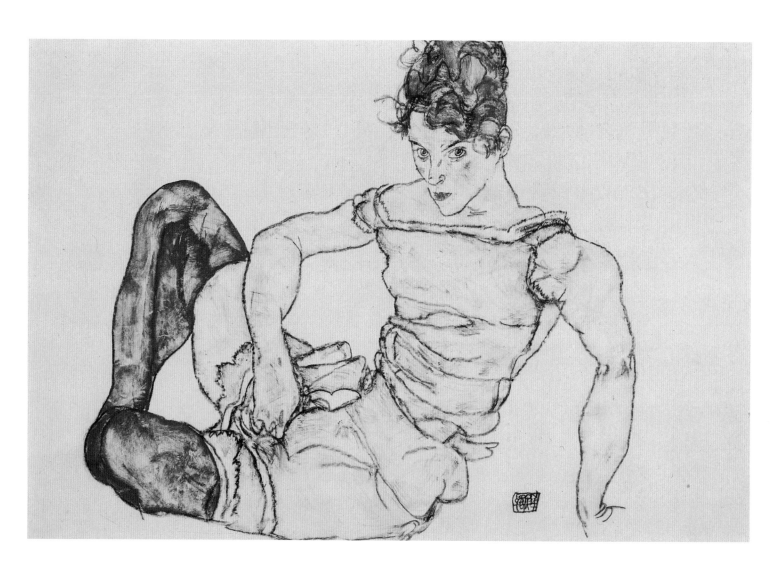

Seated Woman in Violet Stockings, 1917
Sitzende Frau mit violetten Strümpfen
Gouache and black crayon, 29.6 x 44.2 cm
Kallir D 1992; private collection

Edith's elder sister Adele also modelled frequently for her brother-in-law. Here she appears
as more seductive than the rather proper Edith –
though to be drawn in her undergarments, making a hand gesture suggestive of masturbation,
presumably did not come easily to the well-
brought-up middle-class girl. In later years,
though, she claimed that she and Schiele were
having an affair at the time.

across the street from the studio in Hietzinger Hauptstrasse where he had
been living since 1912. He had appeared at his studio window dressed as
an apache and eventually invited the sisters to the cinema (cf. p. 35) – a
daring proposal, in the terms of pre-First World War middle-class morality, which thought the cinema unsuitable for young ladies.

"Dear Miss Ed. & Ad. [Edith and Adele] or Ad. and Ed.," he wrote to the
girls on 10 December 1914. "I feel sure your esteemed mother will give you
permission to go to the cinema or the Apollo with Wally and me, or wher-
ever you like. Rest assured that in reality I am quite different – not an 'apache': that was merely a pose I struck, in the high spirits of the moment…"

And indeed, Schiele used poor Wally as a chaperone as he deliberated
secretly upon a possible future bride. The two attractive sisters replied:
"We shall be very glad to go to the cinema, to the Park Cinema on Monday, to see Ewer's *A Woman of the World*. With Wally, of course. Who
shall get the tickets?" In pencil, one of them added: "My mama must
know nothing of this. A. & E."

The two girls, brought up in a protective middle-class environment that
seems to have impressed Schiele deeply, were the daughters of a property-
owning family. The artist had a strong sense of order and an aversion to
the Bohemian life, unlike others such as Klimt and Kokoschka, and these
will have played a part in his decision to propose to Edith Harms before
very long.

Schiele's organizational ability, and his cool, calculating habit of mind, were apparent not only in his assiduous handling of exhibition deals or contacts with collectors. In everyday matters, from the location of a better studio to his meticulous attention to form in his marriage arrangements, he had a strong sense of purpose. There is a revealing comment in a letter to Roessler of 16 February 1915: "I intend to get married, advantageously, not to Wally."[5] It is conceivable that he thought Wally not suitable to his station.

The wedding took place on 17 June 1915 at the main Lutheran church, in Dorotheergasse. Johann Harms, Schiele's new father-in-law, was a master fitter who originated from northern Germany; his wife Josefine, née Bürzner, from Lower Austria, had been the widow of a man named Erdmann, and it was probably she who had owned the house in Hietzing, a well-to-do residential area, when she married Harms.

The milieu visible in a surviving family photograph is strongly reminiscent of that of the piano-playing Uncle Leopold; in the case of the Harms family, though, everything is a little smaller and more confined. In place of the grand piano they had an upright; otherwise, all the props that were considered *de rigueur* in a Viennese salon were there – grandfather clock and sideboard, a potted palm, and a reproduction of an Old Master, a portrait by Frans Hals.

Of Wally, subsequent to Egon Schiele's entrance into the world of middle-class married life, it remains to be said that, disillusioned and in despair, she volunteered for the Red Cross, went to war as a nurse, and

Reclining Female Nude, 1917
Liegender weiblicher Akt
Gouache, watercolour and charcoal,
29.7 x 46.3 cm
Kallir D 1945; Brno, Moravská Galéri

Is this a portrait of Adele or Edith? The pose is provocative, though the erotic impact is not as direct as in earlier work. Since marrying, Schiele – subdued by the two proper sisters – had become tamer.

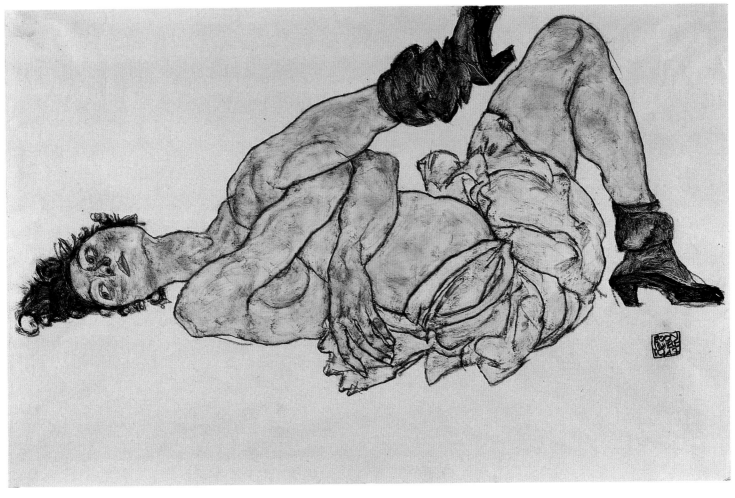

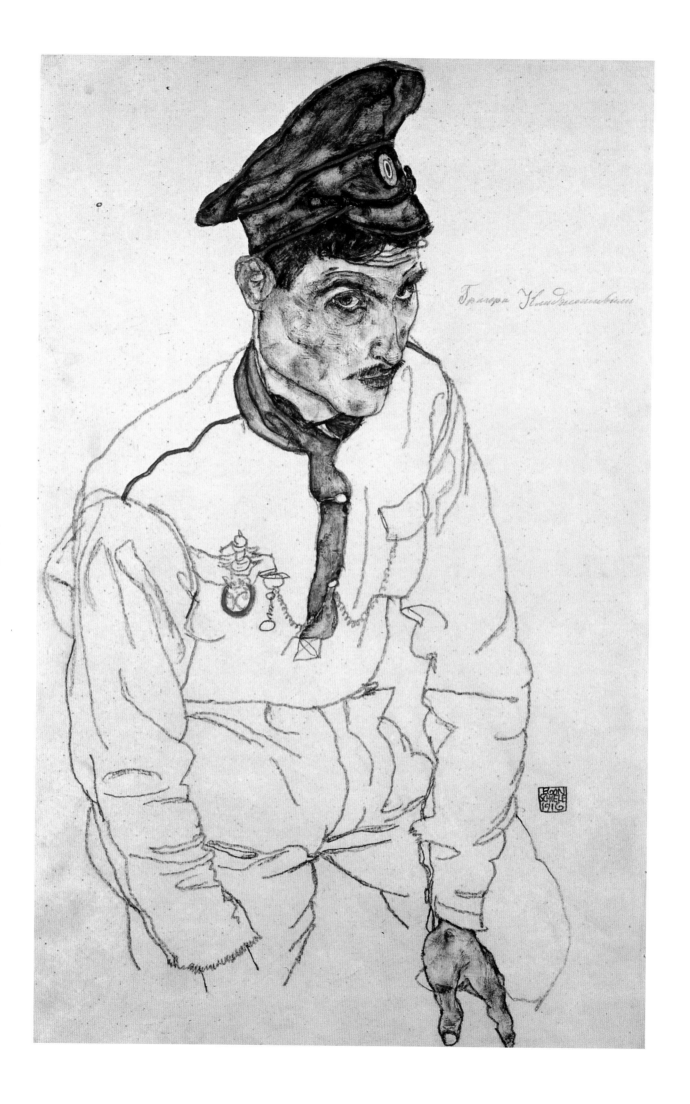

on 23 December 1917 died of scarlet fever in an Austrian military hospital at Sinič, near Split, in Dalmatia.

Four days after the wedding, Schiele was called up: he reported for duty in Prague, and went on to training at Neuhaus in Bohemia. Edith followed, taking a room at the fashionable Hotel Paris in Prague and then at the Hotel Central in Neuhaus, so that she could at least be with him when he was off duty.

By late July Schiele was already back in Vienna, with permission from the army authorities to spend his nights in his Hietzing studio whenever he was not working on entrenchments at the Lainz wildlife park or guarding Russian prisoners of war. In letters, Schiele complained bitterly about his own military service and the army and the war in general. He was far from sharing the enthusiasm of other young men who went to war with fanatical zeal.

The young couple had to forego a honeymoon. However Schiele was spared the front line and the newly-weds were able to see each other regularly. As the war continued, Schiele found it possible to remain behind the lines: in early 1916 he was assigned to unarmed service, first to clerical work near Vienna and then to an officers' POW camp at Mühling in Lower Austria. There he was even given the use of a makeshift studio. In 1917 he was transferred back to Vienna, to the army supply commissary, where one new friend was to be Karl Grünwald, an art dealer who was a supervising officer at the depot. His superior officer, Dr. Hans Rosé, took him under his protective wing, "assigning" him to draw the food supply stores and the branches of the commissary. That autumn Schiele was moved yet again, to the Army Museum, where he continued to be spared active service under arms.

During the First World War, writers and artists in the old imperial army were still accorded privileged status. If at all possible, they were not sent to the front but given tasks in safe institutions such as the Army Museum or War Press Office. The German army, by contrast, was not as protective of artists, and painters such as August Macke and Franz Marc were among those who died early on the battlefields.

In 1916 and 1917, thanks to his privileged position, Schiele was able to continue showing work at exhibitions. He exhibited with the Munich Secession, in Dresden and elsewhere, and in shows of Austrian art that toured neutral countries for propaganda reasons, for instance Amsterdam, Stockholm and Copenhagen.

In 1917, Dr. Franz Martin Haberditzl (1882–1944), director of the Vienna Moderne Galerie (now the Österreichische Galerie), helped Schiele an important step further along the path to official recognition. That spring Haberditzl acquired drawings by Schiele and the oil *Portrait of the Artist's Wife, Seated* for the museum. He objected to the colourful tartan kilt that Edith was wearing in the first version, considering her too unsuitably, Bohemianly dressed to be exhibited in an imperial museum; and Schiele overpainted accordingly (revised version of 1918; p. 36).

In its final year, 1918, the war seemed even remoter from Schiele's life than it previously had. His notebooks recorded no fewer than 117 visits by models in the period from January to November – visits that were often overclouded by the jealousy of his young wife.

Though he had been called up, Schiele was spared the experience of front-line combat. He was assigned to unarmed duties. At a POW camp at Mühling in Lower Austria he sketched Russian officers and soldiers.

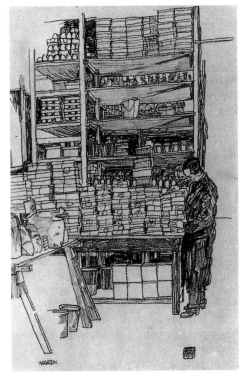

Supply Depot: Storeroom with Civilian Worker in Vienna, Schottenfeldgasse, 1917
Konsumanstalt: Magazin mit Zivilarbeiter in Wien, Schottenfeldgasse
Black crayon, 46.2 x 29.5 cm
Kallir D 2160; private collection

In 1917, well-intentioned superiors ordered Schiele to draw army supply depots. That autumn he was transferred again, to the Army Museum.

Secession poster: Friends at Dinner, small format, 1918
Sezessionsplakat, Die Freunde (Tafelrunde), klein
Colour lithograph
Private collection; Vienna, Historisches Museum
der Stadt Wien

This poster for the 49th Vienna Secession exhibition shows Schiele, at the head of the table, with friends. To his left, probably, are Georg Merkel, Albert Paris von Gütersloh, Georg Kars, and Willi Novak. To his right are Anton Faistauer, Felix Albrecht Harta and possibly Otto Wagner. The chair in the foreground facing Schiele was occupied by Klimt in the oil sketch, but in the final version Schiele left the place for Klimt, who had just died, empty.

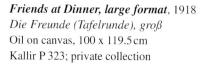

Friends at Dinner, large format, 1918
Die Freunde (Tafelrunde), groß
Oil on canvas, 100 x 119.5 cm
Kallir P 323; private collection

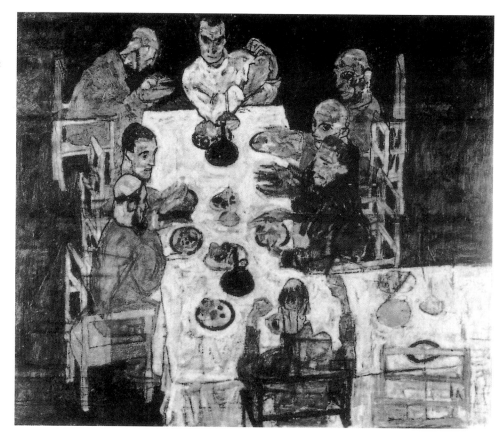

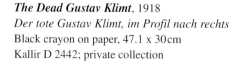

The Dead Gustav Klimt, 1918
Der tote Gustav Klimt, im Profil nach rechts
Black crayon on paper, 47.1 x 30 cm
Kallir D 2442; private collection

Gustav Klimt, the friend and helper so revered by Schiele, died on 6 February 1918.

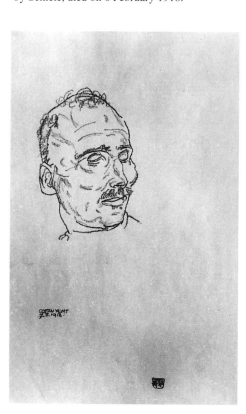

On 6 February 1918, Gustav Klimt died. Klimt had been the idol of Schiele, his supporter, and a fatherly friend. The younger artist drew Klimt on his deathbed, and paid his farewell, with words eloquent of his admiration and profound sense of loss, in the periodical *Der Anbruch* (The Dawn): "Gustav Klimt, an artist of unbelievable perfection, a man of rare profundity, his work a sacred shrine." (15 February 1918)

A month later, in March, Schiele achieved his national breakthrough at the 49th Vienna Secession exhibition, where he showed no fewer than 19 paintings and 29 watercolours. The show was a great artistic and financial success; and Schiele, as if by an unspoken agreement, stepped into the leadership role amongst the Vienna avant-garde that had been made available by Klimt's death. The entire élite of the intellectual and financial communities were now alert to his work and were increasingly wanting to have their portraits painted by him. In July Schiele moved into a new studio at 6, Wattmanngasse, in the Hietzing district, meaning to use it for large-format work; his old studio, he planned, could be transformed into a painting school. At the age of twenty-eight, it now seemed that he had success and fortune ahead of him.

But in autumn 1918 Edith Schiele developed the Spanish influenza that was sweeping Europe, and on 28 October she died, in her sixth month of pregnancy. Schiele caught the same disease, and he too died shortly after, on 31 October.

Only a few days later, the doomed Austro-Hungarian monarchy collapsed. Schiele's visions of death had become reality, with a vengeance. His work, however, not only lived on after his death, but was to find worldwide acclaim by the latter decades of the 20th century.

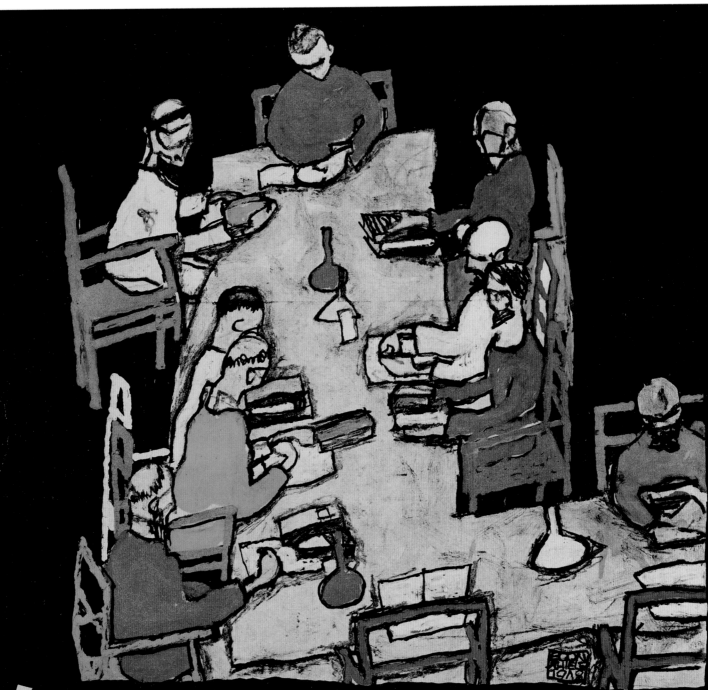

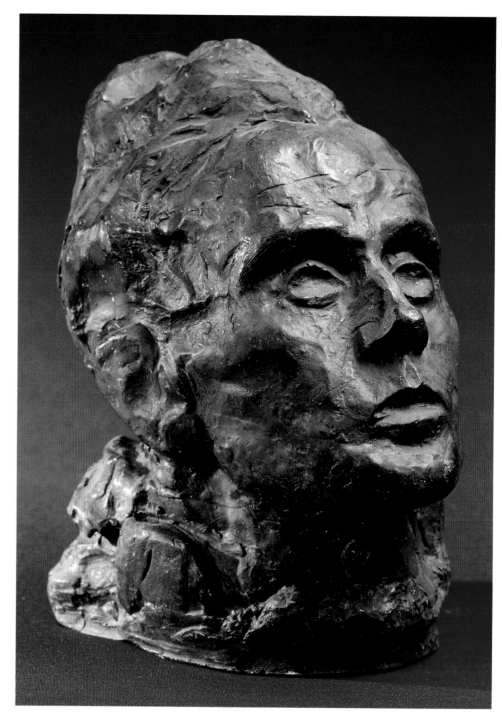

"Dear Mother Schiele," wrote Egon Schiele on 27 October 1918 in his last letter to his mother. "Edith fell ill a week ago yesterday with Spanish influenza and contracted pneumonia on top of it. She is also pregnant, in her sixth month...; I am already preparing for the worst..." Edith died on 28 October; Egon Schiele succumbed to the same illness on 31 October.

Self-Portrait (Bust), 1918
Selbstbildnis (Büste)
Plaster, coloured, height: 28.5 cm
Vienna, Historisches Museum der Stadt Wien

This plaster cast of Schiele's first venture into sculpture was made from a lost clay maquette. Report has it that Schiele did the colouring and working himself.

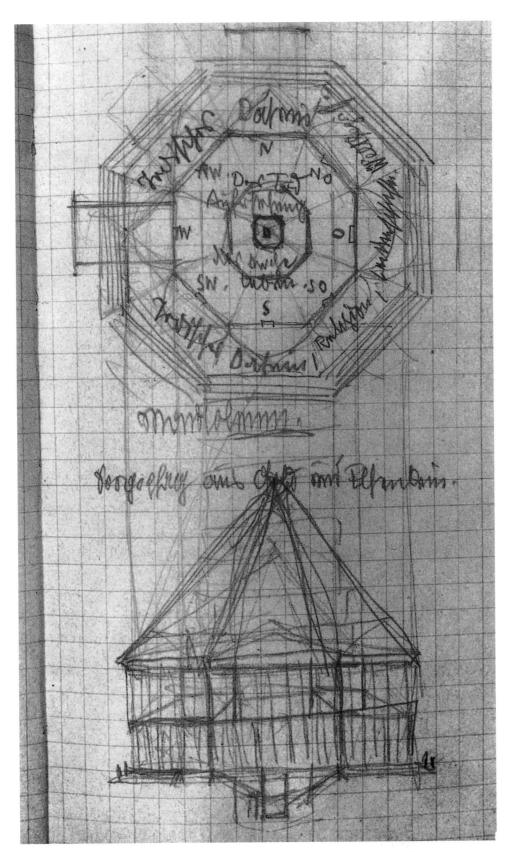

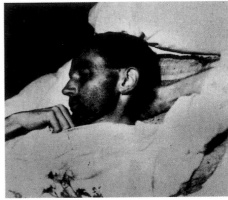

Sketch design of a mausoleum, c. 1918
Entwurf für ein Mausoleum
Pencil on paper
Kallir Sk. 19, p. 31; private collection,
courtesy Galerie St. Etienne, New York

Judging from his diary, Egon Schiele was highly critical of the war. In the last year of his life he planned a mausoleum, a large-scale project for a building in the manner of a temple, decorated with paintings and frescoes.

Schiele on his deathbed, his arm in a stylized pose. Photographer Martha Fein took a number of pictures of the dead Schiele in this unusual posture. He was first buried in the Harms family grave; later he and Edith were reinterred.

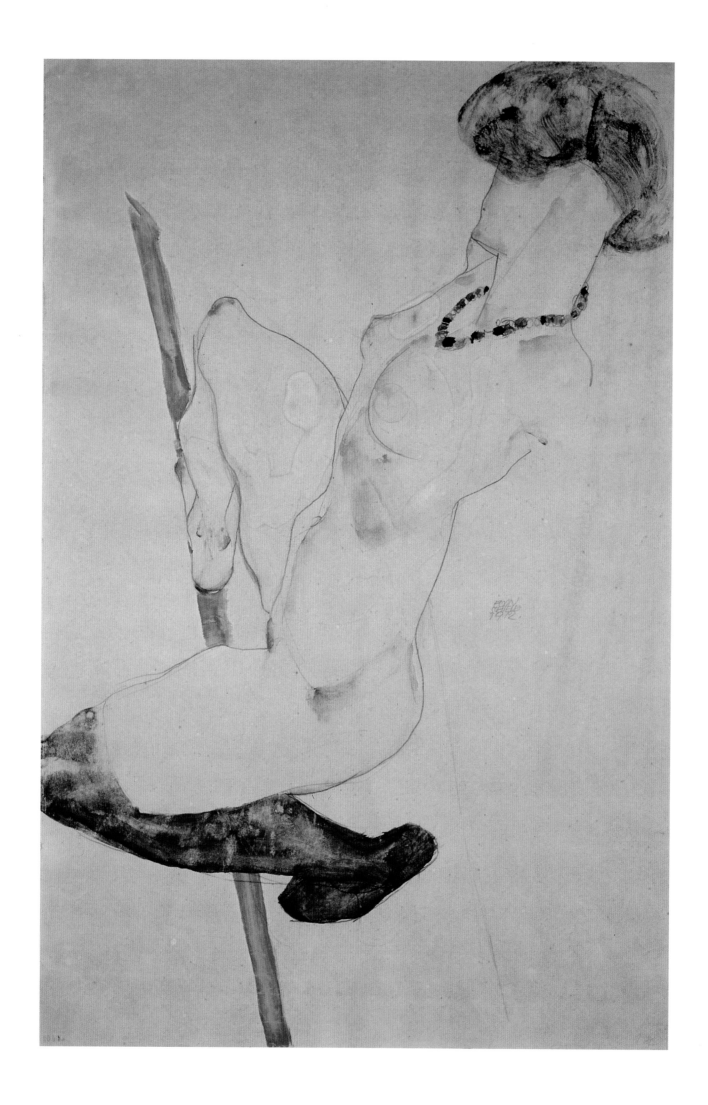

A Bird's-Eye View of the World

Schiele once said that he would like to circle over the city like a bird of prey. And it was from that perspective that he approached the objects of his scrutiny, whether a townscape or a nude model. The object was the victim of Schiele's will: he had to possess it, entire, for himself.

In a sense, Schiele cut his nude models out of their surroundings. Shorn of distracting references to the real, with no indication of available light and shadow, the time of day, or the quality of the air, they serve as vehicles for erotic emotion in the greatest variety of positions, often obscene. The artist was the puppetmaster in an Expressionist *Kama Sutra*, manipulating girls stripped of individuality, their faces often looking carved, with dots for eyes and staring into an undefined distance. The unworked white or brown of the paper served as an empty space, a stage on which things might happen.

Schiele subjected townscapes to his own will in the same way. He transformed architectural shapes and the contours of buildings into an urban being into which he breathed an emotional life of its own, independent of people. People do not appear in his houses, streets and squares. The nature of the city is cloaked in darkness, and the nighttime side of things emerges into the fore – the unsettling quality of windows open without apparent reason, the shutters banging fearfully in a stormy wind, omens of impending menace and danger.

Schiele's living, breathing towns are beings. They are stripped of all incidentals: no passers-by, no children playing, no carriages or horses, no flowerstalls or stray dogs. The towns are themselves the protagonists. There are pointers to times of day or year, hints of historical or topographical coordinates – but reality has been styled into the symbolic.

Schiele combined the internal law of concentration on a single motif – a nude model, group of figures, or town – with the external, formal law of a superior viewpoint, a bird's-eye view. His painter's inquisitiveness seized upon isolated objects as if he were in flight.

It is known that Schiele used a ladder in his studio, and would stand on it in order to obtain the correct, desired angle of view of his model, lying on the floor or a sofa. He would then make his drawing rapidly, setting the lines down in the drawing pad he held balanced. In the case of his townscapes, most of which show the town of Krumau on the river Moldau (Vltava), Schiele took up a vantage point on the hill near the castle, from where he could look down on the Gothic intricacies of rooftops, walls and streets. From above, he could indeed seize hold of the entire world below him with his eye, like a bird of prey.

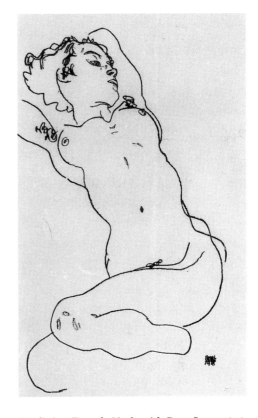

Reclining Female Nude with Bent Legs, 1918
Liegender weiblicher Akt mit angezogenen Beinen
Black crayon, 47.5 x 29.7 cm
Kallir D 2363; Vienna, Graphische Sammlung Albertina

PAGE 46:
Tightrope Walker, 1912
Seiltänzerin
Gouache, watercolour and pencil, 48 x 32 cm
Kallir D 1089; private collection

The skewed angle of vision from above shows the tightrope walker as an armless torso cropped in two places by the picture edge. This unusual angle lends the picture its powerful dynamics.

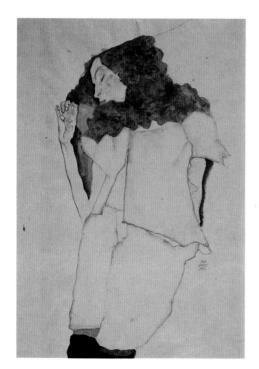

Sleeping Girl (Study of Gerti Schiele), 1911
Schlafendes Mädchen (Studie nach Gerti Schiele)
Watercolour and pencil, 44.5 x 31 cm
Kallir D 866; Vienna, Graphische Sammlung Albertina

Schiele often adopted a bird's-eye perspective, an angle which destabilizes his subjects, as in this portrait of his sister asleep. At first glance we are unsure if she is lying or standing, suspended or reclining.

PAGE 49:
Two Girls on Fringed Blanket, 1911
Zwei Mädchen auf einer Fransendecke
Gouache, watercolour, ink and pencil,
56 x 36.6 cm
Kallir D 849; private collection, courtesy Galerie St. Etienne, New York

Almost abstract, this picture of two girls on a blanket interlocks areas of colour, retaining the faces and legs as highlights in the predominantly brown and green composition. The fringe of tassels provides a rhythmic frame around the two figures.

The key role of the bird's-eye view in Schiele's work had implications for both his form and content. The *Tightrope Walker* (1912; p. 46) makes this particularly clear. We see the diagonal of the tightrope from above, as if from the point of view of another artiste higher up on the metal scaffolding in the big top and watching the girl as she walks the rope. The figure of the naked girl herself resolves into two axes. One runs from her head, in the top right corner, to her stocking-clad foot held suspended in mid-air; her knee is cropped by the picture edge. The other is marked by the right foot, parallel to the rope, with the bent leg above it. The girl's torso is armless, and her face is averted from us. It is a marvellously successful record of a fleeting moment, with a magical unreality that derives from the nakedness of the model and the cropped torso as well as from the colour highlights of her hair, pubic hair, and necklace.

In *Two Girls on Fringed Blanket* (1911; p. 49) we are looking down on two figures lying locked in a lesbian embrace on a brown tasselled blanket. The skirt of the girl seen *en face* has been pulled up to expose black stockings with red garter bands, white thighs, and a red petticoat. The second girl is turned towards the first; she is wrapped almost entirely in a green and brown cloak that has fallen open at the thighs to reveal her sex, in red. The girls' hair, cascading decoratively, defines the centre of the composition, and also bridges the black and brown areas of colour. The girls' clothes are rendered as almost abstract zones, and the shades of black, green, blue, yellow and brown provide a vibrant contrast to the brown background of the blanket – the tasselled fringes of which frame the twosome in a rhythmic manner.

The formal tension is achieved by the polarity between the pale faces and legs, a white with a slight toning of blue, and the dark colours of the clothing, a greenish brown suggestive of decay. The lack of any unambiguous spatial definition is somewhat unsettling; at first glance we are unlikely to be sure whether these girls, with their startled expressions, are standing, sitting or lying. Only on closer inspection do we feel sure that the angle of vision is a slant one from above. Even so: are the two girls really lying, or are they not perhaps hovering on a flying carpet?

If we cover over the economical but intensely rendered pale areas, this world of colours and shapes can in fact be read as abstract. To Schiele's contemporaries it must all have seemed disquietingly unfamiliar. He was casting aside all the conventional rules. The central perspective that had been used ever since the Renaissance to establish the artificial illusion of space; a realistic account of colours and shapes; didactic content, or a regard for social taboos – all of these considerations had become irrelevant in works such as this one.

In *Sleeping Girl (Study of Gerti Schiele)* (1911; p. 48), the contrast of the detailed head, hair and skirt (suggested at the bottom of the sheet) with the areas merely outlined in purple produces a distinctive, trance-like effect. Schiele's sleeping sister Gerti is seen in profile. Her face, with its red lips, is framed by full, lavish curls of chestnut hair.

As so often with Schiele, the colour zones in this study can be seen independent of their function, and are available to free interpretation. It is

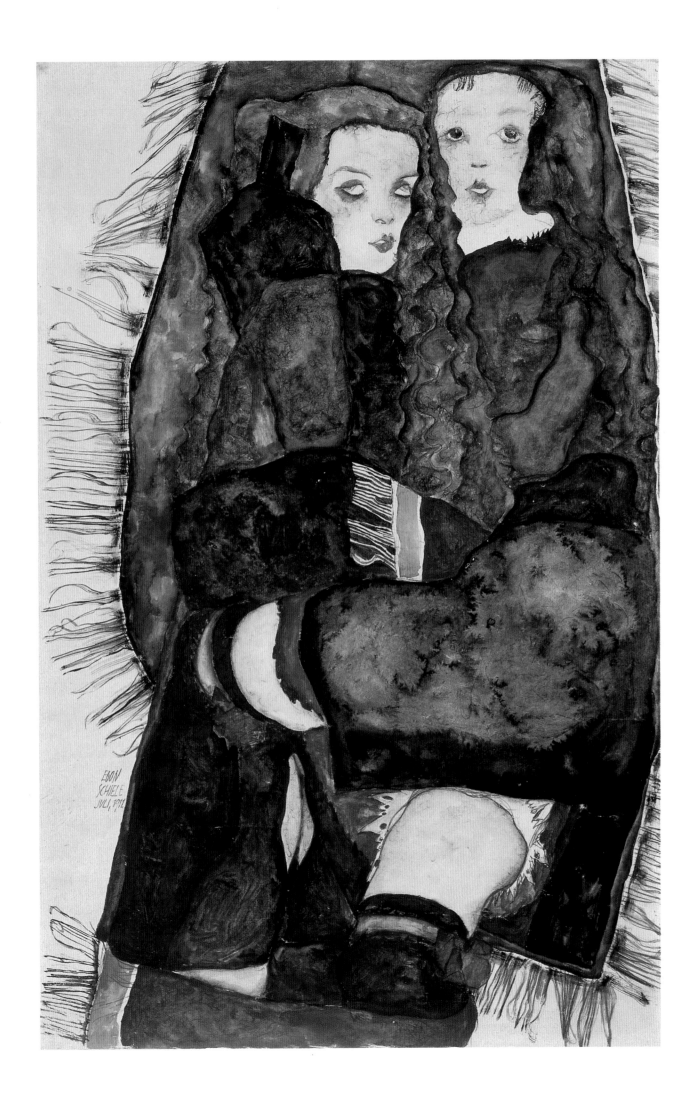

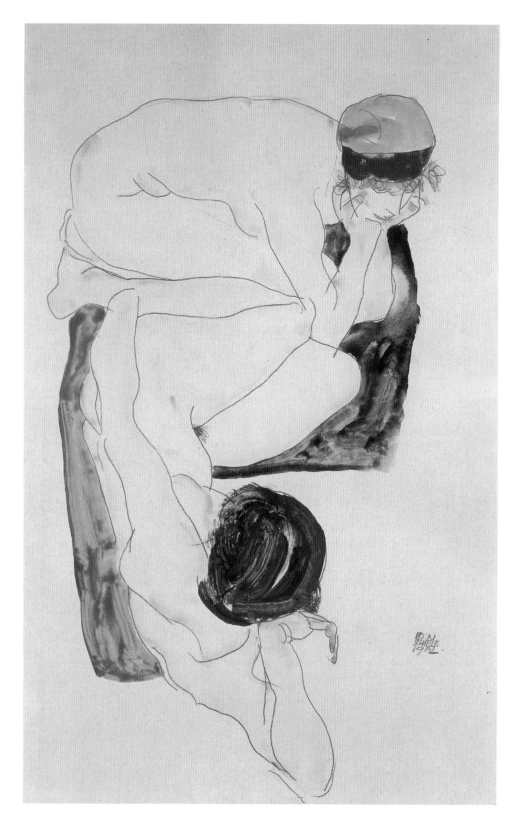

Two Reclining Figures, 1912
Zwei liegende Figuren
Gouache and pencil, 48.3 x 30.5 cm
Kallir D 1114; private collection

The two models are seen from different angles, one from the side and the woman to the fore from above, in a location that remains spatially undefined. The fine, precise brushwork and economic colouring seem to leave them in suspension.

as if we were seeing a fragment of an unreal dream world, as if these were amorphous shapes that might metamorphose at any moment – first resembling a piece of material, then perhaps a lady of the mist, a drape, an architectural detail, or a hazy landscape. For Schiele (and not only for him), sleep, dreams, death, and the spiritual duality of self and alter ego (cf. the oil *The Self-Seers I*, 1910; p. 154), were important symbols. They were key concepts in the work of other contemporaries in Austria too, from the psychoanalytic evaluation of dreams undertaken by Freud to the poetic transformations wrought by the poets and dramatists Hugo von

Hofmannsthal (1874–1929), Arthur Schnitzler (1862–1931) and Georg Trakl (1887–1914).

Did such thinking determine Schiele's use of the purple outlines that set off Gerti's arm, hand and garment, linking them in a second dimension in contradistinction to the realistic part of the figure? Purple is the colour of nightshade, the colour of toxic berries that can be used for sleeping drafts. The sense of suspension is heightened by a spatial ambiguity typical of Schiele: are we in front of a reclining model, or at some higher vantage point, perhaps indeed hovering above her? The brown drawing paper provides all the background we have, devoid of pointers to real circumstances – a reminder that Schiele deliberately avoided unambiguous definition of this order. His title *The Self-Seers I*, used elsewhere for a self-portrait, might readily be adapted to this sheet – Gerti as self-seer. She is dreaming herself (or about herself) as a purple-framed but deliberately undefined space.

If we are looking for a vivid incarnation of the Lolita syndrome, there can be little to match the *Reclining Semi-Nude* (1911) for excitement – a sheet that is shameless in the truest sense. With a skirt striped in red, blue and orange outspread around her, a young girl is presenting her apple-round derrière at the centre of the composition, the cleft of her vagina marked in red. The rosette of her skirt is like the calyx of a flower, framing her newly awakened sense of sexuality. The photos of young girls with which writer Peter Altenberg adorned his wretched room at the Hotel Graben are a mere shadow to this, a thing of faded sepia: Schiele's colours are juxtaposed vividly and decoratively. The moss green of the surface on which she is reclining (a sofa, an armchair?) offsets the patchy colourfulness of her patterned blouse. Again, Schiele eliminates any spatial definition. The girl's body is fragmentary too, the legs being done only as far as the knees, for instance – a trick Schiele used time and again to establish the impression of a fleeting glimpse, caught in suspension, unfinished, sketchy. Here, this fleeting quality stands for emotions, too.

The *Three Girls* (1911; p.53) are gazing with a doll-like, frozen expression that is just as enigmatic. It is possible that this sheet shows one single girl in various states of undress, semi-clad or, as in the central figure, almost totally exposed. The green piece of paper covering the genitals was added later by another hand. The most agitated of the three is the girl on the left, with her arms upraised and partly concealed beneath her hair, and her legs, also bare, bent to the right. This girl's skimpy dress, a mere suggestion of watercolour, covers only her breast and belly; it is as if she were just getting out of her clothing, offering her legs, as high as the waist, to our inspection. The girl in the middle, her eyes almost closed, has raised her clothing so high that it almost reveals her breasts.

In this composition once again, the spatial location is undefined. Are the girls lying on the floor? Or on a sofa? Or are the two on the right standing, while the girl on the left is reclining? Schiele gives us no clear information. As in a dream, a number of asynchronous states may possibly be visible simultaneously. The depersonalized bodies of the girls become a tenuous single entity as we look at them, like a jigsaw assembled from the scraps of dreams – tantalizing but unreal.

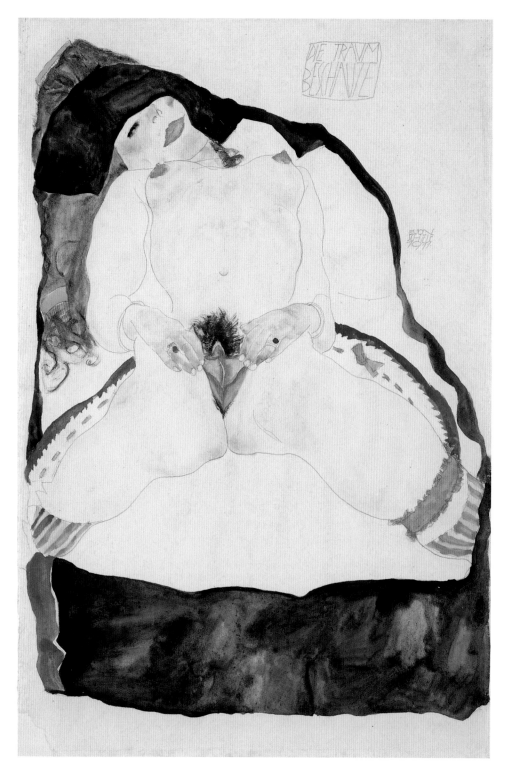

The restlessness in the presentation of the *Two Reclining Figures* (1912; p. 50), and their appeal, derive from the different points of view the artist has used in this gouache drawing. The two nudes are seen from two conflicting perspectives – the woman with the blue headband from the side, her head in three-quarter profile, the other woman from above and behind, allowing us to see her hair, not her face. The two are linked formally by the mat, on which the woman with the headband is kneeling while the angled legs of the other lie on it. The compositional sense of balance is thrown by these two conflicting perspectives; the kneeling nude occupies the topmost third of the picture, while the other, reclining

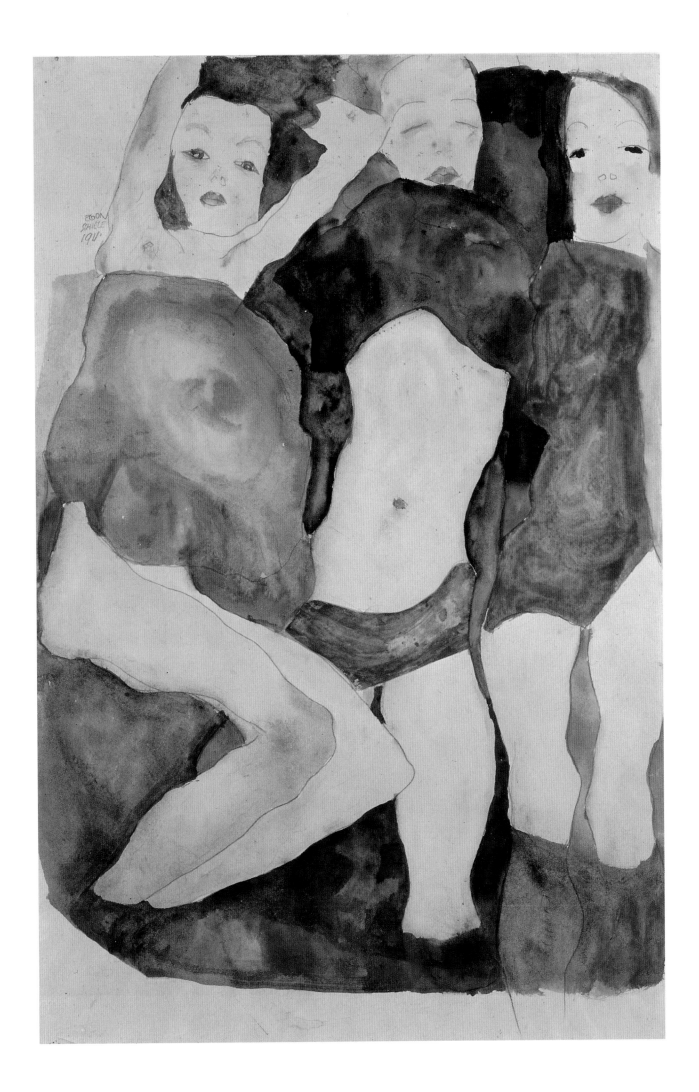

across the remaining two thirds, seems to be slipping down, towards us. Again, as so often in Schiele, it is possible to interpret the picture as showing not two women but one woman viewed from different angles and in different positions. Not that this in any way diminishes the force of the gouache's ludic engagement with the vagaries of the real.

In *Intertwined Nudes (Embrace)* (1912) too, the drama of the formal presentation derives from the conflicting perspectives in which the male and female nudes are presented – the man, a torso with a bush of black hair, frontally, the woman from the side but with her face turned directly to us, and her eyes closed. It is as if the man were rising from the depths, while the woman is on a higher level, closer to us as we view the picture. Both figures are fragmented, without hands, their bodies completed only to the knees. The combination of side and superior viewpoints, and the torso rendering of the figures, produce a certain mannerism in the pose, one distinct from the anatomical mannerism of Amedeo Modigliani or Ernst Ludwig Kirchner, who established new aesthetic values by elongating their figures. Schiele offers unusual perspectives, plays games with movements, and, with a deliberately antithetical sense of stagecraft, places his figural groups on the plain, colourless backgrounds of empty sheets.

In prison at Neulengbach, Schiele drew the things that were available: the cell door, an orange on the blanket, the ante-room, chairs, a water pitcher. In *Organic Movement of Chair and Pitcher* (1912; p. 30), the two

Wally in Red Blouse with Raised Knees, 1913
Wally in roter Bluse mit erhobenen Knien
Gouache, watercolour and pencil, 31.8 x 48cm
Kallir D 1335; private collection

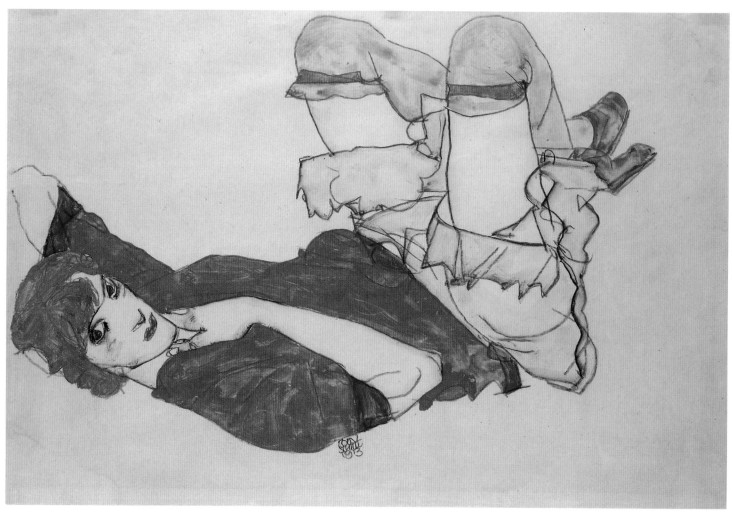

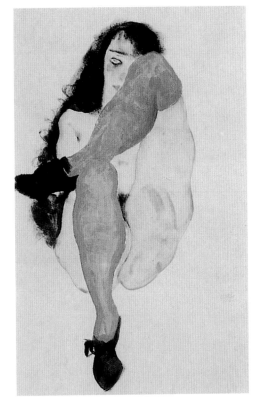

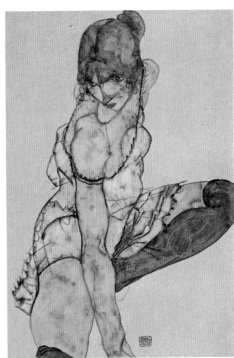

Female Nude in Green Stockings, 1912
Weiblicher Akt in grünen Strümpfen
Gouache, watercolour and pencil, 48.2 x 31.8 cm
Private collection

RIGHT:
Blonde Girl in Green Stockings, 1914
Blondes Mädchen mit grünen Strümpfen
Watercolour and pencil, 48.1 x 32.3 cm
Kallir D 1533; whereabouts unknown

objects seem to be suspended in mid-air. But, as with the graphics of
M. C. Escher, we are free to interpret the background supplied by the
bare sheet as the floor of the cell, with an upturned chair and a pitcher on
it. In that case, consistently enough, the chair would be seen from a superior vantage point and the pitcher from the side – so establishing Schiele's recurrent visual confusion.

Does the adjective "organic" in the title have an exact meaning, or is it
mere wordplay? Does Schiele mean "natural" – in which case the artist
would be able to set the chair and pitcher in motion, using his visual
magic wand? The visual conundrums can be given a further twist if we
turn the sheet to portrait format (as Roessler originally reproduced it).
What is of the essence is the magic, the *Transfiguration* – to borrow the
term from a work of 1915–16 (subtitled *The Blind II*). Realistic representation of ordinary objects and people, drawn accurately to scale, is transformed by stylistic means into unreal dream imagery. Schiele parted company with central perspective, which had presented objects and people in
a mimetic, illusory space that spoke of this world and of experience in it;
Schiele was interested in other, sophisticated visual options. In combining frontal and bird's-eye views, the suspension of objects, isolation of
outline, and bare, unmarked backgrounds, Schiele was not only express-
ing the nervous tension and restlessness of the age but was also articulating his own ravelled psychological condition whilst in custody. His hallu-
cinatory vision of things was the expression of a prisoner's worn emotional state.

The same applies to another of the prison watercolours, *Remembrance
of the Green Socks* (1912). In it, a chair has been subjected to Schiele's
visual sorcery; over its back hang the green socks of the title. The drawing *Seated Woman from Above* (1914), despite its radical point of station
(we can imagine Schiele leaning out of the window to look down on the

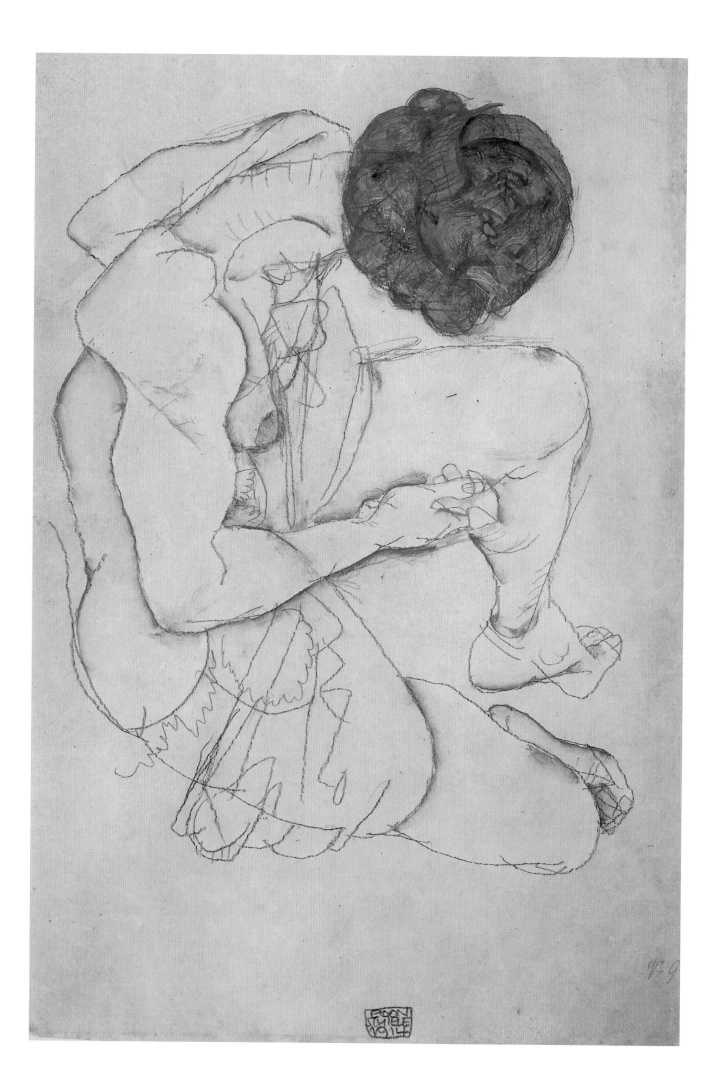

resting girl and draw), almost has the naive appeal of a German Romantic drawing, though only in formal terms. The folded-back skirt, exposing the pubic region, is altogether from the Schiele repertoire, a feature that makes the break from the 19th to the 20th century all the clearer.

Lesbian couples, seen embracing as in the gouaches *Two Women, Embracing* (1914) or *Two Girls (Lovers)* (1914; p.58), are all the more vividly present by virtue of the superior perspective. It is as if the artist, like a reporter bent on exposing every intimate detail, were revealing everything to us – the animal clutch of these embraces, the simplification of movement to the erotic, the facial features remaining wholly unseen in *Two Women, Embracing*. In this gouache, the women are face down; the woman on top is pressing her lover to the floor, and their desire, intensified by this sheer pressure, is heightened still further by the arm gestures, at once reaching out and enfolding.

One of Schiele's finest gouaches, *Two Girls, Lying Entwined* (1915; p.97), affords an example of Schiele's new way of seeing at its purest. The two delirious nudes seem spatially suspended. Schiele combines side and superior views, contrasts the clothed and naked bodies, uses the picture edge for radical cropping, and enlists a traditional repertoire of erotic accessories (garters, black stockings, high-heeled shoes). The impact of the whole is enforced by the baroque sense of movement and the unifying effect of the bright yellow dress. At the same time, the girls' faces frozen with intensity, their unfocused gazes, and the clawed left hand of the nude, suggest that they are at climax. The rigid doll-like appearance of the clothed figure, and the lurid red highlights of the lips and nipples, further heighten this allegory of sexual ecstasy.

Schiele additionally found new means of presentation by combining superior viewpoints with kinds of movement that could be variously interpreted, as in the drawing *Bending Nude Girl with Loosened Hair* (1917) or the gouache *Falling Woman* (1917). Are these nudes kneeling, arms upraised, about to fall out of the picture? Or are we seeing a record of a fleeting moment, as in some circus snapshot of an acrobat on the trapeze? Schiele's images are not acts of realism; rather, the movements he presents are symbolic movement fantasies, just as his erotic nudes and couples articulate sexual fantasies.

In the gouache *Man and Woman* (1917), the motif of the embrace has become symbolic. The faces of the lovers can barely be seen; the girl's head is viewed from above, while the male nude, with his back to us, is seen from below right. The tension again derives from the combination of different perspectives, from cropping at the picture edge, and from the absence of any clear spatial definition. The nudes, robbed of individual personality, have become an allegory of the loving embrace.

The bird's-eye view from a superior vantage point was the most significant artistic resource in Schiele's new approach to townscapes, too. By preference he took his motifs from Krumau, his mother's birthplace near the Austrian border. It was there that he spent the summer of 1911 with Wally – till the conservative townsfolk drove them out. It was there too that he imagined himself circling above the town like a bird of prey. It is the crooked houses and Gothic church spires of Krumau, its walls curving to the bend of the Vltava, its steep rooftops, that Schiele adapted for

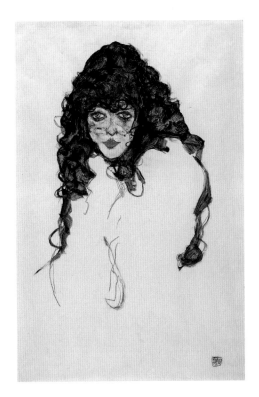

Woman with Black Hair, 1914
Frau mit schwarzem Haar
Gouache, watercolour and pencil, 48.2 x 31.6 cm
Munich, Staatliche Graphische Sammlung

PAGE 56:
Seated Female Nude, 1914
Sitzender Frauenakt
Gouache and pencil, 46.4 x 31.7 cm
Kallir D 1532; private collection

The angle and presentation establish intimacy, as if the nude were being seen by a lover bending to look at her shoulder. But the foreshortening and the economy of outline nonetheless have a distancing effect.

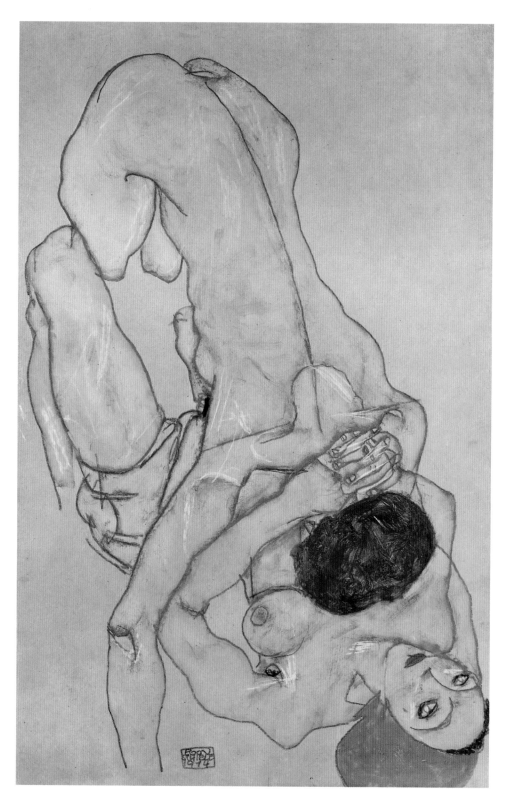

Two Girls (Lovers), 1914
Zwei Mädchen (Liebendes Paar)
Gouache and pencil, 31 x 48cm
Kallir D 1610; private collection

Like Gustav Klimt, who also made erotic drawings of high quality, Schiele liked to draw lesbian couples. Here, the ecstatic movements determine the structure; the faces are either invisible
or puppet-like.

the fantasy town we see in such pictures as *The Small City I (Dead City
VI)* (1912; p. 186), *City on the Blue River II* (1911; p. 62) and *City on the
Blue River I (Dead City I)* (1910). Schiele would take up a position near
the castle on the hill across the river, from where he commanded his
desired bird's-eye view of the town.

In *Krumau Town Crescent I (The Small City V)* (1915/16; p. 182) we
seem to be flying low over the rooftops of the town. Schiele gives us the
courtyards and narrow crooked streets from above; like the old houses
themselves, he follows the course of the Vltava, including the wooden
bridge. He even registers the laundry flapping in the breeze. The win-

PAGE 59:
Two Girls Embracing (Two Friends), 1915
Zwei Mädchen, einander umarmend
Gouache, watercolour and pencil, 48 x 32.7cm
Kallir D 1742; Budapest, Szépmüvészeti
Múzeum

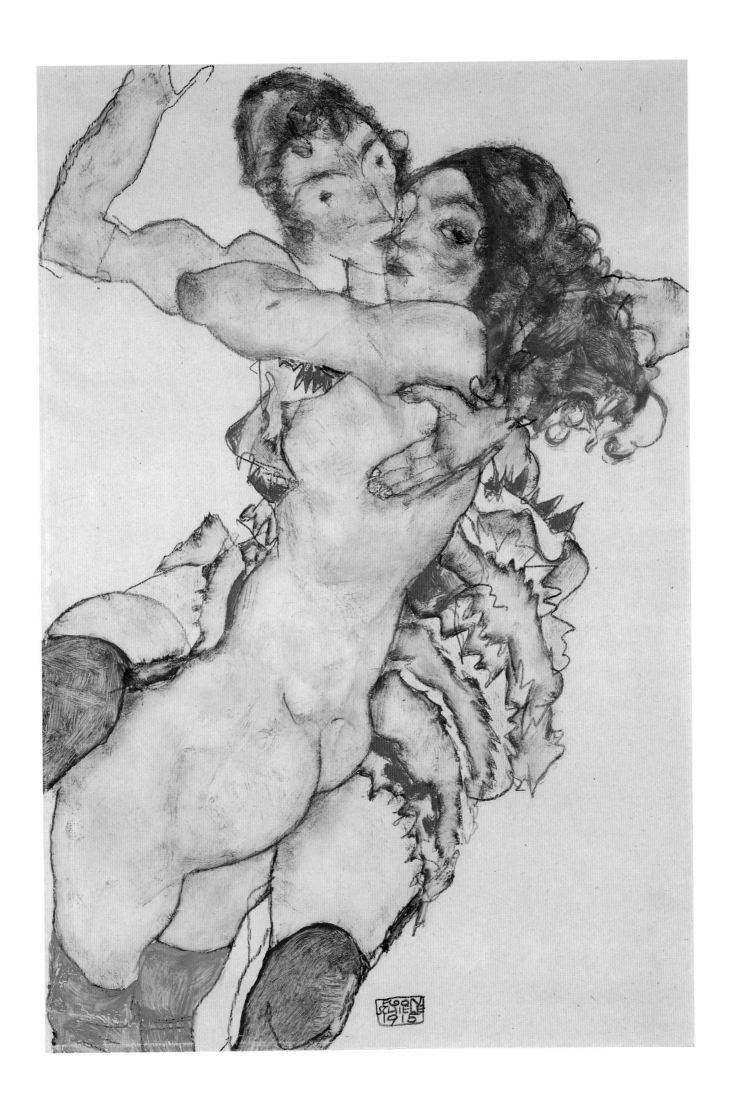

dows of the houses to the fore are open, those to the rear are mainly closed. Not a soul is in sight. Despite the colourful washing on the lines, the town seems deserted. The town itself, however, seems possessed of a secret life of its own. It is as if the very walls were breathing. The closed windows seem to be looking at us, while the open windows are like an alarm signal – warning of fire, storm, war or other disaster? The yellow walls gleam as if illuminated by Bengal lights, and the red chimneys, drains and skylights introduce a note of disquiet. The grubby brown of the rooftops is like a burden upon the houses; the colours present in the laundry are not strong enough to disarm the sensation of danger and menace. It is the toytown of a mute, precocious, anxiety-ridden child.

In the small *City on the Blue River II* (p.62), the river occupies a substantial area of the panel. From the top left to bottom right, the blackish blue of the water takes up a good third of the picture. The houses look as if they are venturing forward on a peninsula; they can even be seen as buildings on a floating island. It is an enchanted and mysterious town, and rightly bears that symbolically-laden adjective so beloved of the German Romantics, "blue". Again the townspeople are conspicuous by their absence, making the independent life of the town itself all the more palpable. As the crystallization point of emotions, the town dissolves into the waters; with a new wave of his emotional magic wand, Schiele confers a whole new meaning upon this being, the town.

In *Dead City III (City on the Blue River III)* (1911; p.63), the town has moved further forward, to the lower edge of the painting. The high, dark roofs and black walls exert a constrictive, oppressive force on the pale walls. In this picture the water surrounds the island of the town on three sides, and precludes any view of the horizon. Schiele shows us a dead town, seemingly on the brink of submerging beneath the waters, as in the Flood. The steep roofs of this ghost town, and the walls with their embrasure-like windows, have become a vision of doom. The town is the image of a dying epoch, a symbol of decay, decline and death. Those who are

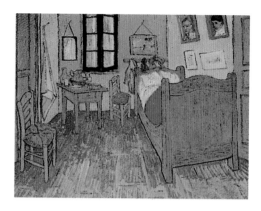

Vincent van Gogh
The Artist's Bedroom at Arles, 1889
Oil on canvas, 57.5 x 74cm
Paris, Musée d'Orsay

Schiele saw this picture at the International Art Show in Vienna in 1908. In 1911 he painted his own room at Neulengbach. While van Gogh's composition is still recognizably a room, Schiele's consists of blocks of colour that almost add up to an abstract pattern.

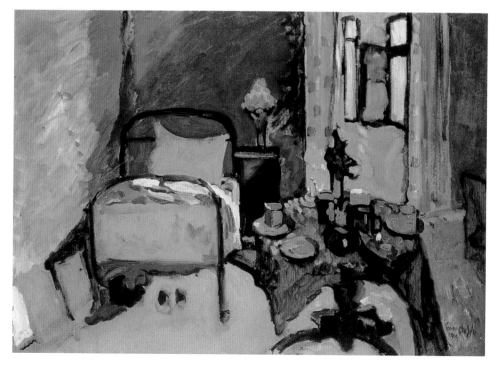

Wassily Kandinsky
Bedroom in Ainmillerstrasse, 1909
Schlafzimmer in der Ainmillerstraße
Oil on card, 48.5 x 69.5cm
Munich, Städtische Galerie im Lenbachhaus

PAGE 61:
**The Artist's Room in Neulengbach
(My Living Room)**, 1911
Das Zimmer des Künstlers in Neulengbach
Oil on wood, 40 x 31.7cm
Kallir P 220; Vienna, Historisches Museum der Stadt Wien

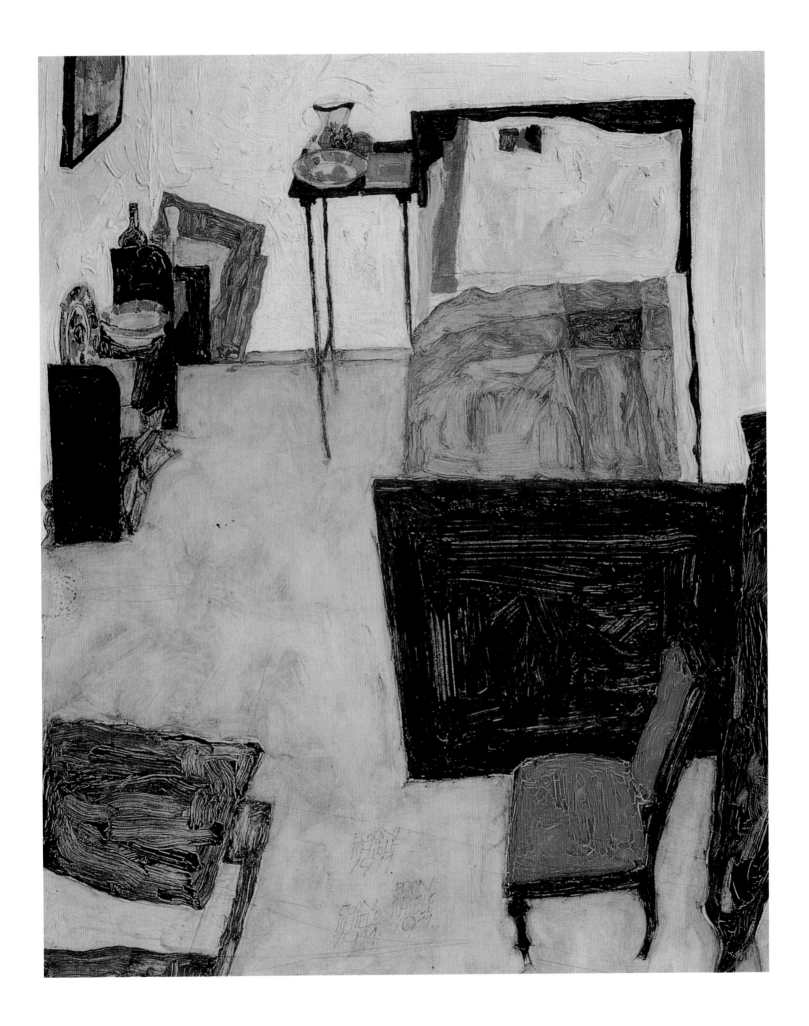

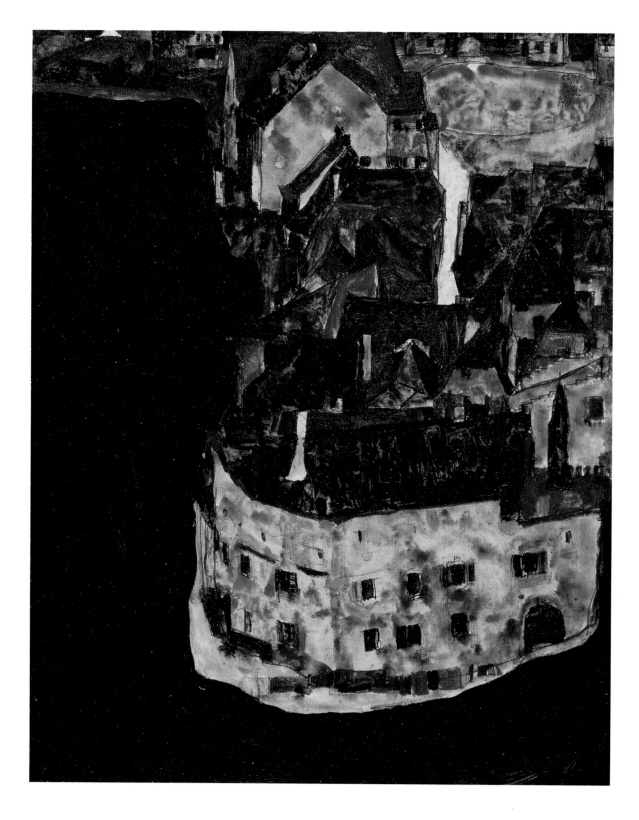

City on the Blue River II, 1911
Stadt am blauen Fluß II
Oil and gouache on wood, 37.2 x 29.8 cm
Kallir P 212; private collection

Egon Schiele wanted to circle above the city like a bird of prey. Krumau in
southern Bohemia was frequently his subject for townscapes. *City on
the Blue River II* shows an urban entity enclosed by water on two sides and
animated solely by colour.

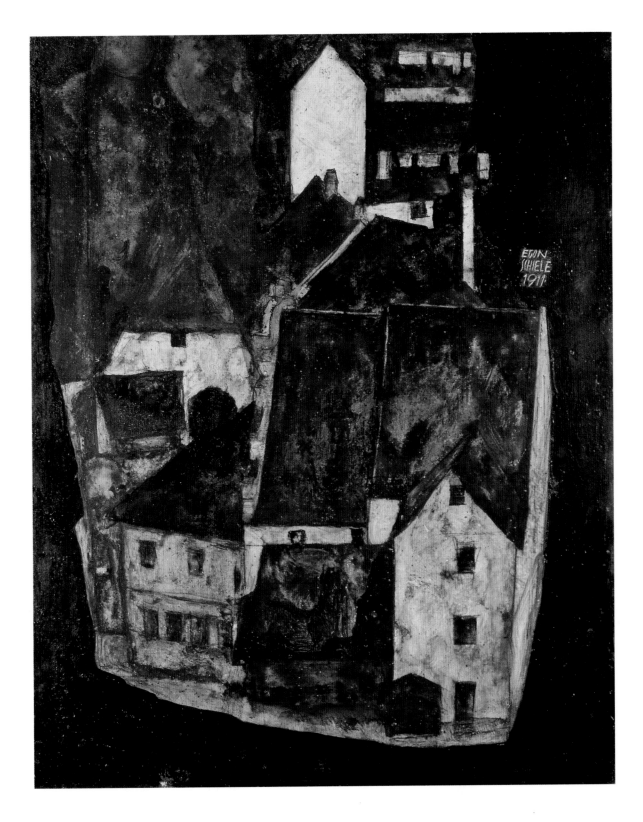

Dead City III (City on the Blue River III), 1911
Tote Stadt III (Stadt am blauen Fluß III)
Oil and gouache on wood, 37.1 x 29.9 cm
Kallir P 213; Vienna, Sammlung Rudolf Leopold

Schiele called a number of his townscapes *Dead City*. In this one, the houses
are surrounded by dark water as if menaced by a new Flood and condemned
to die. The city seems deserted. The only evidence of inhabitation is the
laundry out to dry.

familiar with Austrian literature will recall that it was not very far from the Krumau region that the 19th-century writer Adalbert Stifter lived, whose emphasis was on the harmonic life made possible by a "gentle law"; and from that idea to Schiele's universe it is as vast a step as from Stifter's conception of Nature as the source of all happiness to the solitary desolation of a Franz Kafka.

The small oil *The Artist's Room in Neulengbach* (1911; p.61) suggests eloquently how different an artist's sense of existence had become in the years since van Gogh's *The Artist's Bedroom at Arles* (1889; p.60). The van Gogh was owned in Schiele's day by his own patron, Carl Reininghaus, and Schiele doubtless saw and studied it. Van Gogh gave an arresting account of the poor, cramped accommodation he lived in, but his perspective nevertheless has the effect of emphasizing that it affords shelter and protection. In the Schiele, space has a quite different significance. He has abandoned perspective. The floor and walls are neutral zones of colour occupying most of the picture and serving as a ground for the furniture and other items. The elevated viewpoint permits us (as in the pictures of people and towns that we have already discussed) to cast a brief glance from above, retaining our distance. We see everything but do not feel part of the scene.

The nocturnal aspect of things is once again the dominant feature of *City in Twilight (The Small City II)* (1913). In this painting, Schiele deploys individual Krumau motifs together with buildings of his own invention. The river takes up the lower third of the picture, and the street that divides two blocks of houses meets it at a right angle. The familiar bird's-eye view defamiliarizes this building-block town more than ever. The dim light of dusk somewhat mutes the visionary element, but the impression of dreamy unreality remains, established not least by the dimensions of this toytown, where things do not seem quite right.

Even more curiously defamiliarized is *The Small City III* (1912/13; p.65). The river occupies the lower third of the canvas; and an arm of the river repeats the water motif in the topmost third, spanned by a bridge at top left that links the two banks. In the rows of houses, rank upon rank, open and closed windows alternate irregularly. The effect is to lend the painting a distinctive musical rhythm.

There is an even greater severity in Schiele's ranks of recurring architectural details in *Façade of a House (Windows)* (1914; p.67). The windows are set at uneven distances from each other; they are distinguished in terms of form and colour; and their solemn rhythm contrasts with the lighter, brighter, tauter rhythmic structure of the roof tiles. It is a unique example of the power of the artist to transform three simple motifs – façade, windows and tiles – into an exacting graphic composition of an almost abstract quality. This rhythmic rendering of a façade might be seen, in terms of the synaesthetic relations of art and music, as a homage to both Igor Stravinsky and Wassily Kandinsky.

Schiele's use of high viewpoints, fragmented motifs, the simultaneous presentation of non-simultaneous states, the depersonalization of motifs, and the effect of the empty ground created impressions of disquiet, of an unfinished state, of distance in the viewer, and of deliberate remoteness from the real. It also heightened the allegorical and symbolic impact of

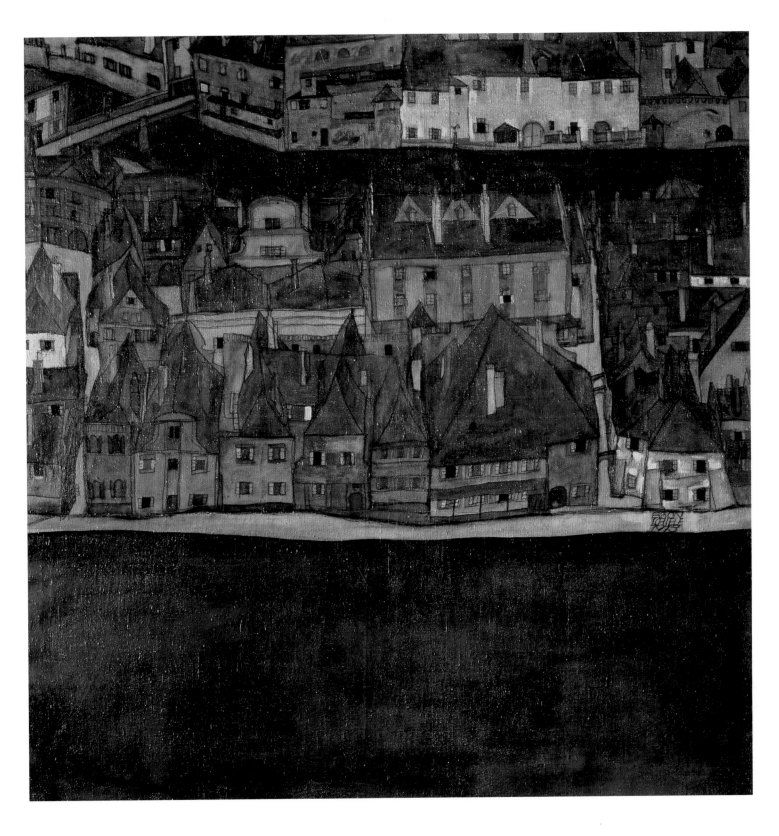

The Small City III, 1912/13
Die kleine Stadt III
Oil on canvas, 98.5 x 90.5 cm
Kallir P 261; Vienna, private collection

Here, the façades are bright – but the dark water enforces the mood of menace
nonetheless, and the opened windows reveal nothing but blackness.

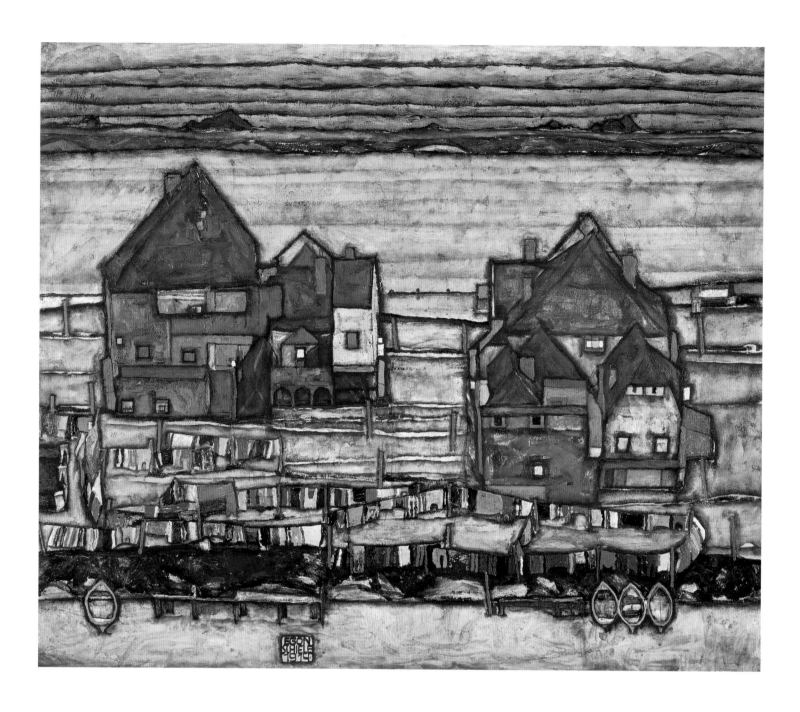

Houses with Laundry (Suburb II), 1914
Häuser mit Wäsche (Vorstadt II)
Oil on canvas, 100.5 x 120.5 cm
Kallir P 283; Vienna, Sammlung Rudolf Leopold

his work. His use of light – dusk or nighttime light in his townscapes, for example, and elsewhere the shadowless brightness of studio scenes with no apparent light source – intensified the symbolic implication of fear, of being exposed.

In contrast to the luridly lit nudes are Schiele's dark townscapes, "views of old German towns with their countless rooftops, as if from some sad picture book, some desolate, melancholy box of tricks" as the critic M. R. put it in the *Illustriertes Wiener Extrablatt* (Vienna Illustrated Extra) of 11 March 1918.

Above his motifs circled the bird of prey that Schiele identified with, and which became one with the painter's eye. What that eye saw, as it circled above, was so new a vision of the world that the likes of Professor Griepenkerl, and the world he lived in, would necessarily be profoundly shocked. Even so, it was the visual world of the rebellious student that endured, whereas Griepenkerl's did not – because Schiele's visionary view, as he himself put it, "pointed forward to what was to come".

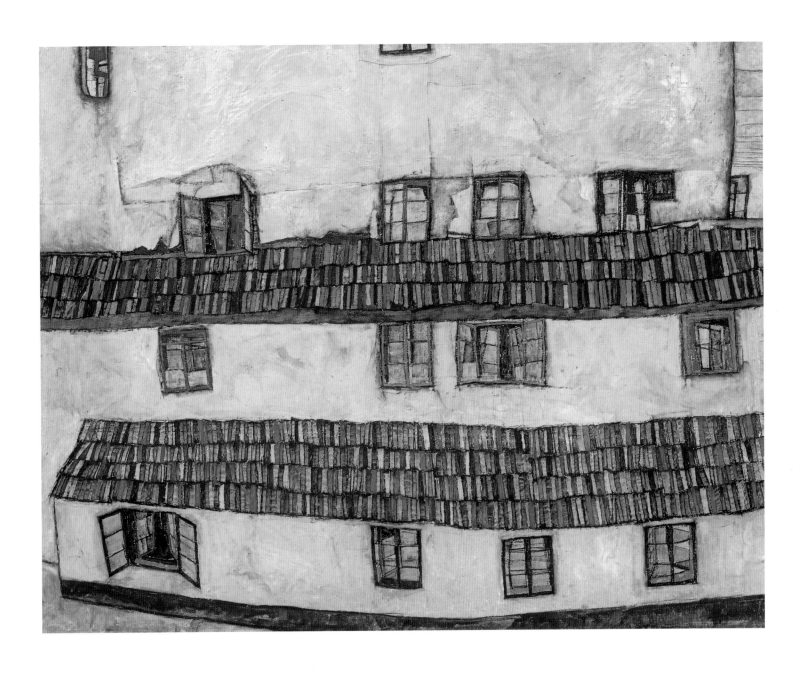

Façade of a House (Windows), 1914
Hauswand (Fenster)
Oil and gouache, 110 x 140 cm
Kallir P 284; Vienna, Österreichische Galerie.
Belvedere

In *Façade of a House (Windows)* Egon Schiele takes the strict graphic structuring
of his canvas to its extreme. The windows and frames, walls and tiles
provide the artist with an occasion for rhythmic juxtaposition
of lines and flat spaces.

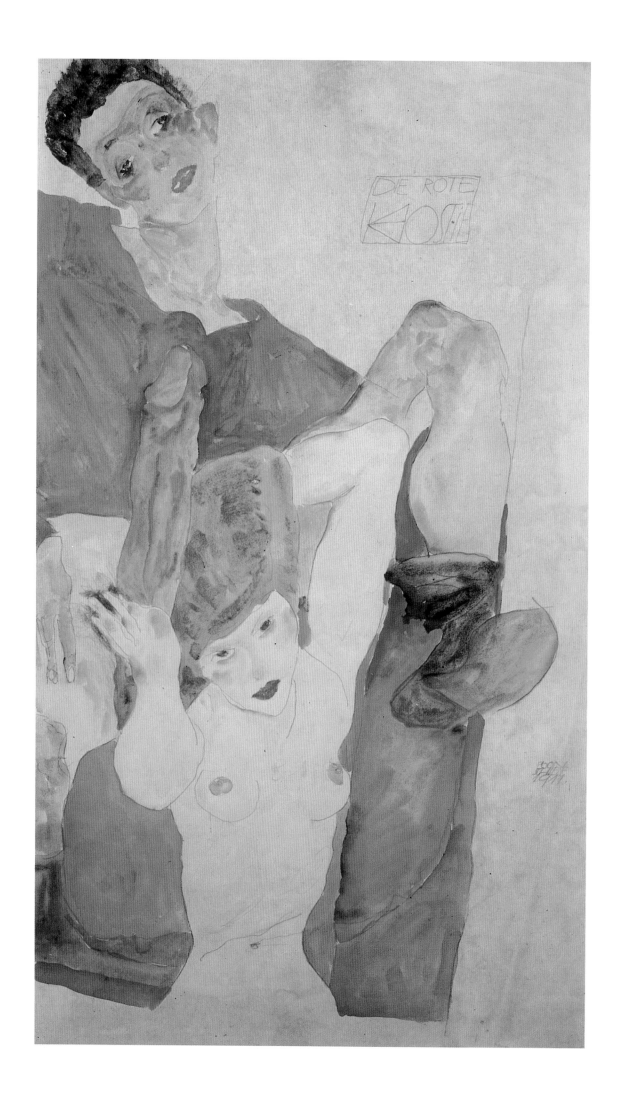

From Girl Child to *Grande Dame*

Schiele's earliest portraits of women were still conceived wholly in the spirit of the late 19th century, be it in the manner of Henri de Toulouse-Lautrec or the early Klimt. In the *Portrait of Bertha von Wiktorin* (1907; p.69) we see a young woman in profile, her hair pinned up. Her eyes are almost closed, and at the left corner of her mouth a cigarette is burning – an unusual and daring motif in a picture of a woman at the time. The portrait is done in the style of late Impressionism, and we might pardonably think it a detail from a Lautrec figure composition.

In form and content, Schiele's *Danae* (1909; p.70) is a homage to Klimt, who had painted the subject the previous year. Schiele's nude, well-lit and bending forward, is done in flowing, spatially generous form and presented in front of a background of decorative vegetation that spreads across the centre of the picture, its coiling tendrils framing the woman.

In the portrait of his sister Gerti, known as *Portrait of a Woman with Black Hat (Gertrude Schiele)* (1909), the influence of Klimt is still apparent, though new departures in style are in evidence too. The heavily decorative dress, the wavily silhouetted outline of the coat and hat, and the use of planar areas, are elements borrowed from the Klimt repertoire; but the expressiveness of the hands already indicates the path that Schiele will take away from Klimt.

The following year marked the change. The *Portrait of Poldi Lodzinsky* (1910; p.72) bears characteristic features that clearly point forward to Schiele's later, inimitable Expressionist style: the enlarged and coarsened hands, the mask-like ugliness of the face, sharply contrasted areas of colour in the clothing, and the vertical format, well-suited to ornamental treatment of spaces, in marked opposition to the expressive qualities of the figure.

Schiele's new departure is even more clearly apparent in other drawings, watercolours and gouaches done in that same year. In the gouache *Proletarian Girl in Black* (1910) the expressive features of style are intensified by the enlargement of the head, the skeletal presentation of the legs, and the jagged, nervous outline. This girl is a rickety creature with no claim to beauty, but Schiele's account of her nonetheless has real emotional force.

In the gouache *Reclining Girl in Dark Blue Dress* (1910; p.73), crude sexuality arrives in Schiele's art as a new form of expression. The girl has hauled her skirt up to reveal her carmine privates, high-

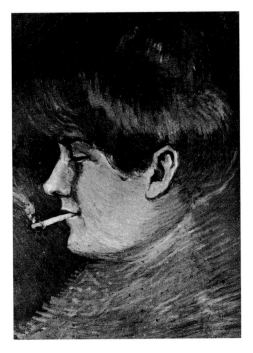

Portrait of Bertha von Wiktorin, 1907
Bildnis Bertha von Wiktorin
Oil on card, 40 x 30.8 cm
Kallir P 9; private collection, courtesy Galerie
St. Etienne, New York

Provocation was important in Schiele's early work. He was in revolt against uncomprehending members of the family and teachers. This portrait defies convention in showing a woman smoking, a highly unusual motif for the day.

PAGE 68:
The Red Host, 1911
Die rote Hostie
Watercolour and pencil, 48.2 x 28.2 cm
Kallir D 972; private collection, courtesy Galerie
St. Etienne, New York

In this watercolour Schiele carries provocation to its extreme. Not only was the subject daring, but he added a title taken from the everyday life of the church. It belongs to Schiele's series of ecstatic and unsparing self-portraits.

Danae, 1909
Pencil and white crayon, 30.6 x 44.3cm
Kallir D 298; Vienna, Graphische Sammlung
Albertina

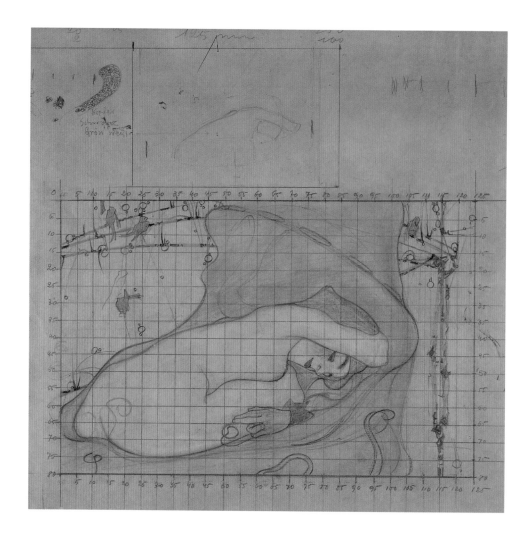

lighted in white, to our voyeuristic gaze. It is impossible to defend this picture against the charge of pornography. Even so, Schiele's radicalism of form places him beyond too simplistic a categorisation. He was not merely out to satisfy a shallow voyeurist impulse. Pubescent lust and delight in discovery, the naive symbolism of distinguishing sexual features, and boyish stratagems for looking up girls' skirts are combined in the twenty-year-old artist's way of viewing the world with the invention of ingenious new forms, which took the Schiele of 1910 a step forward, out of the world of teachers and uncles and into the radical world view of the Expressionist avant-garde. In the years ahead, Schiele pursued this distinctive combination obsessively. His unsparing passion was not only brought to bear on female nudes, though; his scrutiny of male nudes, and particularly of his own body, recorded in countless drawings, gouaches and watercolours, was equally unremitting. "The erotic work of art is sacred too", he wrote in 1911 to his uncomprehending uncle.[6]

In *Seated Nude Girl* (1910; p.78) the Expressionist insistence on realistic presentation, even if it involves the unbeautiful, is particularly apparent. The girl, staring warily out at us, has all the fearful, chilled rigour of a patient awaiting medical examination. Her shoulder, elbows and knees are angular, her hair uncombed, her head and body bony. It is a wretched, emaciated body that recalls the work of Edvard Munch and looks forward to that of Käthe Kollwitz; and it shows Schiele already at a great distance from the hedonistic middle-class world of Klimt.

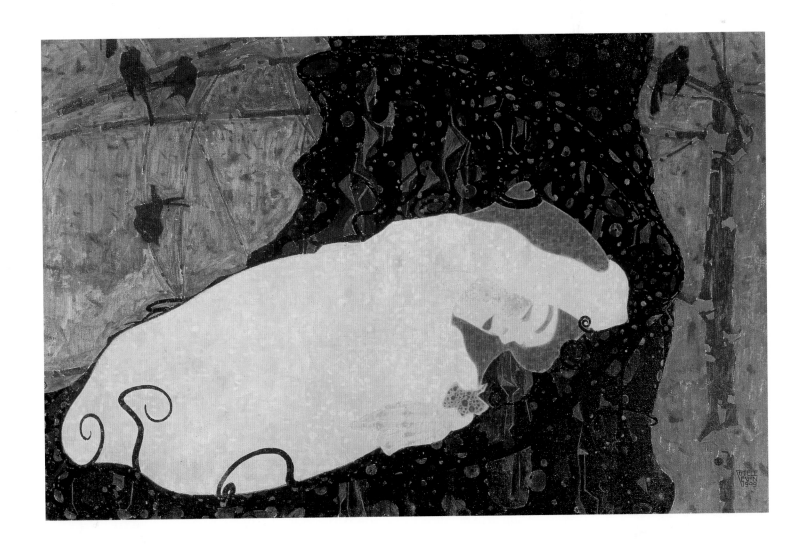

Danae, 1909
Oil and metallic paint, 80.6 x 125.4 cm
Kallir P 148; private collection

In early pictures of women, Schiele tended to take his bearings from Gustav Klimt, as in this mythological *Danae*, in which he abides closely by the manner of Art Nouveau, with its decorative arabesques. Like Klimt's *Danae*, Schiele's is a creature of ornament.

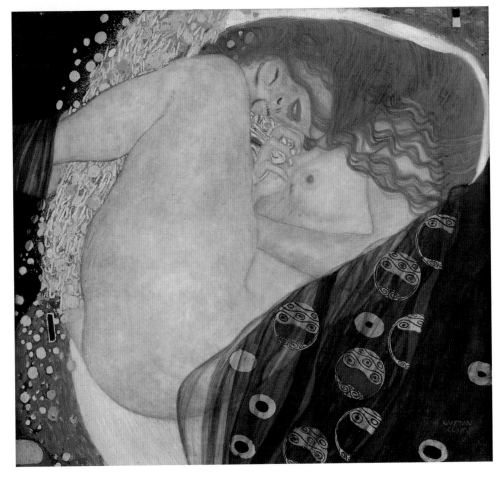

Gustav Klimt
Danae, 1907/08
Oil on canvas, 77 x 83 cm
Private collection

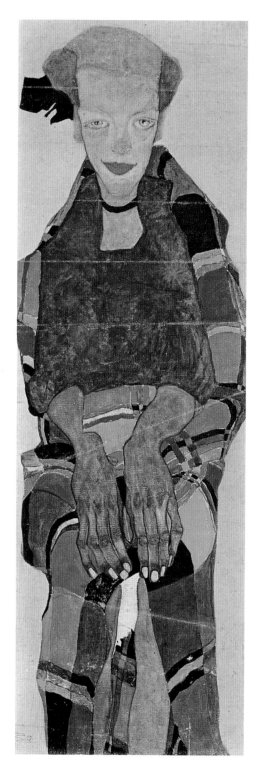

The watercolour *Nude Girl with Folded Arms (Gertrude Schiele)* (1910; p.79) again centres upon the elongated and angular body of a young girl, but this time the plaintiveness that prompts compassion in *Seated Nude Girl* is absent. Schiele's sister is standing nude, her head turned to her right, her arms crossed protectively over her chest. The right hand is fragmented, its outline merely suggested. Her hair and legs are both cropped by the picture's edges. It is a shorthand record of a fleeting moment, given life by the rapidity of the watercolouring, done purely in orange and red – an especially striking example of Expressionist aesthetics, which were indifferent to colours as realistic representation and preferred them to have an autonomous, expressive life of their own. This autonomy was quite at odds with the subsidiary function that the tradition of academic painting assigned to colour.

The autonomy of colour and form is again apparent in *Seated Female Nude with Blue Garter, Back View* (1910; p.76). The woman's head, trunk and behind are merely sketched in, as if in shorthand, and the rapidly-applied colouring is patchy; but from above the knees to the feet we are given a detailed, realistic account that records the exact pattern of the stockings, complete with the garter tied in a bow. The impression is of a nude seen from the rear by two different cameras, one establishing a precise close-up of the part that is rendered realistically, the other giving an unfocussed image of parts of the body that are slightly further away. This optical trick also creates an interesting polarity between two- and three-dimensional areas. Merely to describe the phenomenon is to intuit the artistic surprises Schiele still has in store for us.

In another watercolour, *Red Nude, Pregnant* (1910; p.77), showing a seated girl with her hands clasped on her pregnant belly, the surprise lies more in the subject matter, the provocativeness of which is heightened by the lurid red watercolouring. Klimt had occasioned a scandal by portraying a pregnant woman; the unconventional subject hit a nerve in hypocritical middle-class society, where the fact of a real, nude pregnant body had no place in the aesthetic code. The nymphs and caryatids of the Ringstrasse's stylish buildings were almost sexless creatures, with neither pubic hair nor breasts worth mentioning; in that world, to draw a pregnant woman, who might easily have been a penniless model carrying an illegitimate child, was a daring act. Klimt took the risk in mature years; Schiele seized it at the age of twenty.

A gouache showing Schiele's sister almost as a witch, her nose screwed up and expression derisive, also ran counter to prevailing notions of beauty. In *The Scornful Woman (Gertrude Schiele)* (1910; p.75), Gerti is wearing a huge and magnificent yellow hat that contrasts startlingly with her naked body, arms crossed beneath her breasts, and the black skirt. The outline of the whole has been highlighted in white brushwork against the brown of the paper. The arms, breasts and distorted facial features have also been highlighted in white, albeit not as heavily. Well might one think of the Walpurgis Night witches' sabbath of German lore. Schiele here employs features reminiscent of Toulouse-Lautrec which were entirely new to the Vienna scene, and which go hand in hand with the young Kokoschka's portrait work. He caricatures; he uses the distortion of the clown; he remains unsentimental; he focuses on society's out-

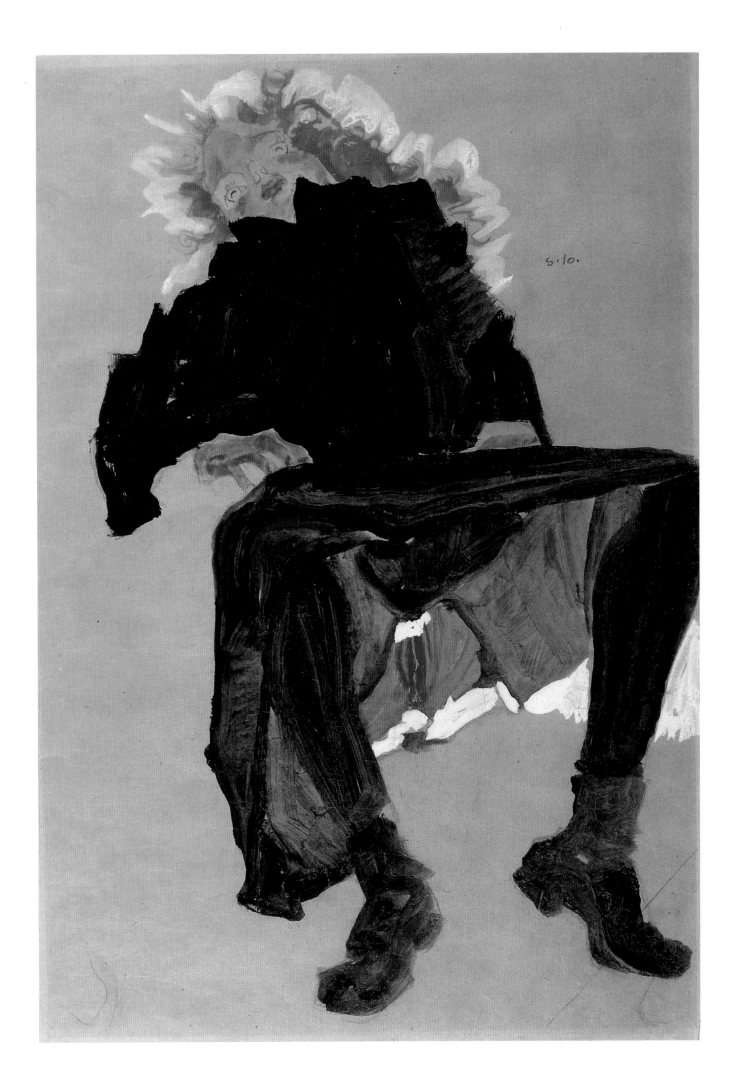

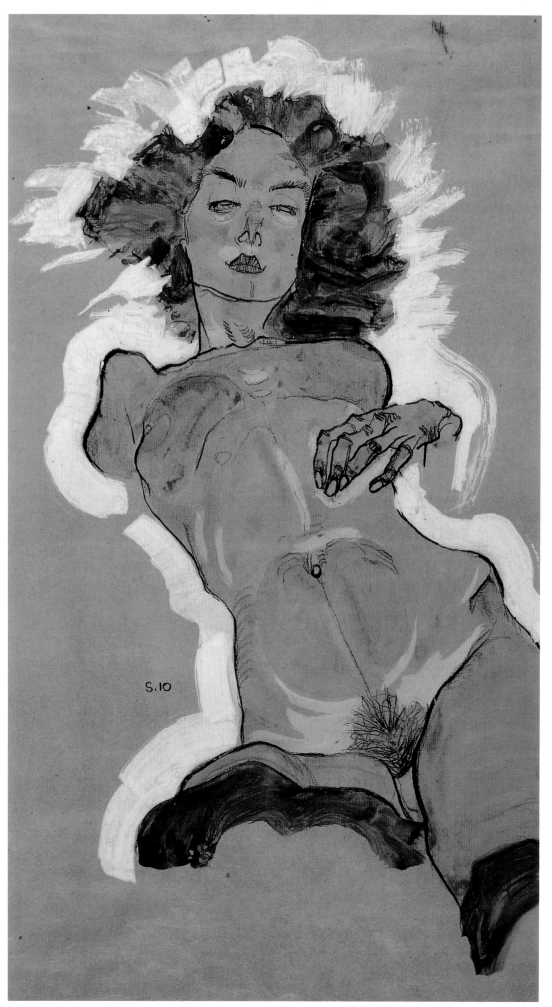

Female Nude, 1910
Weiblicher Akt
Gouache, watercolour and black crayon with white highlighting,
44.3 x 30.6 cm
Kallir D 555; Vienna, Graphische Sammlung Albertina

The mere torso of the body, the eloquent colours, the hair on end and the white contouring make this nude explosively aggressive.

PAGE 75:
The Scornful Woman (Gertrude Schiele), 1910
Die Hämische (Gertrude Schiele)
Gouache, watercolour and charcoal with white highlighting,
45 x 31.4 cm
Kallir D 546; private collection

Egon Schiele, once he put the style of beauty cultivated by Viennese Art Nouveau behind him, deliberately aimed at ugliness and extremes. Here he presents his sister with distorted, contemptuous features.

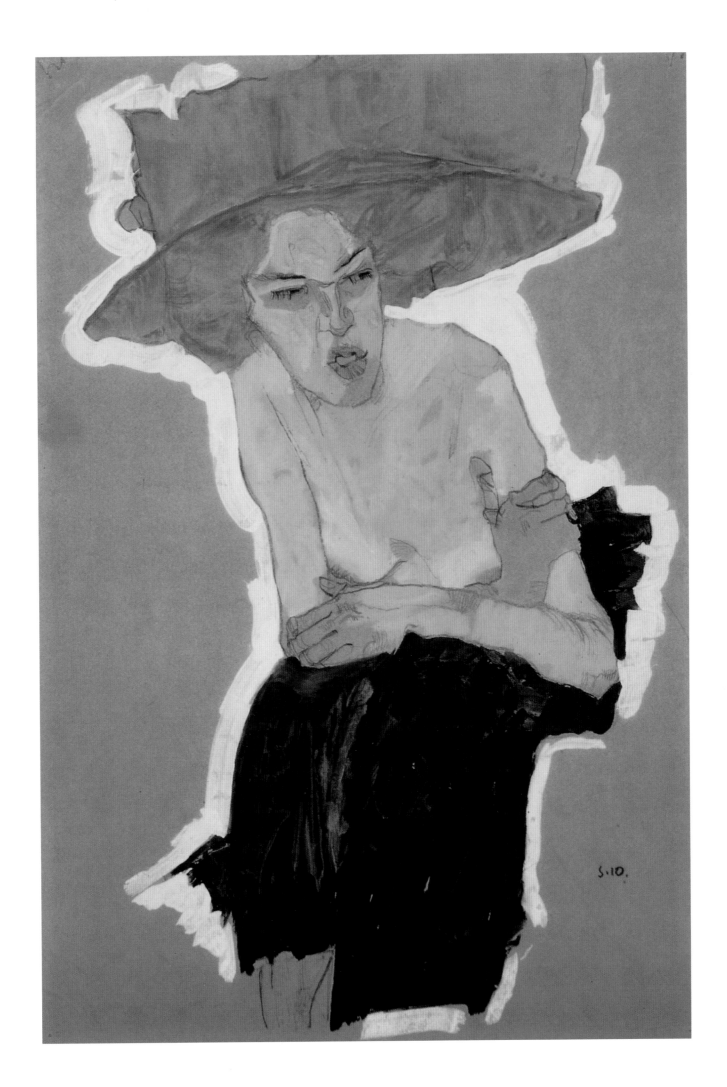

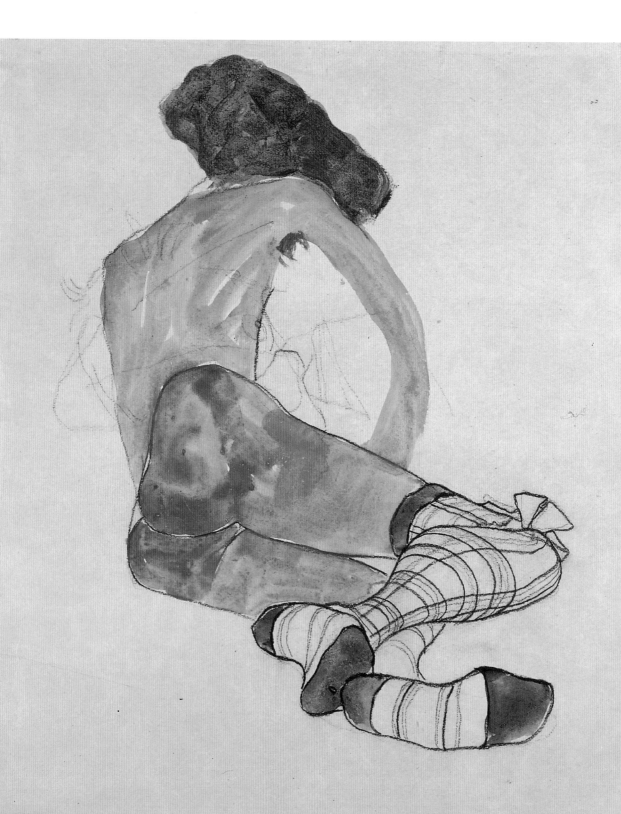

**Seated Female Nude with Blue Garter,
Back View**, 1910
*Sitzender weiblicher Akt mit blauem Strumpf-
band, vom Rücken gesehen*
Gouache, watercolour and charcoal, 45 x 31.5 cm
Kallir D 523; private collection

Schiele took a growing interest in unusual positions. Here, the stockings seem to have interested him most – the woman is merely a few
patches of watercolour.

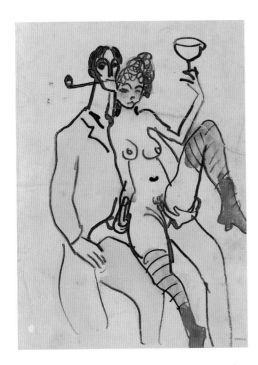

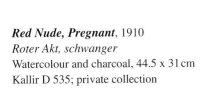

Pablo Picasso
Angel Fernández de Soto with a Woman,
1902/03
Angel Fernández de Soto avec une femme
Watercolour and Indian ink, 21 x 15.2 cm
Barcelona, Museo Picasso

Red Nude, Pregnant, 1910
Roter Akt, schwanger
Watercolour and charcoal, 44.5 x 31 cm
Kallir D 535; private collection

Klimt had already caused a scandal by painting a
pregnant woman. In seizing the same nettle,
Schiele was not out to create a transcendent or
prettified image.

siders. The portrait is reduced to simple outline, as in a poster, and a few
blocks of colour; in this, Schiele evidenced a palpable affinity with Pari-
sian artists of his time.

The reflection and framing of the body's outline with thick white
gouache is a device which recurs in various pictures of this period. One
very striking example is the gouache *Female Nude* (1910; p. 74). Unlike
The Scornful Woman it emphasizes Expressionist characteristics. It is as
if the body had been divided into four separate parts: the head and neck,
the torso, the cropped legs, and the hand, which seems too large in relation to the rest of the woman's body and appears to have materialized out
of nowhere. The chalk-white framing has the effect of conjoining these
four parts into a unified whole. Nevertheless, the fragmented impression

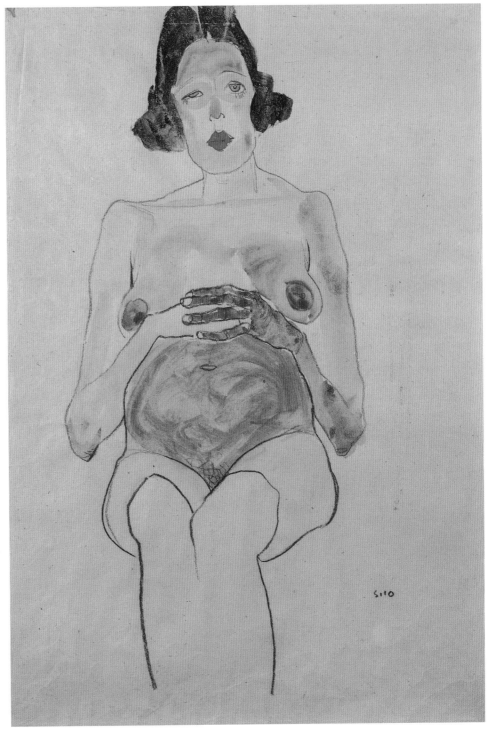

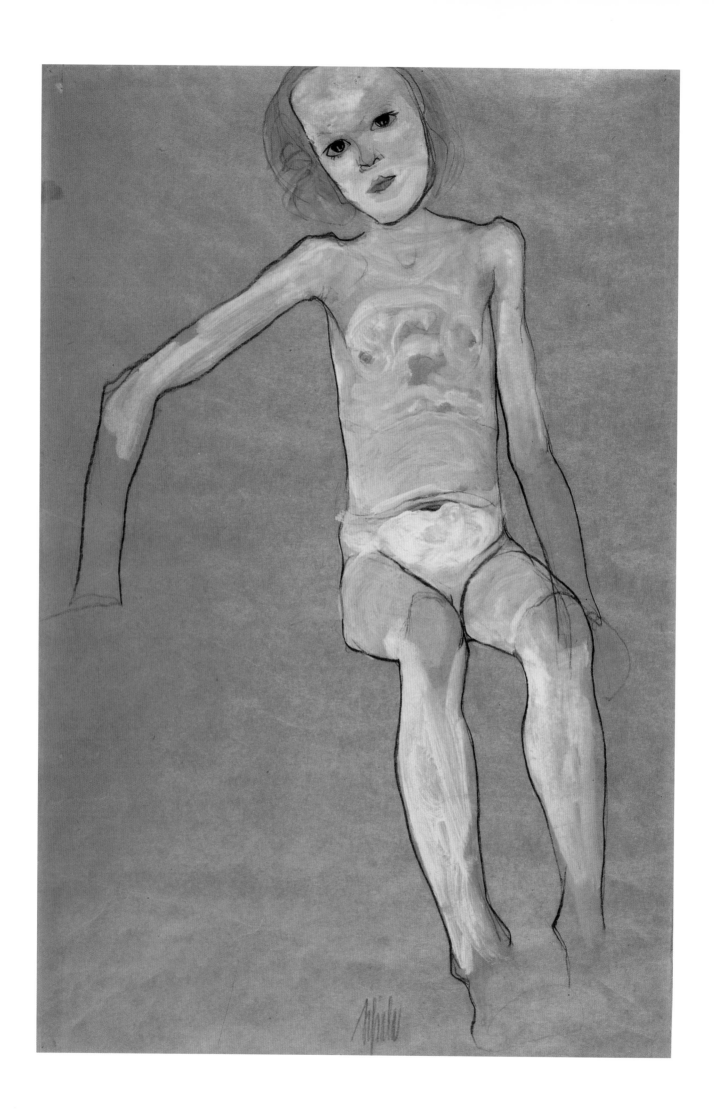

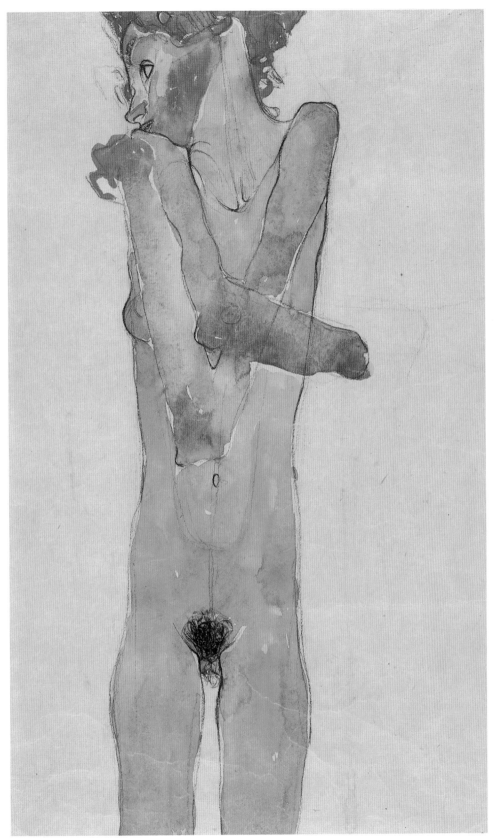

Seated Nude Girl, 1910
Sitzender Mädchenakt
Gouache and black crayon with white
highlighting, 44.8 x 29.9 cm
Kallir D 426; Vienna, Graphische Sammlung
Albertina

Schiele was particularly interested in the angu-
larity of young girls not yet come to the full-
blown womanhood traditionally celebrated in
art. Here we see the bony limbs and skinny
frame of a child.

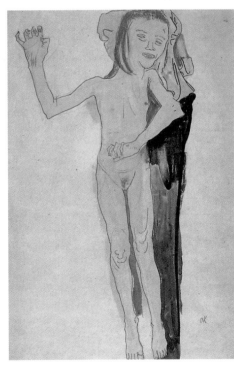

**Nude Girl with Folded Arms (Gertrude
Schiele)**, 1910
*Mädchenakt mit verschränkten Armen (Ger-
trude Schiele)*
Watercolour and black crayon, 48.8 x 28 cm
Kallir D 516; Vienna, Graphische Sammlung
Albertina

The picture of Schiele's sister Gerti shows her
making a touching, perhaps naive movement,
maybe one of shame or because she is cold. The
elongated limbs of this child girl emphasize a
need for protection.

Oskar Kokoschka
Standing Female Nude, 1909/10
Stehender weiblicher Akt
Pencil with watercolour and body colour,
44.5 x 30.5 cm
Private collection

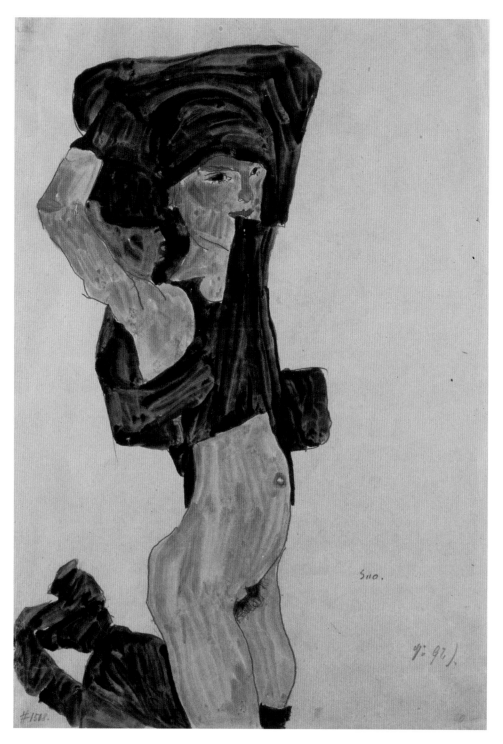

Kneeling Girl, Disrobing, 1910
Kniendes Mädchen, sich den Rock über den Kopf ziehend
Gouache, watercolour and pencil, 44.8 x 31 cm
Kallir D 561; private collection

Much of Schiele's work is not only provocative but also marked by the quest for new formal strategies. Here he is exploring the contrasts between lascivious movement and crude representation, between the unsensual black of the clothing and the sensual red of the body.

PAGE 81:
Black-Haired Nude Girl, Standing, 1910
Schwarzhaariger Mädchenakt, stehend
Watercolour and pencil with white highlighting,
54.3 x 30.7 cm
Kallir D 575; Vienna, Graphische Sammlung Albertina

PAGE 82:
Nude on Coloured Fabric, 1911
Akt gegen farbigen Stoff
Watercolour and pencil with white highlighting,
48 x 31 cm
Kallir D 776; private collection

PAGE 83:
Two Girls (Lovers), 1911
Zwei Mädchen (Liebespaar)
Gouache, watercolour and pencil, 48.3 x 30.5 cm
Kallir D 774; private collection

makes an arresting impact that is typical of Expressionist art. The woman's torso seems all the more plastic by virtue of a number of features: the lacking arms, the exaggerated curves of belly and breast, the patterning of the pubic hair, and the aureoling of the face in a frame of wild red hair and an outer halo of white highlighting. The head, indeed, looks like a portrait sketch in its own right, independent of the body. As for the outsize, skeletal hand, it too has a quality of independence; and the fact that it looks rather like a male hand merely serves to heighten our sense that the individual body parts do not quite add up to a whole. The legs, with their purple garter bands, are cropped; even so, they form the lower part of the curving S shape which, with the white highlighting, gives the composition its coherence.

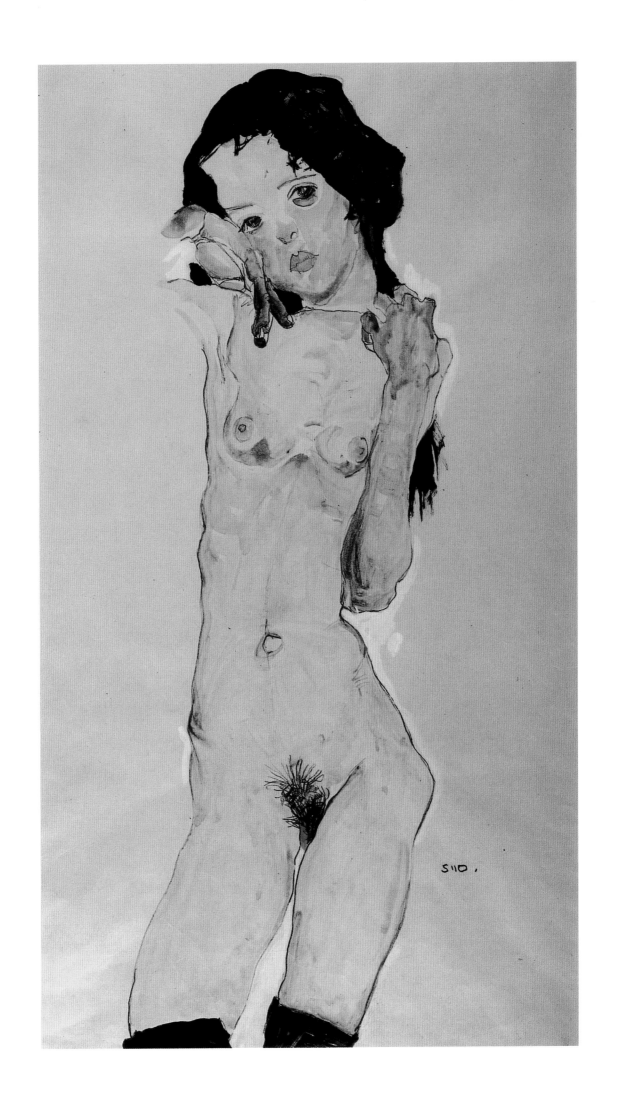

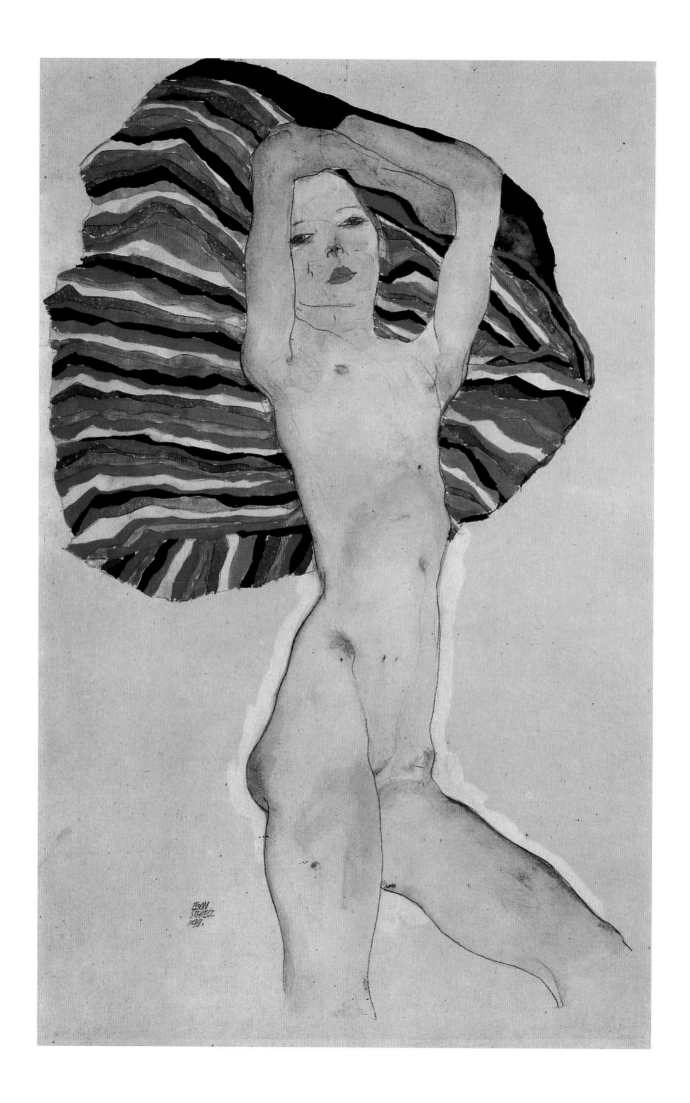

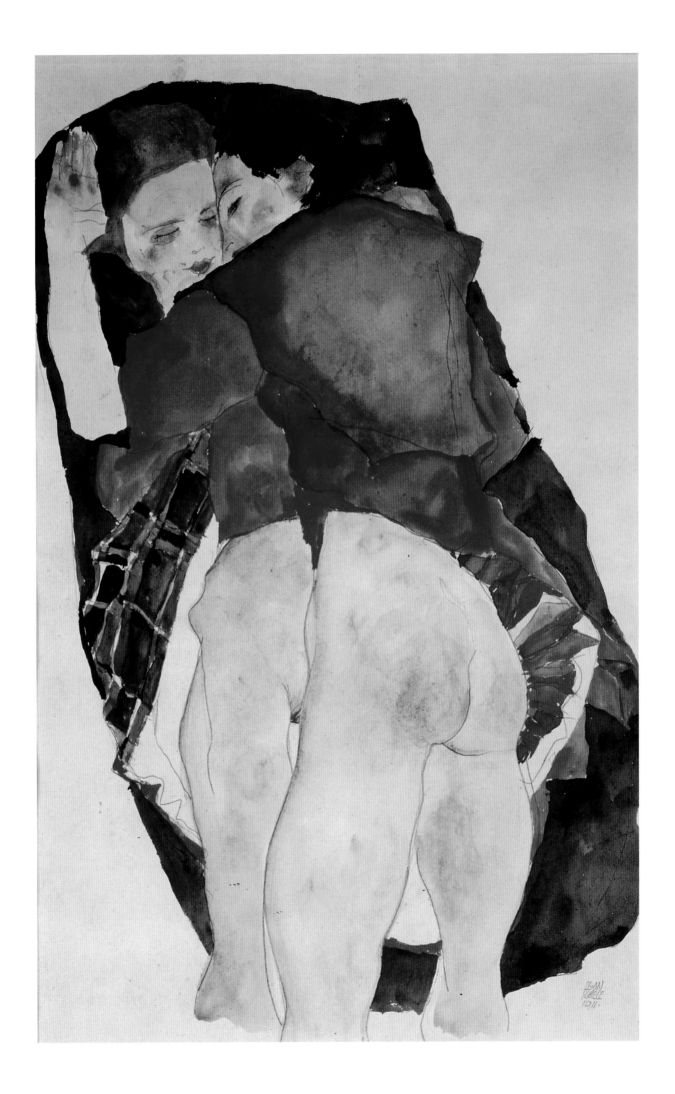

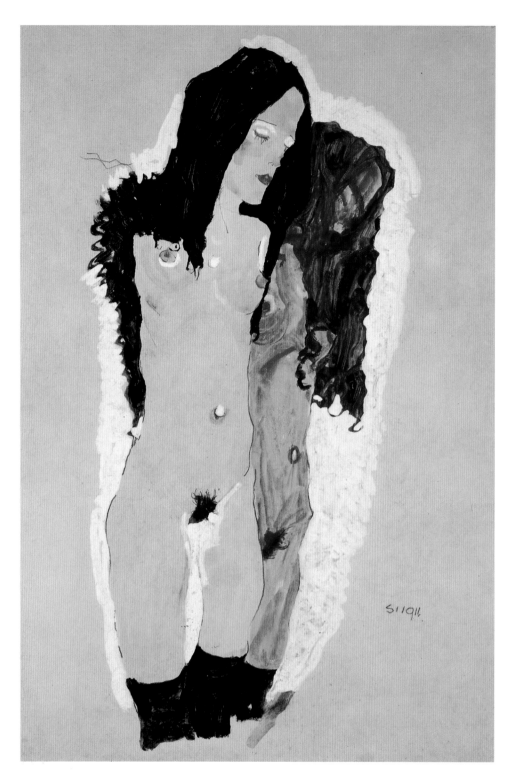

Two Reclining Girls, 1911
Zwei liegende Mädchen
Gouache, watercolour and pencil,
52.5 x 35.1 cm
Kallir D 807; private collection

Schiele's angle from above, together with the
title, may lead to confusion, since at first glance
the girls look as if they are standing. They also
have an air of image and mirror reflection. But
the ambiguity is altogether to Schiele's purpose.

Schiele's alternation between dissonance, shock effects and deliberate
provocation, on the one hand, and a need, on the other, to retain the
melody of the line as a means of establishing harmony, underpinned his
entire work, and marks the difference between his art and that of contemporaries such as Ernst Ludwig Kirchner or George Grosz.

Two more pictures will serve nicely to illustrate the evolution of Schiele's art in that year of 1910. *Kneeling Girl, Disrobing* (1910; p. 80) repre-
sents his radical, Expressionist vein; the watercolour *Black-Haired Nude
Girl, Standing* (1910; p. 81) is Schiele in harmonious mood. In the picture
of the kneeling girl pulling her skirt over her head, the lascivious gesture,
angular brushwork, lurid red colouring, and cropping, all suggest why

PAGE 85:
Standing Nude, 1911
Stehender Akt
Watercolour, gouache and black crayon,
53.3 x 28cm
Kallir D 791; private collection, courtesy Galerie
St. Etienne, New York

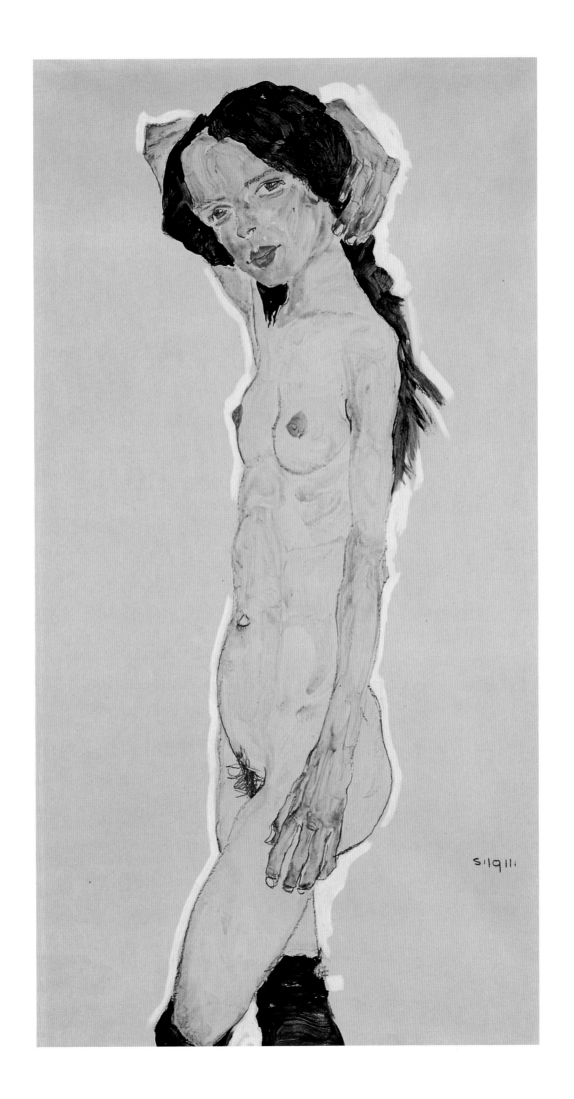

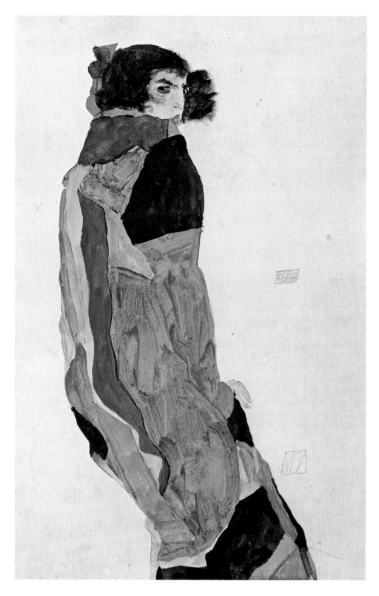

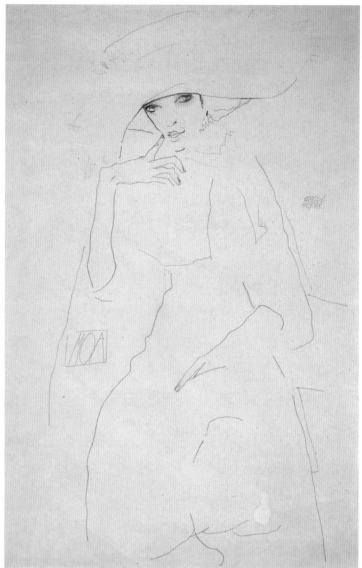

Schiele was seen as an avant-garde artist at odds with the middle-class state of things. The watercolour of the standing girl places greater emphasis on relatively classical features, such as the decorative quality of the lines, their unity, and a certain passive grace, almost academic in character, in the gesture the girl child is making with her right hand.

In 1911, Schiele developed his watercolour technique to a point of greater sophistication – though he was never to abide wholly by the classical repertoire of watercolour work, tending to mix graphic media (watercolour, gouache, pencil, crayon and so forth) in his pictures.

Working-class girls from proletarian districts, who became aware of their own seductive, sexual power at an earlier date than his own sister, a middle-class girl protected by governesses, were of great interest to Schiele (as were street youths of the same age). This was not only a question of the kind of youngster these girls and youths represented; it must also have been easier to persuade working-class kids to model nude than well-to-do middle-class girls. Whether the details of their nudity were always as we see them, or Schiele allowed his erotic imagination to adapt at will, it is hard to say; but it is certain that his models genuinely were flesh-and-blood pubescents and teenagers, and not mere products of an idle fantasy.

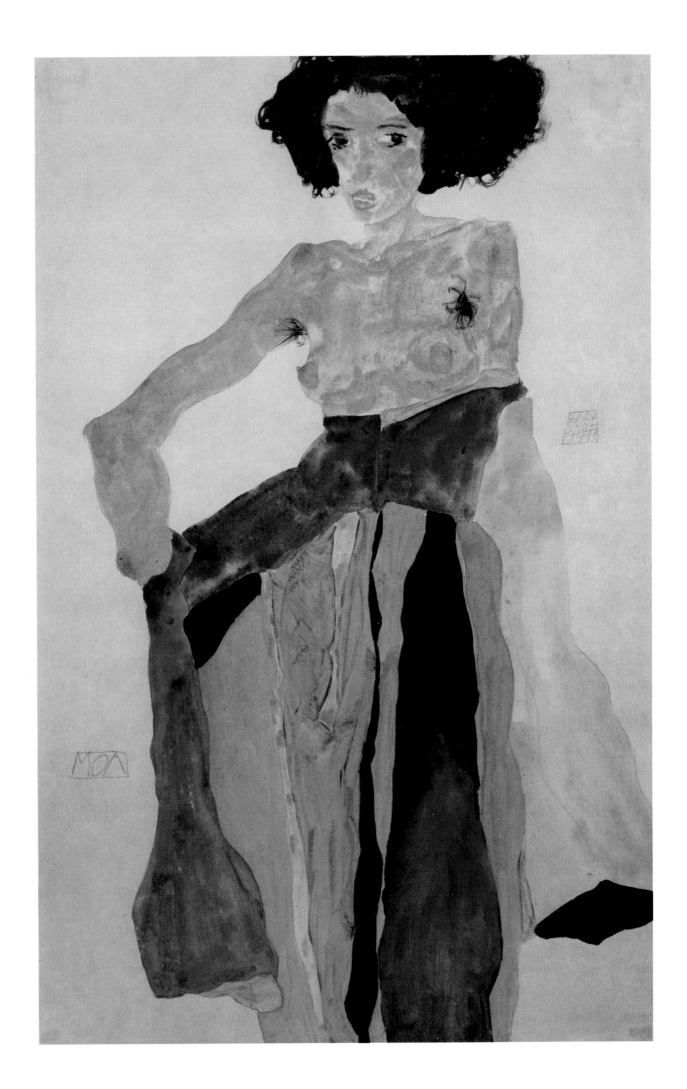

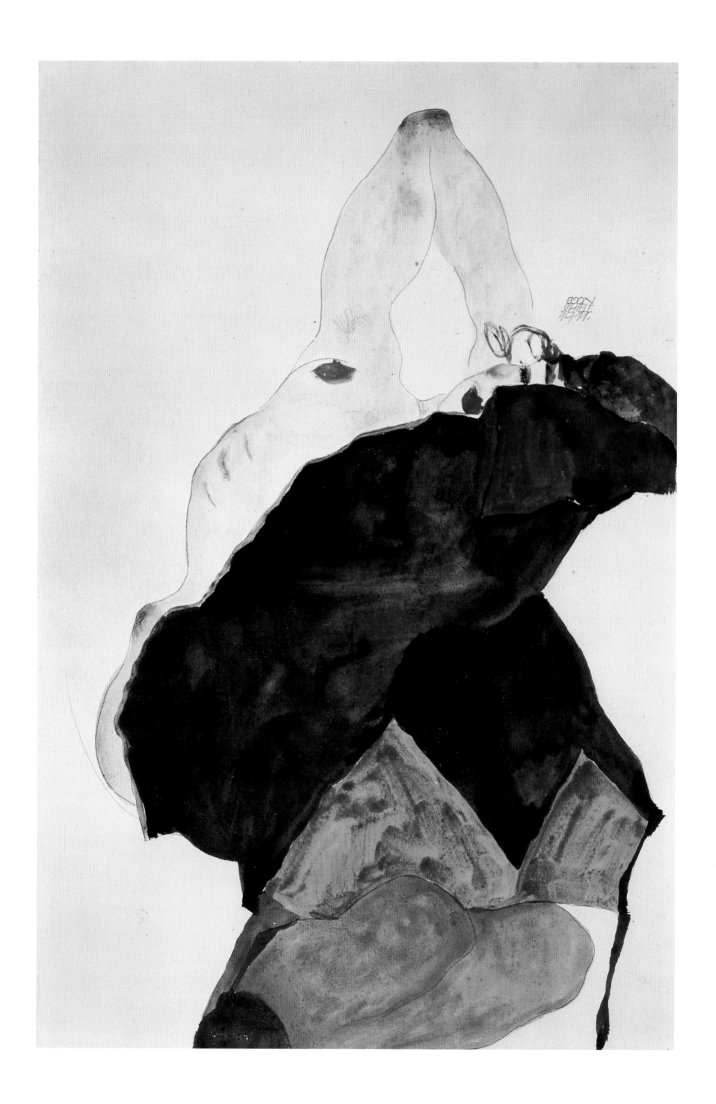

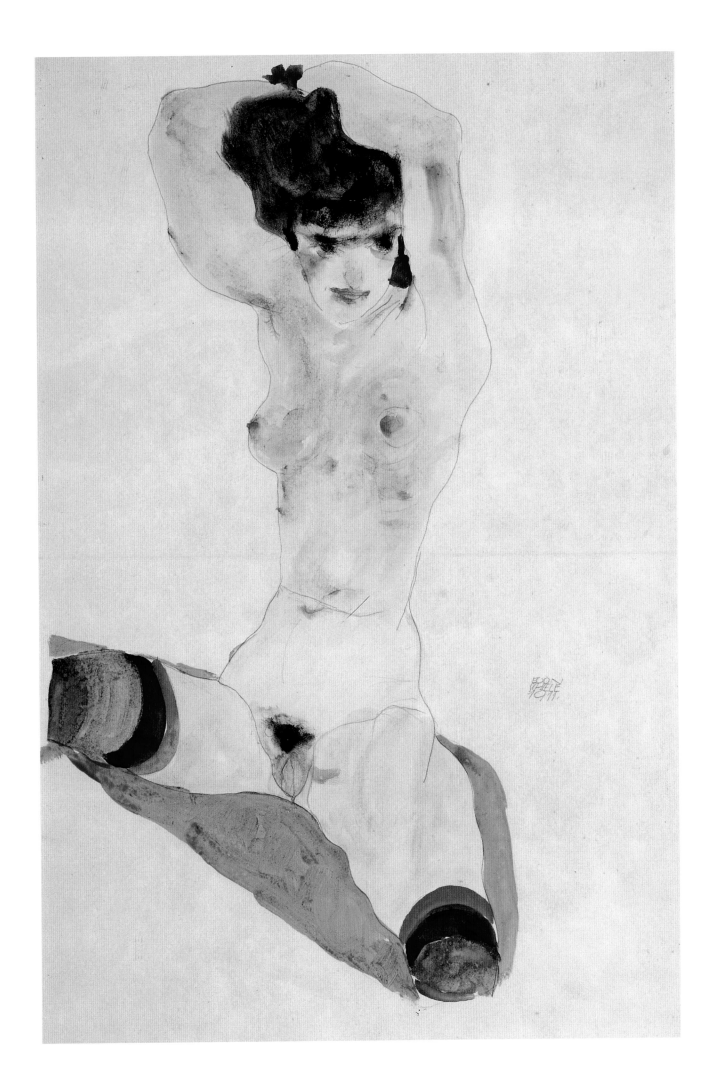

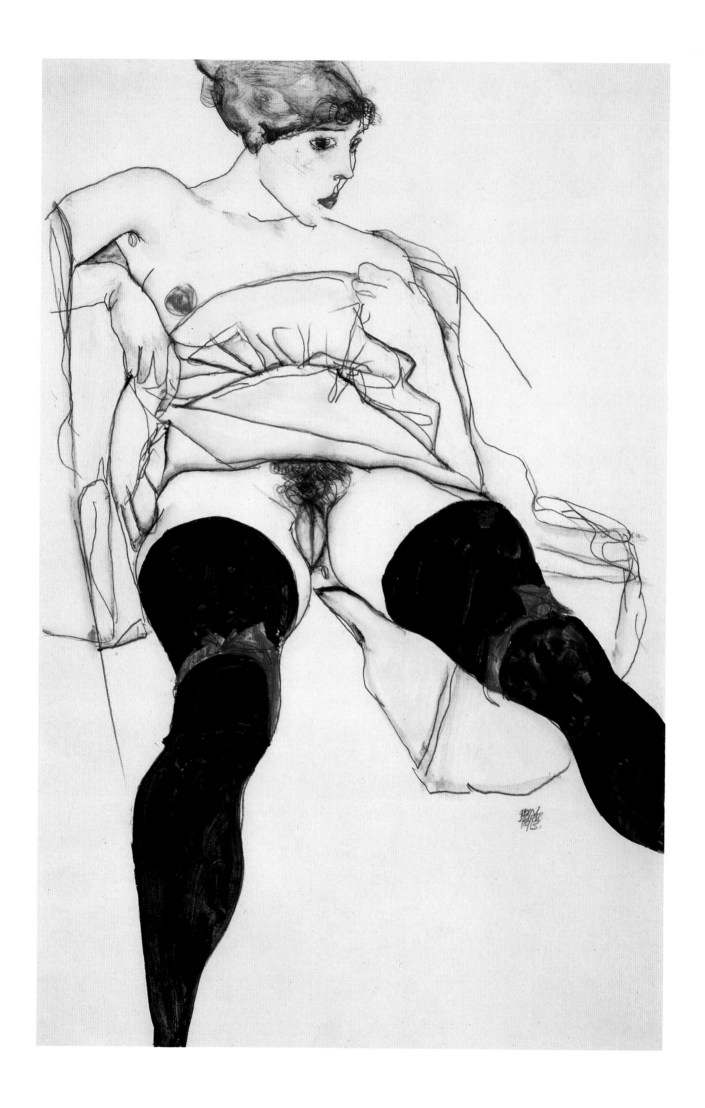

PAGE 88:
Girl with Elbow Raised, 1911
Mädchen mit erhobenem Ellenbogen
Watercolour and pencil, 47.9 x 29.8cm
Kallir D 923; private collection

PAGE 89:
Seated Nude Girl with Arms Raised Over Head, 1911
Sitzendes nacktes Mädchen mit über dem Kopf verschränkten Armen
Watercolour and pencil, 48.2 x 31.4cm
Kallir D 927; private collection

Schiele's use of colour was economical but effective. The contrast of the complementaries blue and yellow is particularly well deployed. The composition also serves to draw attention primarily to the genitals.

PAGE 90:
Woman with Black Stockings, 1913
Frau mit schwarzen Strümpfen
Gouache, watercolour and pencil, 48.3 x 31.8cm
Kallir D 1245; private collection, courtesy Galerie St. Etienne, New York

Egon Schiele was also a master of direct confrontation, as in *Woman with Black Stockings*, where the black-stockinged legs guide our line of vision – as in a perspective drawing – to the centre of the composition, and thus to the woman's genitals.

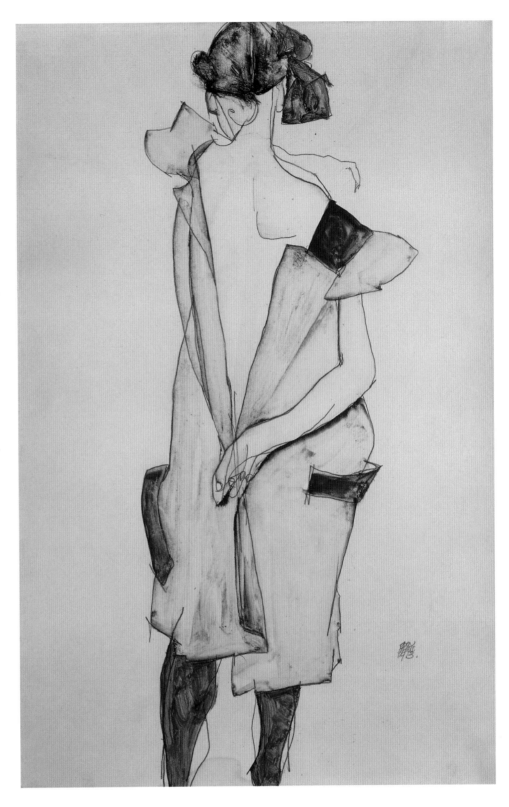

Standing Girl in Blue Dress and Green Stockings, Back View, 1913
Stehendes Mädchen in blauem Kleid und grünen Socken, Rückenansicht
Watercolour and pencil, 47 x 31 cm
Kallir D 1271; private collection

This drawing almost has an air of high society to it. Schiele generally tended to the coarse, but here the outlines and proportions remain harmonious, and the green and blue have the freshness of a spring day.

91

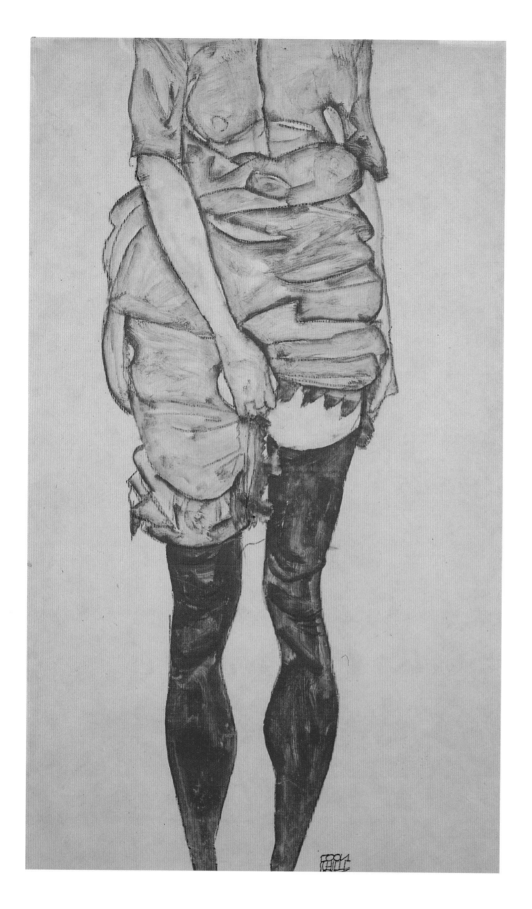

Standing Woman in Red, 1913
Stehende Frau in Rot
Gouache, watercolour and pencil, 48.3 x 29.2cm
Kallir D 1347; private collection, courtesy
Galerie St. Etienne, New York

A work on the subject of explicit sexual gestures.
This woman, all body and no face, seems to be
placing her hand between her thighs as if under
some compulsion. The skirt, hauled up, still con-
ceals the body, and the woman's identity remains
elusive, with only arms and legs to give her
presence.

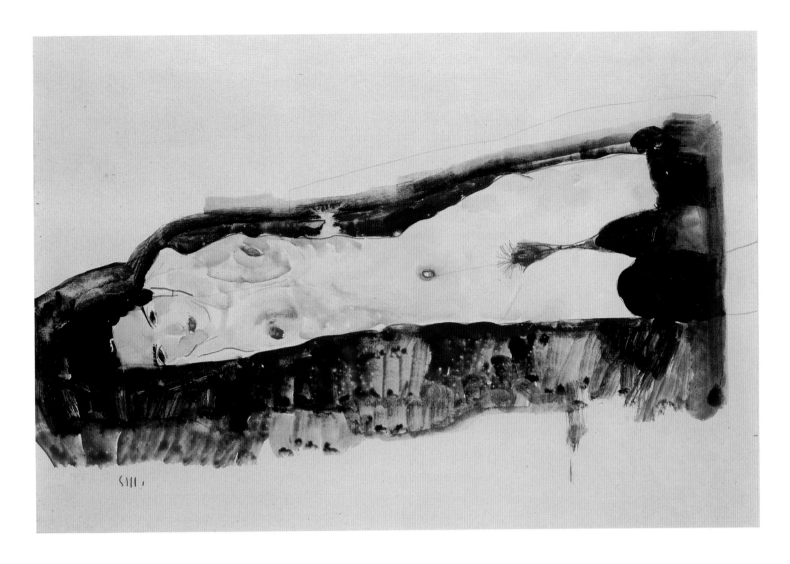

Schiele's lesbian couples, as in *Two Girls (Lovers)* (1911; p. 83), were doubtless drawn from the Bohemian world on the margins of society. Such pictures breached taboos as well. To identify or portray sexual modes that were seen as perverse, such as male or female homosexuality, or indeed masturbation, was seen as an offence against good taste, or even branded as sinful.

In pictures such as *Two Girls*, Schiele made careful use of a textile background, not only to highlight the main figure or figures but also to bring out the colourfulness of the clothing. In *Nude on Coloured Fabric* (1911; p. 82) or *Young Girl with Blue Ribbon* (1911), textile becomes a significant albeit subsidiary motif. The nude is holding the billowing striped material like a flag behind her head and chest. In the second work, the young girl's body is encased in the dress (established with broad brushstrokes) like a cocoon. In relation to her dress and hair, tied in two looped, blue-ribboned plaits which stick out like octopus tentacles one over each ear, the girl's head, neck and hands look too small. Usually Schiele enlarged, but here he has achieved his expressive defamiliarization by the reverse strategy.

In *Standing Nude* (1911; p. 85) too, features such as the girl's black hair held in her right hand reaching from the rear to the fore, and her black stockings, are as crucial to the vitality of the presentation as the red of the mouth and nipples. The girl's body itself is almost exactly the same colour as the paper; only a few brush-strokes have been added to the pal-

Reclining Nude with Black Stockings, 1911
Liegender Akt mit schwarzen Strümpfen
Watercolour and pencil, 29.2 x 43.5 cm
Kallir D 795; private collection

Individuality and physical presence are reduced to an essential minimum. The elongation of the torso is emphasized by the absence of arms. The thin, pale body is framed in blue, and the ground the woman is lying on is merely suggested by a few brief brushstrokes.

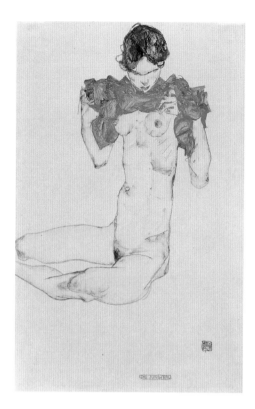

The Virgin, 1913
Die Jungfrau
Gouache and pencil, 48.8 x 31.2cm
Kallir D 1361; Zurich, Graphische Sammlung
der Eidgenössischen Technischen Hochschule

The virgin is girlish, quite free of the seductiveness that Schiele usually presents in his women.
Her eyes are downcast and she seems to be dressing rather than undressing. Schiele's exact eye
for gesture records the essence of character.

PAGE 95:
Standing Female Nude with Blue Cloth, 1914
Stehender weiblicher Akt mit blauem Tuch
Gouache, watercolour and pencil, 48.3 x 32.2cm
Kallir D 1496; Nuremberg, Germanisches
Nationalmuseum

lid grey-white to suggest the moulding of living flesh, while white contouring again highlights the figure against the background. The effect of
the colouring is eerie, though this is countered by the fresh, expressive
plasticity of the girl's newly awakened body.

In *Two Reclining Girls* (1911; p.84), the hair and stockings again afford keynotes and important contours, the more eloquent for being dupli-
cated. At first glance we might well take this for image and mirrored reflection – though a closer look naturally dispels this notion. There is,
however, a characteristic motif of duplication in the work of Schiele, especially his portraits, that creates a ghostly, dream-like impression; and
this other dimension is clearly established by the sychronisation of movement in this picture and the way in which the hair of the two girls seems
to fall in the same rhythm, as it were.

These motifs are supplemented by the abstraction of the textile background in a watercolour that seems to record the artist's sister unob-
served: *Sleeping Girl (Study of Gerti Schiele)* (1911; p.48). Gerti's undergarments are shown as four rectangular shapes. They are lightly watercoloured at the edges and, in formal terms, have a function entirely their
own. These abstract spaces, comprising a good three-quarters of the
figure, interpose between the realistic head, hair, hand and stockings. It is
tempting, when we consider them, to speculate that Schiele, in a less conservative artistic environment such as Paris or Munich, might well have
taken the step into completely abstract art.

The purple contouring, following the pencil outlines, is a reference to
sleep and dreams. In this respect, the purple-edged abstract planes might
also be interpreted as symbolic of the natural or animal, and of the unconscious. In 1911 in particular, the motif of sleep and dreaming was very
important to Schiele, and here it is illustrated on a twofold level, both in
colour symbolism and in realism, through the exact observation of a
sleeping girl.

Schiele's method of presenting planes in an almost abstract manner,
using different colouring, and contrasting them with realistically rendered
parts of a figure, was very important in formal terms. It can be seen in
Two Girls on Fringed Blanket (1911; p.49), which we have already discussed, as strikingly as in the *Sleeping Girl*.

In Schiele's many drawings of a dancer named Moa, the most arresting
quality is their vividness. Moa was the companion of Erwin Dominik
Osen, the eccentric mime and artist of whom mention has already been
made, whose mime performances and fanciful tales of imaginary travels
made an extraordinarily deep impression on Schiele. In one light pencil
drawing we see Moa standing, wearing a broad-brimmed Wiener Werkstätte hat set stylishly low atop her eyeline. In this drawing, Moa's right
forefinger is against her cheek, her lips are parted, and she is gazing at us
with dark eyes. We are all familiar with the allure, garb and poses of
demi-mondaines of this kind, not least from literary sources such as
Arthur Schnitzler's play *Der Reigen* (later filmed as *La Ronde*).

The name MOA, inscribed beside the figure in capitals in this and
other drawings of the dancer, is like a code word in some secret erotic
language. It appears again, for instance, in a gouache and watercolour
portrait of the dancer in three-quarter profile. As in *Nude on Coloured*

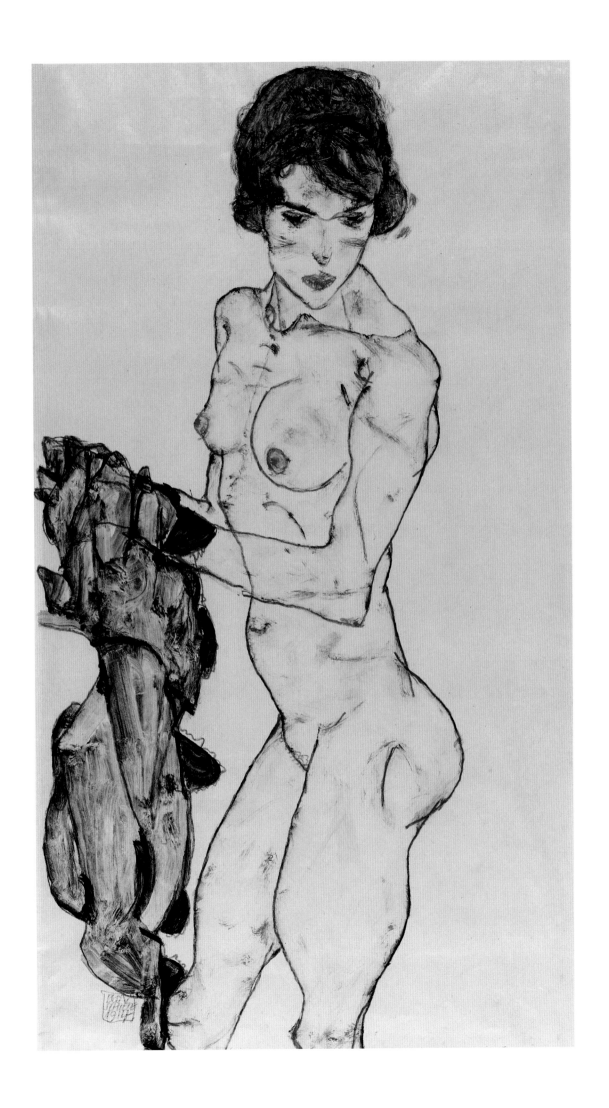

Fabric (p. 82) or *Young Girl with Blue Ribbon* (both 1911), the colours – the brown, yellow, blue, black and orange stripes of her dress and coat, applied with a broad brush – have an Expressionist force beyond mere representation, a presence almost abstract in character. On the other hand, the fluttering ribbons and flying black hair suggest the wild, emphatic rhythm of the dancer whirling across a stage. Klimt's ornamental principle of composition has been displaced by glaring colour and dizzy movement, to create an Expressionist snapshot of great force.

The exotic Moa was one of those many pre-1914 dancers who cultivated eloquent emotional expressiveness, and in *Moa* (1911; p.87), which shows her bare-breasted, the full untamed presence of her fantastic nature appears before us. With its coarse tufts of black hair at the armpits, her upper body seems suspended above the red, blue and green material of her skirt, held in place by the over-long right arm alone. The compositional principle of juxtaposing brightly coloured textiles with the tender tonalities of flesh was used to perfection in the watercolour *Girl with Elbow Raised* (1911; p.88).

In the watercolour *Seated Nude Girl with Arms Raised Over Head* (1911; p.89) the sitter is more vehemently viewed in sexual terms: her legs are splayed, her genitals emphasized. Sometimes Schiele would display and glorify the female genitals still more assertively by placing them centrally in a composition. In *Woman with Black Stockings* (1913; p.90), for instance, the subject's straddled black-stockinged legs draw our gaze to this centre with all the inexorable power of central perspective.

This aside, in the years 1912 and 1913 the figures in Schiele's work became visibly more rounded and plastic. He used arm movements, or the position of arms, to establish space, as in *Standing Girl in Blue Dress and Green Stockings, Back View* (1913; p.91). At the same time, however, he also inclined to a Gothic (as it were) elongation of figures in works such as *Mother and Daughter* (1913), *Kneeling Girl, Back View* (1913) and *Standing Woman in Red* (1913; p.92). The woman in this last picture

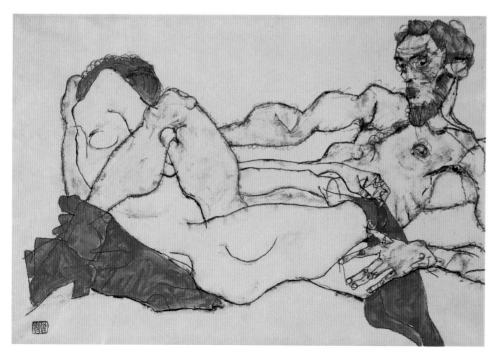

Reclining Male and Female Nude, Entwined, 1913
Weiblicher und männlicher Akt, verschränkt liegend
Gouache, watercolour and pencil, 31.3 x 46.7cm
Kallir D 1453; Vienna, Graphische Sammlung Albertina

Schiele's picture has been read as an image of gender relations. The man is probably his friend Felix Albrecht Harta. The woman is little more than an almost abstract outline.

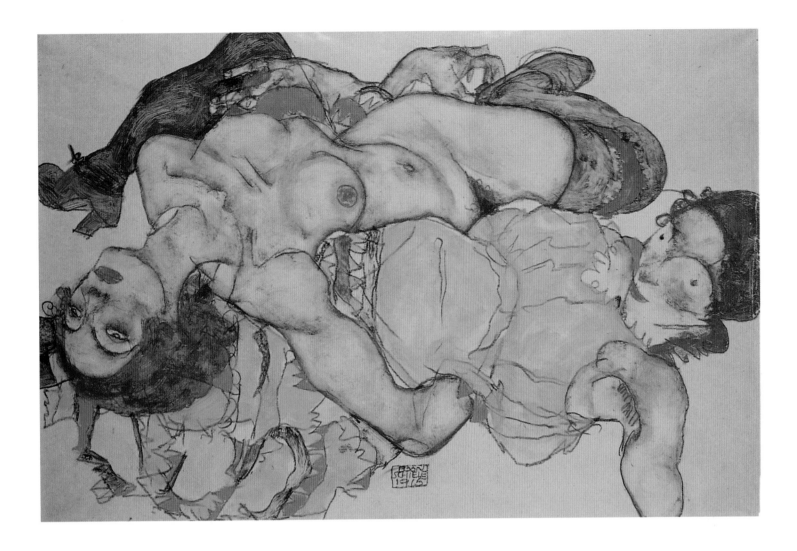

makes a strangely fragmented and restless impression, not only because
of this distortion but also because of the cropping, and because of the
hand she is holding to her sex. The same constituents, in content and
form, can be seen in the watercolour *Reclining Nude with Black Stockings* (1911; p. 93), in which the effect of elongating the torso is heightened by the absence of arms.

   A wonderful gouache of 1913, ambivalently titled *Friendship*, seems
to have given offence to contemporaries; it was turned down for the Munich Secession exhibition in December 1913, on moral grounds. The
two female nudes are seated one behind the other. One girl's face is
turned straight to us, the other is in profile. The rearward girl is reaching an arm across to her companion's upper thigh. The understatement
of the title is itself meant provocatively, since the two young women are
evidently a lesbian couple locked in a hot embrace. Convention dictated
what was permissible; and *The Virgin* (1913; p. 94) remained more com-
fortably within that unspoken code. The girl is sitting almost chastely on
the floor, her legs not opened as flagrantly as in other Schiele works.
She is gazing downward and is in the act of slipping her chemise over
her body.

   Another gouache, *Reclining Male and Female Nude, Entwined* (1913;
p. 96), conveys a many-sided image of human relations. The couple, reclining on a sofa merely suggested in orange, are not embracing; rather
their heads are separated by the lengths of their bodies. The raised leg of

Two Girls, Lying Entwined, 1915
*Zwei Mädchen, in verschränkter Stellung
liegend*
Gouache and pencil, 32.8 x 49.7 cm
Kallir D 1743; Vienna, Graphische Sammlung
Albertina

Around 1914, Egon Schiele's art became more
three-dimensional and plastic. The curves and
fleshiness of his bodies became more explicit as
he paid more attention to effects of shading and
contour.

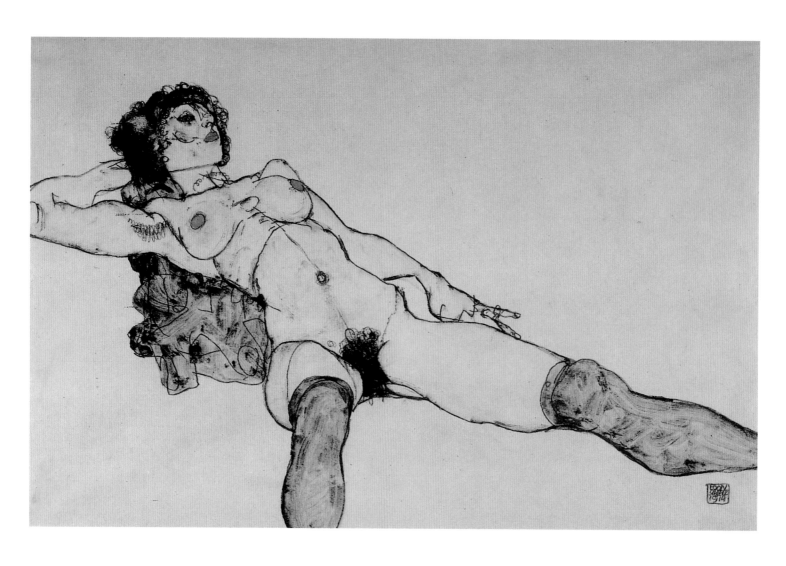

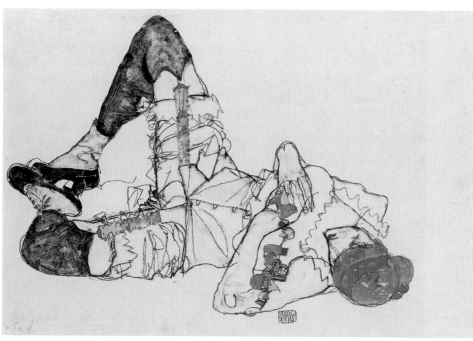

Reclining Female Nude with Legs Spread Apart, 1914
Liegender weiblicher Akt mit gespreizten Beinen
Gouache and pencil, 30.4 x 47.2cm
Kallir D 1484; Vienna, Graphische Sammlung Albertina

Again, this body is more three-dimensional than in many of Schiele's earlier works. He is in the process of eliminating the element of caricature in his drawings.

Woman Reclining on Her Back, 1914
Auf dem Rücken liegende Frau
Watercolour and pencil, 31.7 x 48.2cm
Kallir D 1478; Basle, Öffentliche Kunstsammlung, Kupferstichkabinett

This lolling woman clearly exemplifies a compositional principle that Schiele had hitherto only glanced at: the classical triangular form is twice used, in the legs and in the arms.

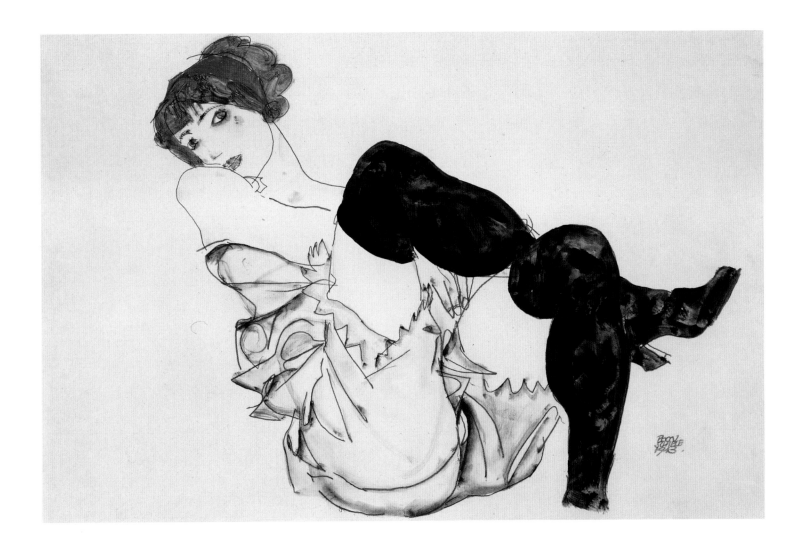

the bearded man is between the woman's legs. The woman, turned away from us, appears to be playing with her lover's genitals. With her left hand she is slipping off her red garter band. It is a daring scene of sexual congress, a picture seen through the keyhole, as it were; yet it is also a melancholy image of loneliness.

The man has not even removed his glasses, and is gazing contemplatively into nowhere. The woman is a mere body; her face is turned away and thus invisible. Amidst the prevailing shades of brown, orange and yellow there are blue outlines and green dabs that introduce an element of chill to the picture, implying that this sexual desire is no more than a clinical act. Whether the man's features are those of Schiele's patron Erich Lederer or, as often supposed, those of his fellow artist Felix Albrecht Harta, is of secondary importance. What matters is that the artist has succeeded so forcefully in presenting the sad isolation of two people whose souls cannot conjoin despite their physical closeness. Kokoschka gave an account of similar feelings in *The Tempest* (1914; p. 128).

Along with the models whose identities we can only guess, or who remain anonymous, the unmistakable face of Schiele's partner Wally (Valerie) Neuzil occurs with greater frequency in his work of this period. With its pointed chin and the eyes enlarged as in an icon, her face appears in drawings, watercolours and gouaches such as *Crouching Figure (Valerie Neuzil)* (1913), *Wally in Red Blouse with Raised Knees* (1913; p. 54) and *Woman in Black Stockings (Valerie Neuzil)* (1913; p. 99).

Woman in Black Stockings (Valerie Neuzil), 1913
Frau in schwarzen Strümpfen (Valerie Neuzil)
Gouache, watercolour and pencil, 32.2 x 48 cm
Kallir D 1240; private collection, courtesy
Galerie St. Etienne, New York

The face of Valerie Neuzil, his partner and model, began to appear regularly in Schiele's art around 1913. He later left her, but paid his tribute in his own way while they were together.

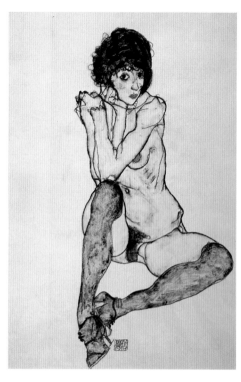

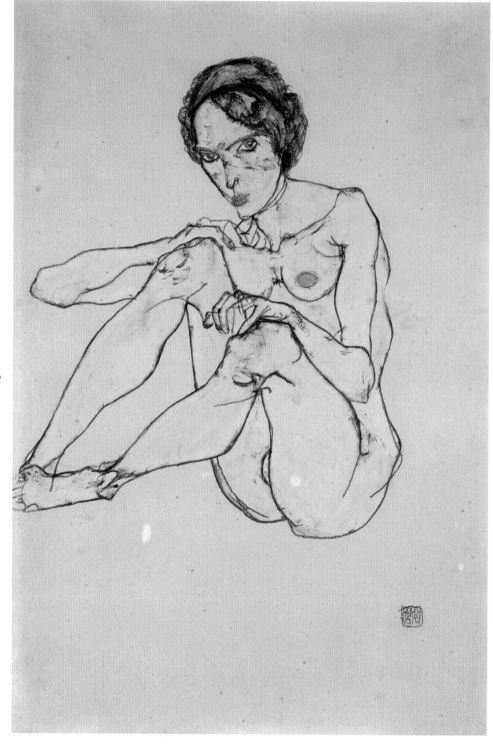

Seated Female Nude, Elbows Resting on Right Knee, 1914
Sitzender Mädchenakt, die Ellenbogen auf das rechte Knie gestützt
Gouache and pencil, 48.3 x 32 cm
Kallir D 1490; Vienna, Graphische Sammlung Albertina

Nude Woman, 1914
Sitzender Akt (Junge nackte Wienerin)
Gouache, watercolour and pencil, 48 x 32.2 cm
Kallir D 1509; London, Fischer Fine Art

PAGE 101:
Standing Woman in Green Shirt, 1914
Stehende Frau in grünem Hemd
Gouache, watercolour and pencil, 48.2 x 32 cm
Kallir D 1544; private collection

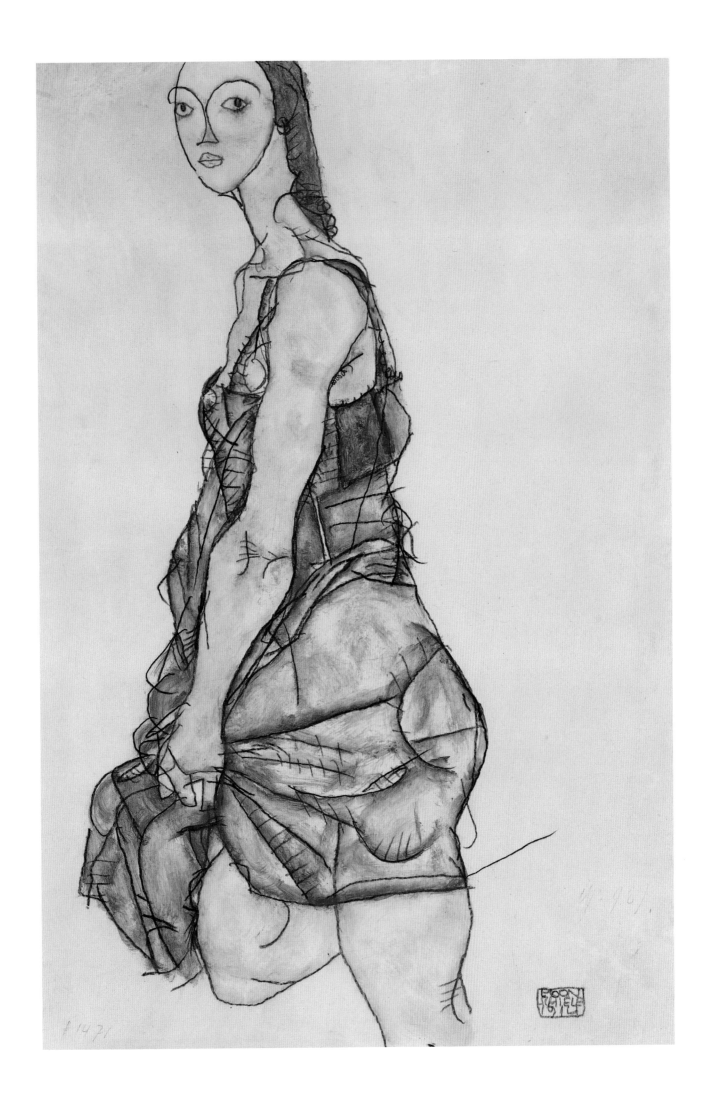

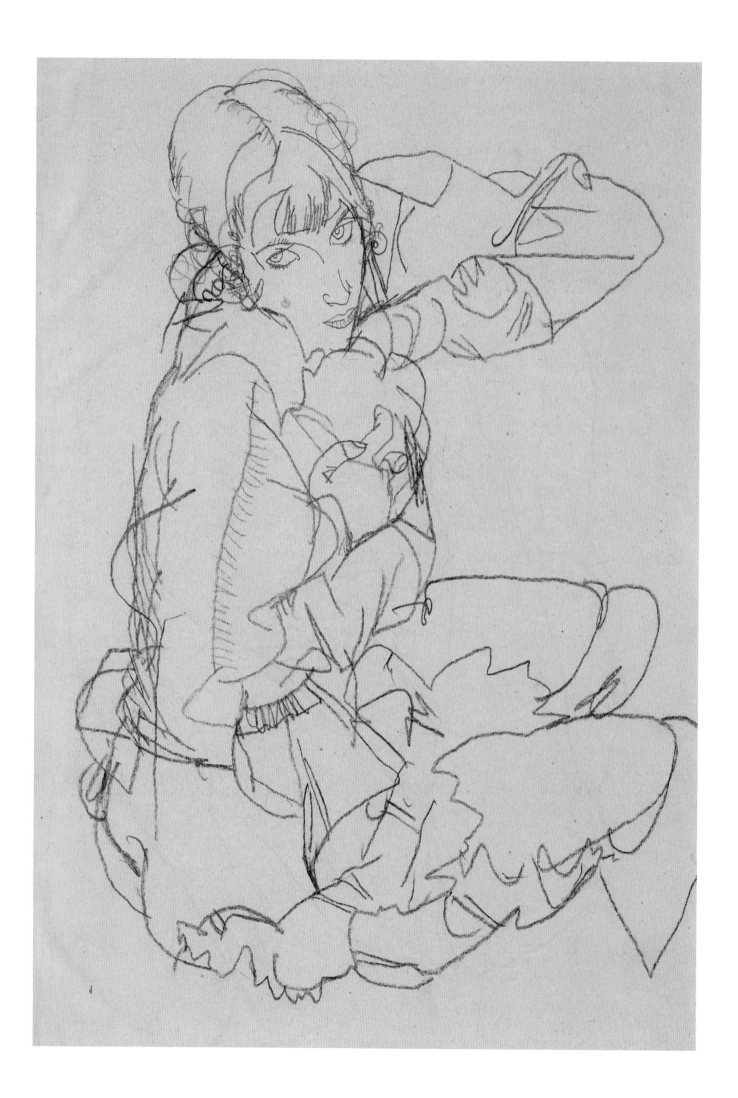

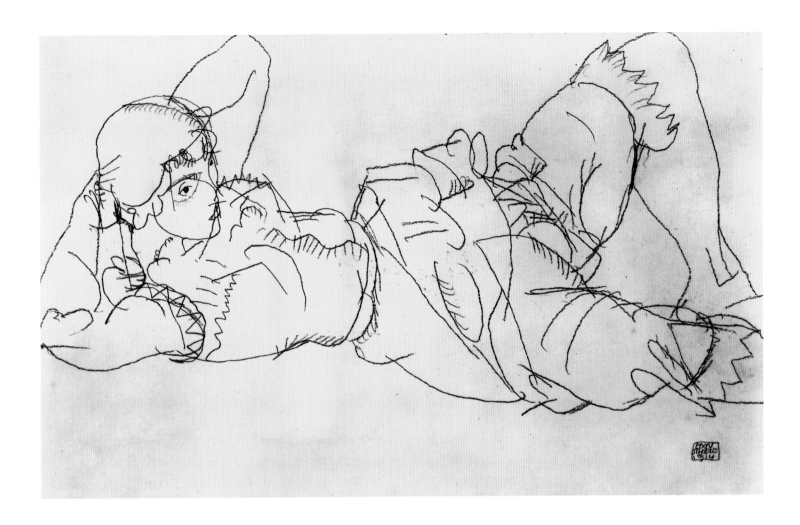

The outbreak of the First World War in 1914 did not at first interrupt Schiele's work or the course of his life. The female nude remained his main subject, followed by the self-scrutiny that was expressed in his numerous self-portraits. Schiele also continued to paint landscapes and townscapes. While the dramatic events at the front became bloodier and more destructive, the artist's style became calmer and softer and even took on classical features.

In the watercolour *Woman Reclining on Her Back* (1914; p.98) and the gouache *Reclining Female Nude with Legs Spread Apart* (1914; p.98), the classical triangle is the basis of the composition. In both pictures, the structural underpinning is even reduplicated. In the first, the legs, bent at the knees but meeting at the soles of the feet, form one triangle, while the arms, with hands clasped on the woman's breast, form a second with the head. In the gouache, the red highlights on the mouth and nipples mark the corners of one triangle, while the other is denoted by the legs. The larger form thus follows classical principles, while the detail work within the drawings, with their nervous hatchings and crisscrossings, makes for visual restlessness.

The triangle is once again the compositional foundation of the unusual *Seated Female Nude, Elbows Resting on Right Knee* (1914; p.100), in which the hands have been drawn in two different positions. Here, the two triangular forms are inverted, their points downward; the lower point of one is the woman's right shoe, of the other her propped elbows.

Reclining Figure, 1914
Liegende Figur
Pencil, 26.7 x 45.7 cm
Kallir D 1545; private collection

In 1914 a new style of drawing entered Schiele's work. As in *Seated Girl* and *Reclining Figure*, such drawings are executed in nervous strokes, whereby the motif is characterized by wavy lines and hatching. Even as the models lose their identity, they are elevated by the artist's confident hand to the status of ideal.

PAGE 102:
Seated Girl, 1914
Sitzendes Mädchen
Pencil, 43 x 30 cm
Kallir D 1575; Munich, Staatliche Graphische Sammlung

The increasing conservatism of Schiele's visual approach is also evident in *Standing Female Nude with Blue Cloth* (1914; p. 95), which has the richly plastic quality of a sculptor's drawing. Here, in contrast to the drawings we have been looking at, the pubic region is concealed by the left leg, in a concession to prudishness, and the agitated detail crisscrossing is almost completely absent.

Schiele's growing use of classical form is also apparent in *Nude Woman* (1914; p. 100), where we can readily view the entire figure of the Viennese girl on the floor as being framed by a notional triangle. Nevertheless, elements of thematic and formal disquiet have been introduced in the stressing of the pubic region and the cropping of the feet.

The uncoloured drawings dating from the first year of the war are predominantly restless and nervous, thanks to their prominent cross-hatching and seismographically wavy lines, that the figures seem trapped in patterns like barbed wire, as it were, their bodies tormented by some sadistic power. The nervously scrawled working overlays the basically geometrical forms. It is as if, in the majority of Schiele's 1914 drawings, the Romantic aesthetic, with its focus on passing moods and torturous dissatisfaction with the here and now, were repressing the forces of formal harmony.

The models Schiele drew in this manner, often half-clothed and with their underskirts hauled up, are charged with a kind of electricity – a power which does not promise hedonistic pleasures so much as a pre-

Nude with Green Turban, 1914
Akt mit grünem Turban
Gouache and pencil, 32 x 48 cm
Kallir D 1563; private collection

The body is thoroughly rendered but the face of the model is a mere puppet-like sketch. Her arms and legs, even her shoes, are done in careful detail compared with the mere hint of a nose and the hasty arc of the eyebrows: the face is a depersonalized mask.

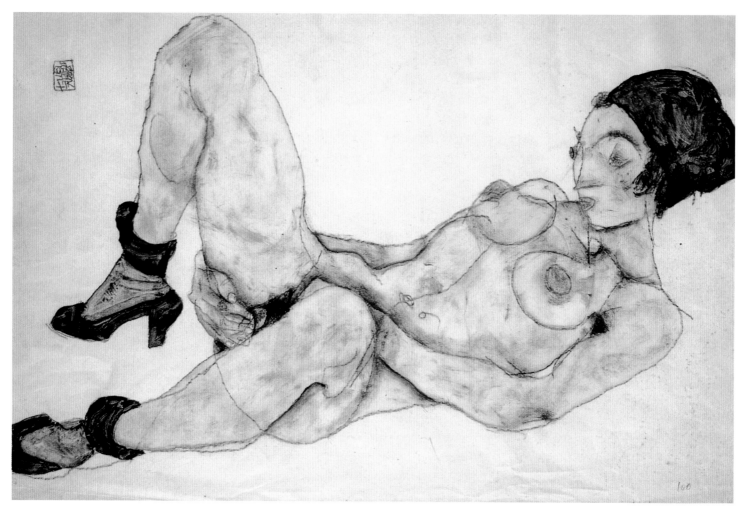

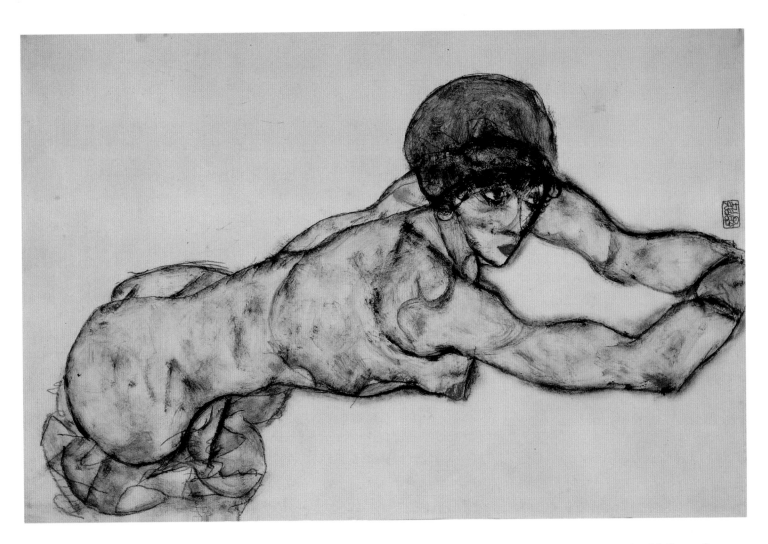

monition of dark things to come. *Reclining Figure* (1914; p. 103), *Seated Woman* (1914) and *Seated Girl* (1914; p. 102) are good examples of this.

This negative sense of being at the mercy of erotic and sexual attractions, rather than simply rejoicing in pleasure and vitality, is often confirmed by the faces, which are deprived of their individuality. The eyes that Schiele was drawing were now no more than staring dots. The faces were styled like those of carved puppets. In some pictures, the models' eyes were closed, which only heightened the sense that they were puppets to be manipulated. The portraits of women became less individualized, stripped of personality, till they came to seem like a catalogue definition of a species, as in *Nude with Green Turban* (1914; p. 104).

And yet this method of suppressing any representationally faithful portrait account of the model's features could often heighten the breathtaking presence of the body itself, most particularly when the colours were used for emphasis. Colour was indeed the true content and subject of Schiele's nudes. It is the juxtaposition of areas of solid or shaded-in colour, representing clothed or naked parts of a model's body, that gives dramatic life to a picture such as *Female Model in Bright Red Jacket and Pants* (1914; p. 106).

Schiele's new way of dispensing with individualizing features went hand in hand with a greater emphasis on aspects of the body's physical presence that created spatial dimension: his colouring grew more economical even as the plasticity of the figures increased. Sculptors such as

Reclining Female Nude with Green Cap, Leaning to the Right, 1914
Nach rechts liegender Frauenakt mit grüner Haube
Watercolour and pencil, 32 x 48.5 cm
Kallir D 1609; Vienna, Graphische Sammlung Albertina

Despite its emphatic three-dimensionality, there is a rigid, frozen quality to this nude. At this time, Schiele was moving from almost abstract two-dimensionality to a fuller three-dimensionality that looks well suited to sculptural work.

Female Model in Bright Red Jacket and Pants, 1914
Weibliches Modell in feuerroter Jacke und Hose
Gouache and pencil, 46.5 x 29.7cm
Kallir D 1593; Vienna, Graphische Sammlung Albertina

In work done between 1914 and 1917 we can see new features in Schiele's art. His – usually powerful – female figures are outlined with dark contours and draped in colourful garments, as in *The Green Stocking*. The emphasis is no longer on the genitals but on the entire physical presence of these women.

Seated Woman with Left Hand in Hair, 1914
Sitzende Frau mit linker Hand im Haar
Gouache and pencil, 48.5 x 31.4cm
Kallir D 1592; Vienna, Graphische Sammlung Albertina

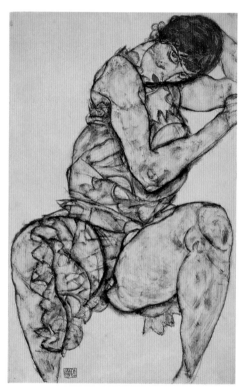

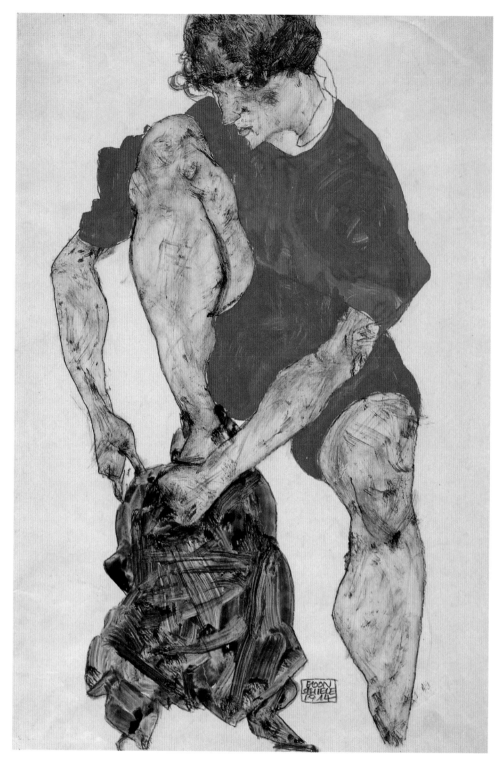

PAGE 107:
The Green Stocking, 1914
Der grüne Strumpf
Gouache and pencil, 47 x 29.2cm
Kallir D 1591; private collection

Auguste Rodin or Georges Minne may be seen as precedents for this. Schiele's nudes, seemingly arrested or indeed frozen, dramatic by virtue of their position and volume rather than the artist's colouring or brushwork, seem perfect for a transfer to stone, wood or bronze – as *Reclining Female Nude with Green Cap, Leaning to the Right* (1914; p. 105) well illustrates.

The large oil *Portrait of Friederike Maria Beer* (1914; p. 113) exemplifies all of these features. The pose is a deliberate one, such as a choreographer might require. The composition is at heart geometrical, but derives a dramatic flair from the juxtaposition of bright monochrome colours and unusual perspectives.

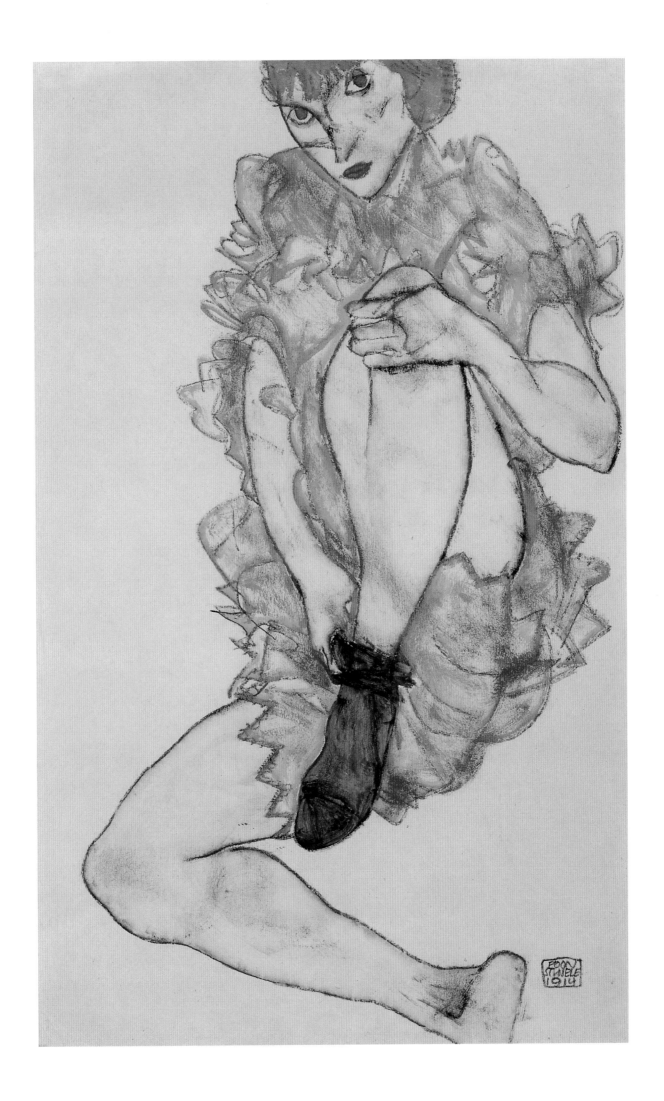

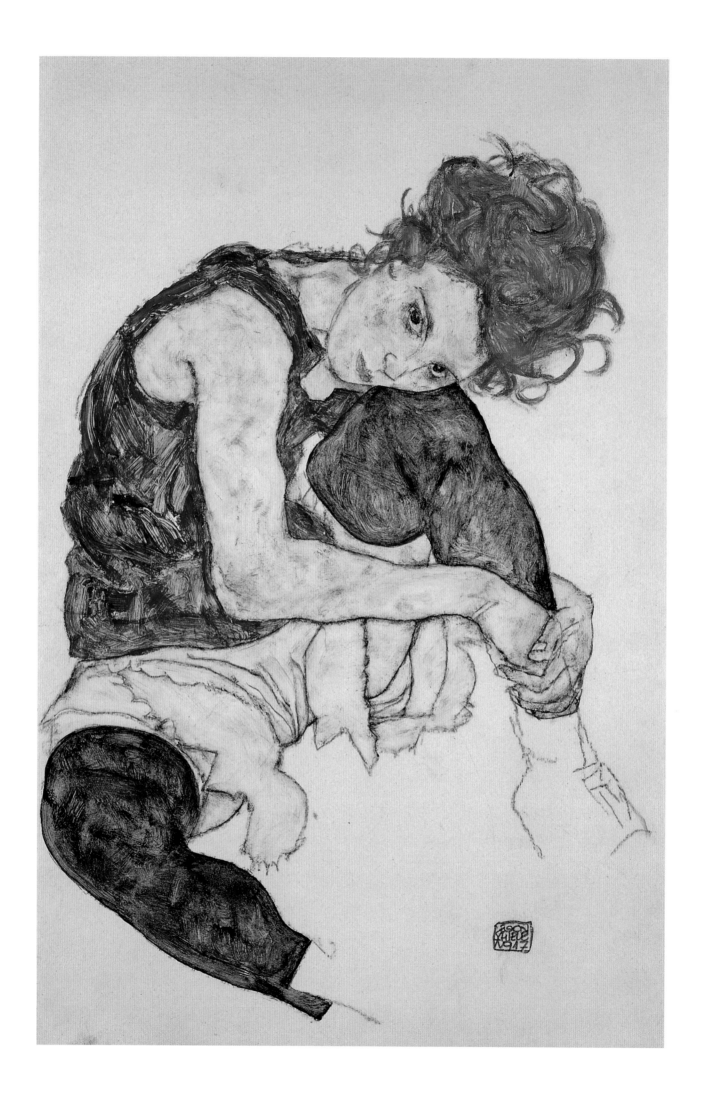

Friederike Beer was the same age as Schiele. Her father owned two of Vienna's most fashionable night clubs, the Gelbe Bar and the Kaiser Bar. Friederike was of the educated Jewish upper middle classes to which the patrons of the Wiener Werkstätte also belonged, and was herself an ardent admirer of the Werkstätte's products. She wore only clothes and hats made by them and had her apartment furnished and decorated in the Werkstätte style. She was the only woman from those circles to sit for both Schiele and Klimt. Though Klimt's *Portrait of Friederike Maria Beer* (1916; p. 112) was in fact painted two years after Schiele's, it remains a product of Art Nouveau, a style that was by then a thing of the past; it is a static, decorative piece of work, a mosaic of colours, like a tapestry.

Friederike Beer had been able to afford the portrait by Schiele herself, since his name was not yet a widely known one; but for the picture by the famous Klimt she turned to her affluent artist friend Hans Böhler, who had proposed to give her jewels for her birthday, and asked him to commission the portrait instead.

Schiele positioned Friederike on a blanket on the studio floor, and had her grasp the cushion behind her head. On her harlequin dress, which

PAGE 108:
Seated Woman with Bent Knee, 1917
Sitzende Frau mit hochgezogenem Knie
Gouache, watercolour and black crayon,
46 x 30.5 cm
Kallir D 1979; Prague, Národni Galeri

Crouching Nude Girl with Cheek Resting on Right Knee, 1917
Kauernder Mädchenakt, die Wange auf das rechte Knie gelehnt
Gouache and black crayon, 45.7 x 29.7 cm
Kallir D 1978; Vienna, Hans-Dichand-Stiftung / Galerie Würthle

Seated Girl in Slip, 1917
Sitzendes Mädchen im Unterkleid
Gouache, watercolour and black crayon,
45.7 x 29.5 cm
Kallir D 1977; private collection

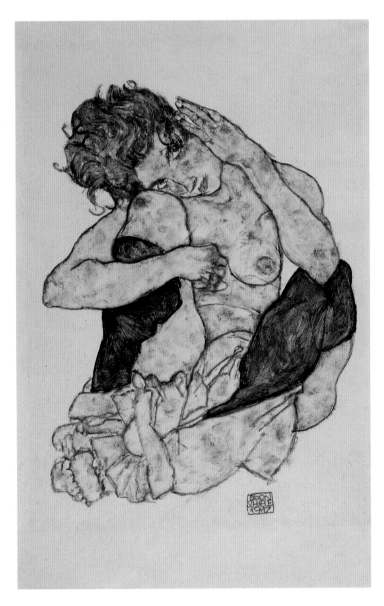

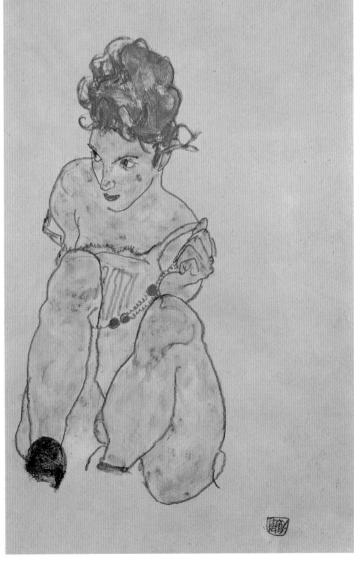

looks more like a Wiener Werkstätte carnival costume than a garment that might be worn in the street, he placed five colourful rag-dolls that Friederike had brought back from a visit to South America. The red-green and orange-yellow zig-zags and the haphazard interpolation of the doll motifs are a homage to the naive and still vigorous power of folk art, such as we still see in colourful costumes; the Blauer Reiter, the Munich group of artists, were celebrating this unspoilt source at the same period. Schiele asked Friederike to remove her shoes; with the feet bare and slightly raised, the hands raised and fingers spread, the figure is a decided S shape. And the overall effect is one of suspension rather than reclining.

Schiele suggested that the picture be hung on the ceiling rather than a wall, and for a while Friederike followed his advice. Her maid is said to have commented that it looked as if her mistress were in her grave. The comment hit the nail on the head, directing our attention, as it does, to the second level present in the painting. This flashy, avant-garde and distinctly unusual portrait of a fashion-conscious young woman is at bottom a devotional or holy picture, the woman a saint whom we might expect to look down at us from the ceiling of a church. Once we have seen the religious, iconographic flavour to the portrait, we can also see the motif of resurrection in the secular clothing.

Schiele's picture of Friederike Beer is not only an eccentric portrait, it is also a modern icon. The conservative-minded in art circles would have

Nude on Her Stomach, 1917
Am Bauch liegender weiblicher Akt
Gouache and black crayon, 29.8 x 46.1 cm
Kallir D 1951; Vienna, Graphische Sammlung
Albertina

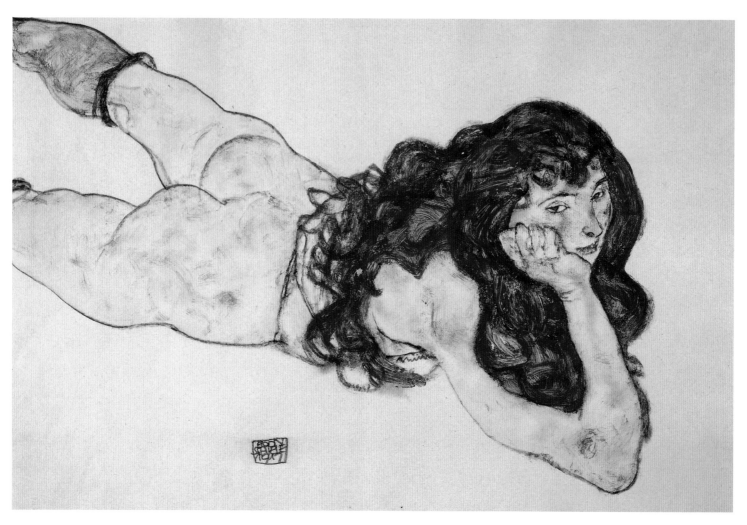

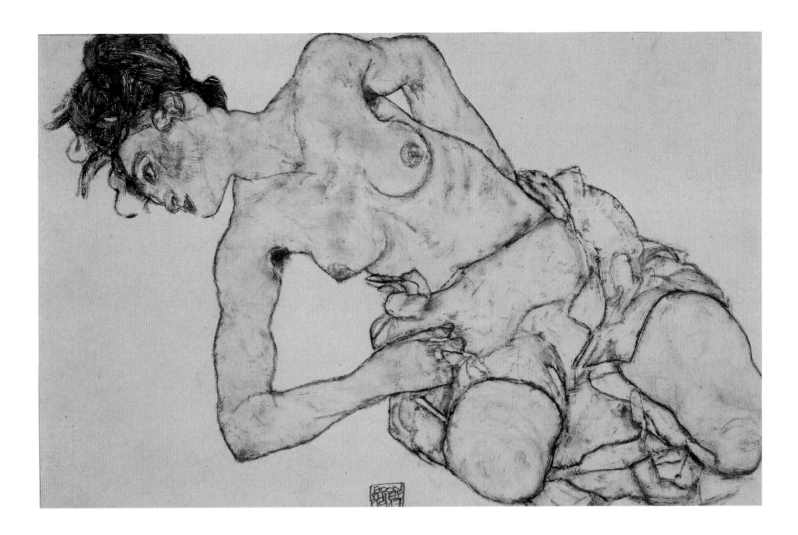

Kneeling Female Semi-Nude, 1917
Kniender weiblicher Halbakt
Gouache, black crayon and pencil, 28 x 42.5 cm
Kallir D 1946; private collection

Schiele has clearly scaled down the seductiveness of his nudes in work such as this. The woman – with no apparent reason beyond the artist's request – is leaning to one side, and Schiele has captured the pose in a fine three-dimensional drawing.

found it blasphemous to speak of "resurrection" or "icon" in conjunction with a subject so worldly; the translation of venerable Christian subjects and forms into a temporal idiom was something beyond their comprehension. But in fact the step from religious iconography to secular allegory is not a great one. In the oil *Death and Maiden (Man and Girl)* (1915–16; p. 129), Schiele paraphrases one of the major themes of Romanticism. He himself is the dark figure of Death, the man in the brown habit, while the girl is Wally. We see her holding Death in a close embrace. The picture has often been seen as a painting of farewell to Schiele's love of Wally; and certainly, in the way the two figures cling together, there seems fear – at the passing of passion, or of the unknown future.

For Schiele, the future, as we have seen, soon took on concrete definition with his marriage to Edith Harms on 17 June 1915. She was of good family, had been well educated at a convent school, and could speak English and French as well as correct high German; and she emerged victorious over the poor girl from the common people, Wally. Still, Schiele does not seem to have been on cloud nine, to judge by *Seated Couple (Egon and Edith Schiele)* (1915). Edith is holding her half-naked husband from behind, and he, eyes wide open and an expression of despair on his face, seems (from the position of his arms and legs) to be trying to break free. Schiele's partners were different – now Wally, now Edith – but the fear remained the same: of farewell, or of the new attachment. All that really changed was the key, from the muted minor of browns to the shrill dissonance of the picture with Edith.

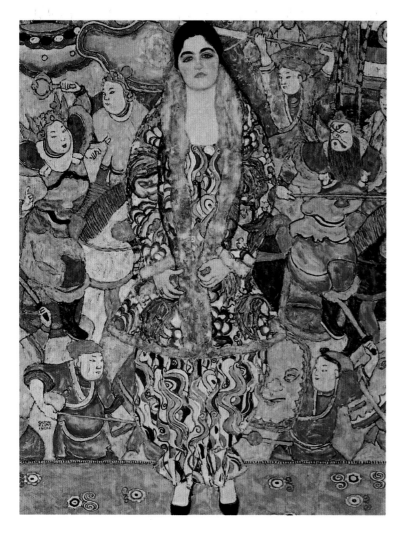

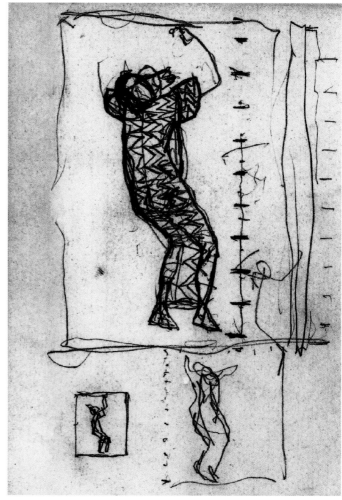

As well as these documents of love's despair, there were a number of
drawings in the first year of Schiele's marriage that showed Edith in the
role of a young and gentle wife, somewhat melancholy. Perhaps the most
impressive is the gouache *Edith Schiele, Seated* (1915; p. 115), in which
the sitter is looking inquiringly at us, her hands modestly folded in the
lap of her striped dress. The colour of her blonde hair is echoed in her
jacket, the blue stone in her ring contrasts with the green stone at her
neck, and the red of her lips is picked up along the edges of her collar.
Everything except for the striped pattern of her dress conspires to contain
emotion and establish formal harmony.

Much the same can be said of the oil *Portrait of the Artist's Wife, Standing (Edith Schiele in Striped Dress)* (1915; p. 114). Here, though, a border
has been crossed, from harmonious containment to rigidity. Edith seems
some monstrous dummy, or an impassive mannequin showing off a cre-
ation of the Wiener Werkstätte. (In point of fact the dress was made from
the curtains in her husband's studio.) It is as if Klimt's typical *grande
dame* had been parodically restated in a folk idiom.

Soon after his marriage in June 1915, Schiele was called up; after training in Bohemia (in Prague and Neuhaus) he was assigned to guard duties
and then clerical work near Vienna, and was even given permission to
spend his nights at his Hietzing studio. Despite this generosity on the part
of the authorities, military service – which he detested – together with the
necessary change in his circumstances as a married man cast a shadow

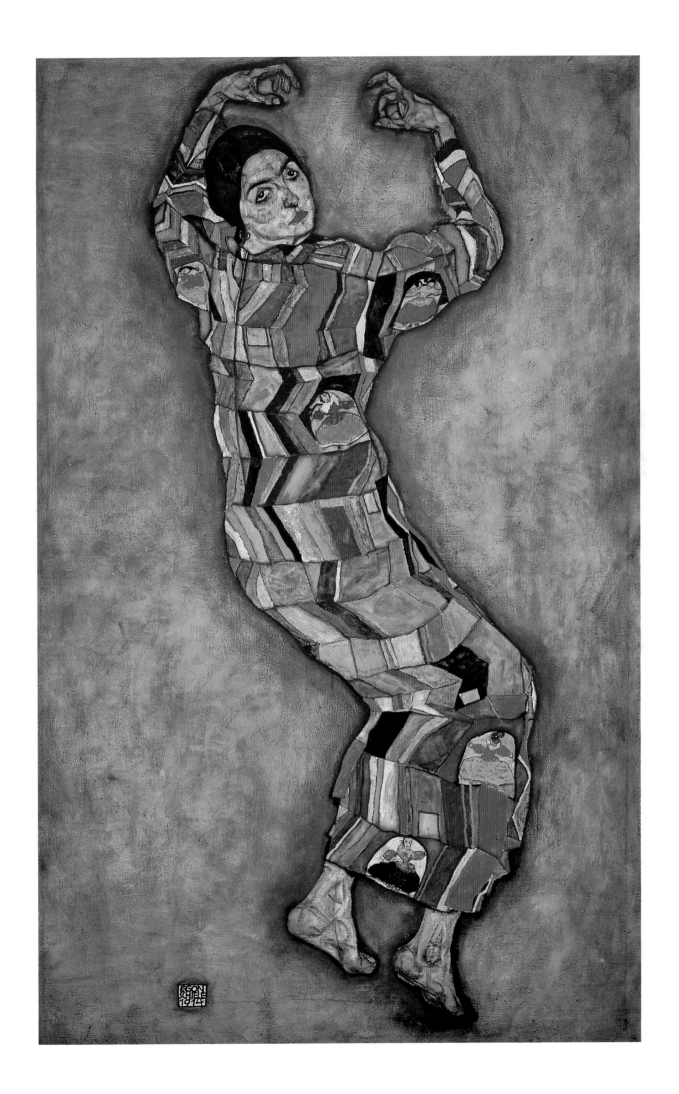

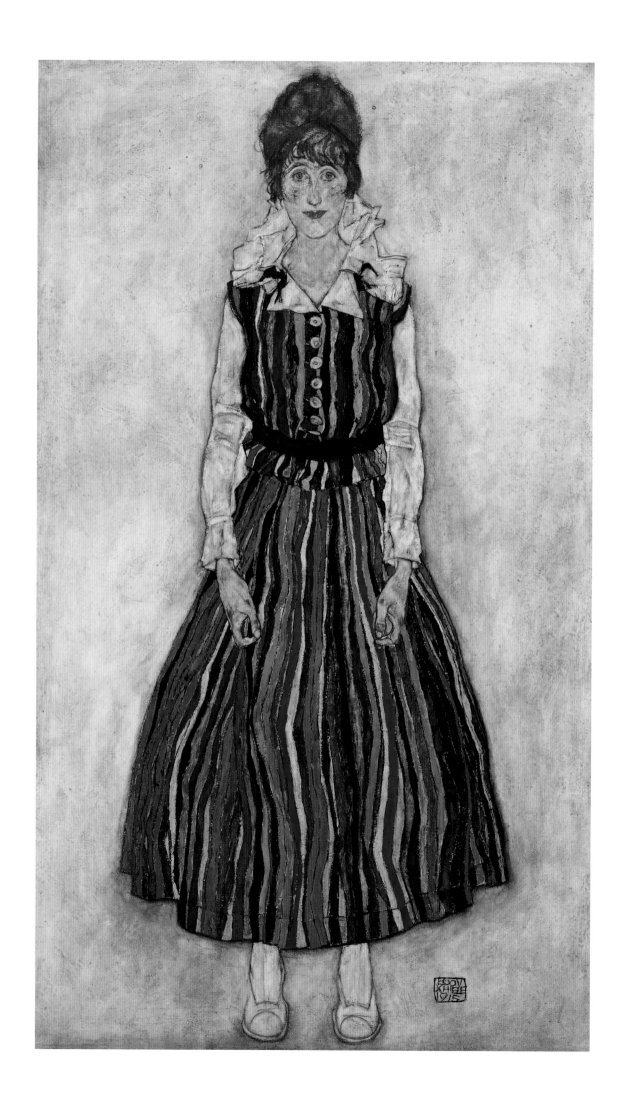

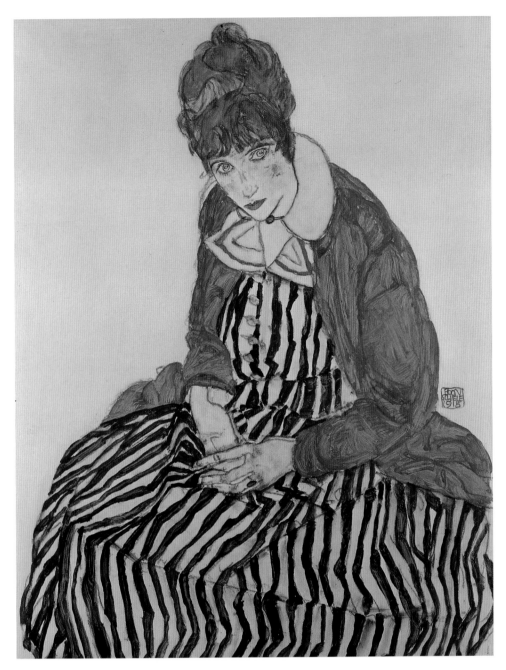

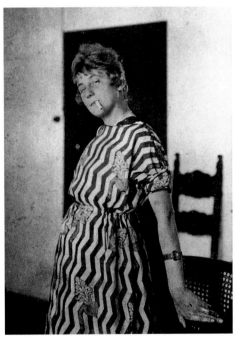

Edith Schiele, Seated, 1915
Edith Schiele, sitzend
Gouache, watercolour and black crayon,
50.5 x 38.5 cm
Kallir D 1717; private collection

Schiele's first painting of his wife has had the
greatest influence on subsequent views of Edith
Schiele.

Edith Schiele with a cigarette, no doubt borrowed for this 1916 photograph from her husband, who smoked heavily.

PAGE 114:
*Portrait of the Artist's Wife, Standing (Edith
Schiele in Striped Dress)*, 1915
*Bildnis der Frau des Künstlers, stehend (Edith
Schiele in gestreiftem Kleid)*
Oil on canvas, 180 x 110cm
Kallir P 290; The Hague, Haags Gemeente-
museum

From 1915, the year he married, Schiele's princi-
pal model was his wife Edith, whom he drew
and painted time and again in various poses and
clothes.

over Schiele's life as an artist. 1916 was his least productive year. All he did were a number of portraits of Russian prisoners of war, Austrian officers, fellow soldiers in his regiment, and family members.

The period of rebellion, when Schiele breached social taboos and was forever looking for new formal strategies, was drawing to a close. From 1916 to 1918 his art simplified, as he consolidated and calmed the approach he had already arrived at. The classical traits we have already remarked on became still more pronounced – as far as this is possible in an Expressionist temperament.

Nude on Her Stomach (1917; p. 110) is a good example of this development. It is as if the characteristic exactions of Schiele's earlier style had been robbed of their edge. The crayon outlines are soft and the figure has been three-dimensionally contoured, with a fleshy softness. The colour highlights are reticently deployed and have been muted by the prevalent unifying brown. The model, chin cupped in her hand, is gazing thoughtfully; the provocative sexuality of Schiele's challenging earlier nudes is gone, and indeed all his 1917 nudes look as if a professor had posed them in the life class.

The culmination and peak of Schiele's tussle with Woman in his new classical style comes with the two large oils *Embrace (Lovers II)* (1917; p. 118/119) and *Portrait of the Artist's Wife, Seated* (1918; p. 36). The former can be seen as a positive, Expressionist paraphrase – in contrast to the negative which Schiele had supplied in *Cardinal and Nun* (1912; p. 164) of Klimt's *The Kiss* (1907/08; p. 164). Details such as the turbulent folds of the cloth the lovers are lying on, or the woman's tumbling, seemingly windswept hair, serve to heighten the dramatic impact, as in Kokoschka's *The Tempest* (1914; p. 128). Schiele's voyeuristic, provocative portrayals of sexual congress in earlier work have been replaced by a sweeping symbolic gesture: we are being invited to experience for ourselves, with the lovers, the physical and spiritual implications of an embrace. And again, the sexual act contains within it the fear of loneliness.

Schiele prepared for the painting of *Portrait of the Artist's Wife, Seated* meticulously, in many a drawing and sketch. In one gouache, *Portrait of the Artist's Wife* (1917; p. 37), the colouring and detail working are clearly subordinate to the larger sense of form. Our attention is being drawn to the portrait head and the sitter's hands. In the painting, Schiele presented his wife full-figure, posed in mirror image to her position in the drawing. Her facial expression is less clearly defined, her gaze less focused, her bearing more withdrawn. Her hands are clasped, and with the arms they form an oval. The colours are subdued. In other words, a degree of compromise with the conventional idea of portraiture is in evidence. And it is even clearer if we compare the first version of the portrait, in which Edith was wearing a brightly chequered skirt. Schiele painted over this skirt for the later, final version, apparently at the suggestion of Franz Martin Haberditzl, director of what was to become the Österreichische Galerie, who wanted to acquire the painting for the museum but felt the original skirt to be too loud or daring. Public collections, though they were cautiously opening up to modern artists, still saw themselves as the custodians of official taste, as their name (till 1918) made clear: "Collections of the Most Exalted Imperial House".

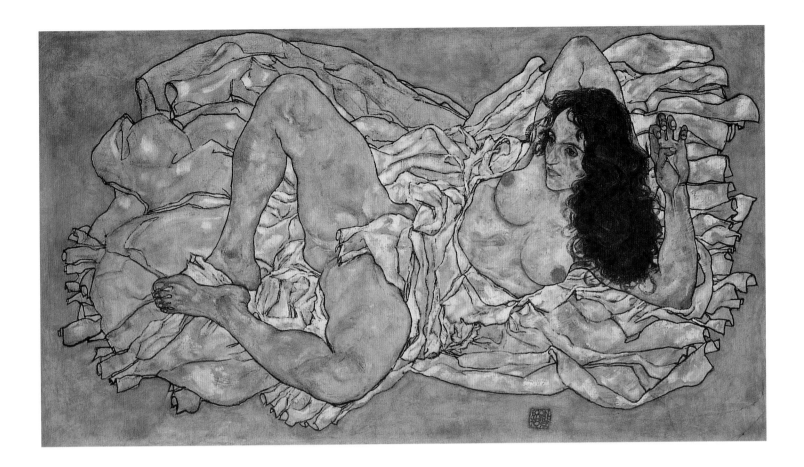

For one of his works to be acquired by the museum (the only time this happened in his lifetime) was an honour that Schiele was not anxious to forego, so he overpainted the bright check in a neutral, indefinable grey. To retain a little of the original liveliness he added a black neckband at the collar blouse, with a red tassel. And so the portrait set the seal on a development towards a more sober form of expression that had been in progress since 1916.

In the eight short years since 1910, Schiele explored the image of Woman from many and various angles – from the budding, awkward body of the pubescent girl via the models in seductive, explicit poses to the portrait of his wife Edith, fit for a museum. In the early years he had been willing to articulate his provocations and his assaults on taboos in angular, aggressively expressive modes that were not wary of ugliness. Then, as he developed, Schiele returned to the unity of line and the fundamentals of classical composition. On the map of modern art, Schiele the Austrian stands midway between Ernst Ludwig Kirchner and Amedeo Modigliani, between the North and the South, between the dramatic, angular style of the German and the soft, melodious manner of the Italian.

Reclining Woman, 1917
Liegende Frau
Oil on canvas, 95.5 x 171 cm
Kallir P 306; Vienna, Sammlung Rudolf Leopold

PAGE 118/119:
Embrace (Lovers II), 1917
Umarmung (Liebespaar II)
Oil on canvas, 100 x 170.2 cm
Kallir P 304; Vienna, Österreichische Galerie. Belvedere

It is primarily the turbulent brushwork that conveys the passion of this embrace. The woman's hair is tumbled and the sheet crumpled. As in Kokoschka's *The Tempest* (1914, p. 128), which shows the artist and Alma Mahler, Schiele's lovers seem afloat on a sea of their own solitude.

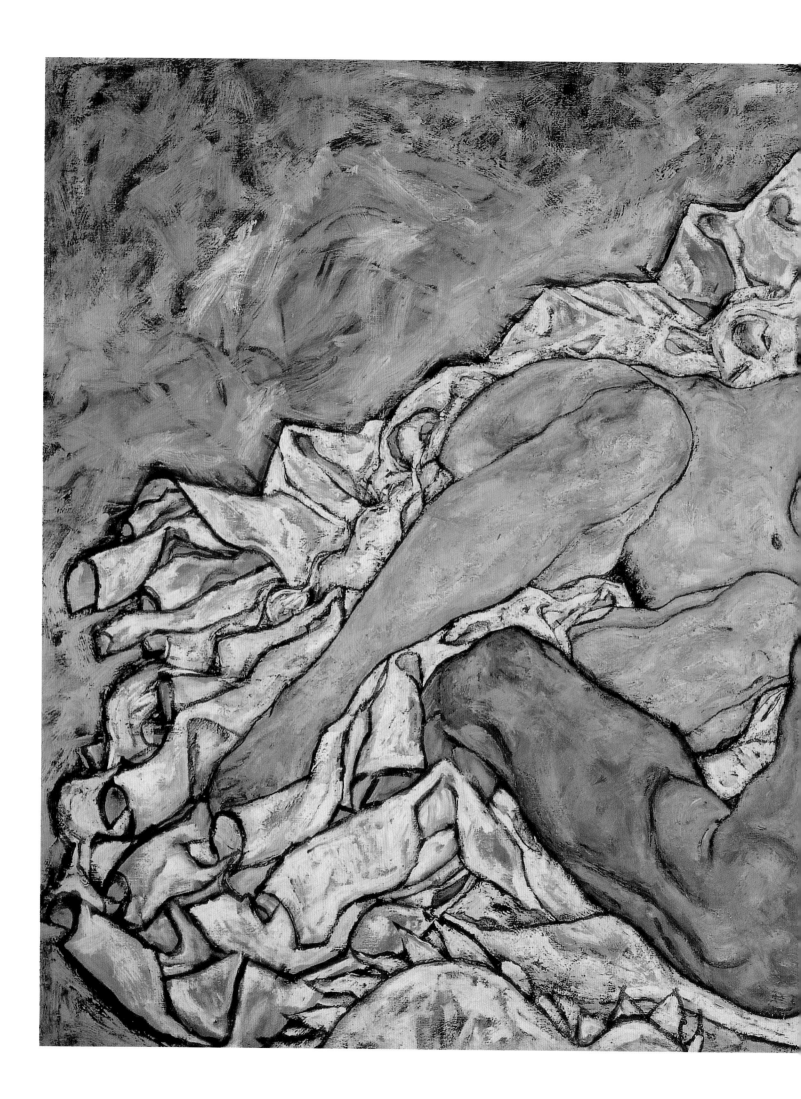

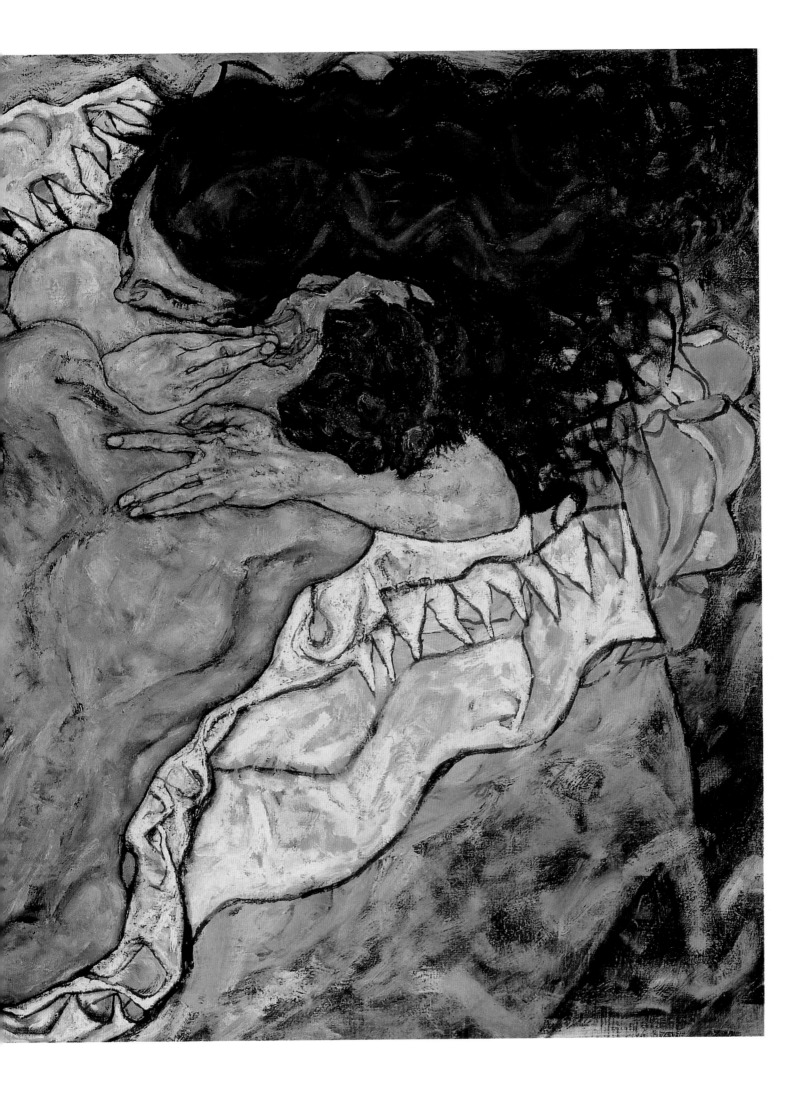

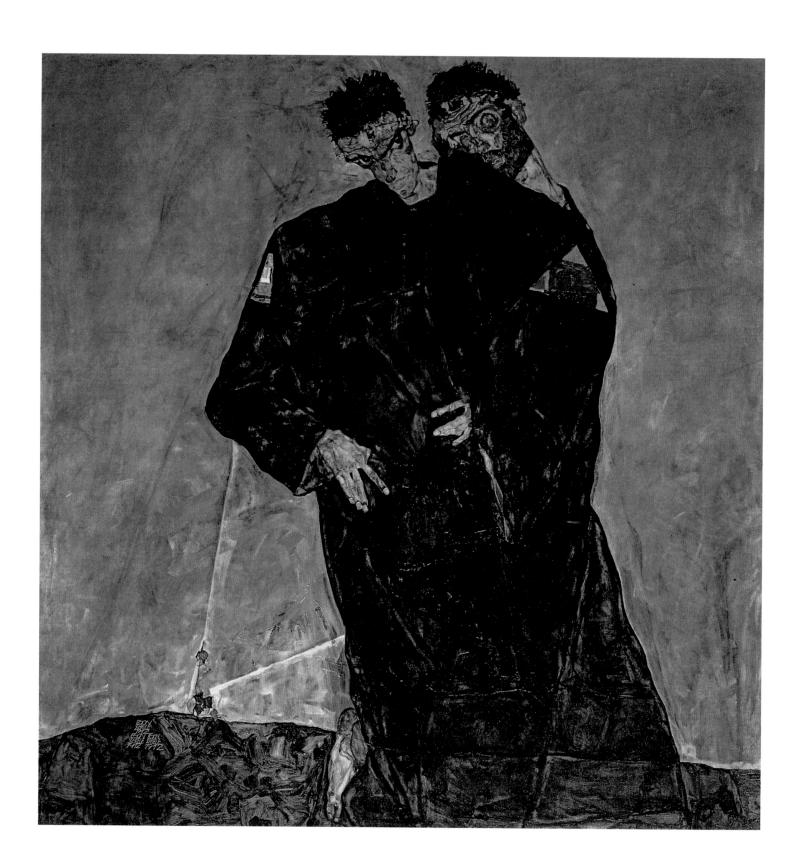

The Image of Humanity: Allegory and Unmasking

For his intimate portrayals of women, Schiele usually worked in small formats, in the chamber music techniques of the artist: drawings, watercolours, gouaches. He tended to keep oil for larger existential issues, for images of life and death, loneliness or conversion. Oil provided Schiele a platform on which to present his ideas in highly individual allegories that combined religious and secular traditions with the passion of the Expressionist artist.

One key picture in this vein is *Agony* (1912; p. 123). We see the heads of two monks; one, the bearded elder, is in profile, the younger *en face*. The elder is looking with concern at the younger, and making an imploring gesture. The younger, his head like a skull with red hollows for eyes, is holding his left hand to his heart, while his right hand, bearing stigmata, is raised as if crippled with pain. The immediate subject of this painting – an elder monk witnessing the pain and death agony of a younger – is surely of secondary significance. Of greater importance is the father-son relation, in religious mode. The hypnotic, governing power of the elder man seems to be transferred by look and gesture to the younger. It is only when we examine this second level, not at first apparent, that we perceive Schiele's distinctive way of transforming a general subject into a personal allegory.

As in *The Hermits* (1912; p. 120), what we are seeing is a religiously-styled rendering of the relation of father Klimt to Schiele the son. Power is transmitted from the father or master to the younger man. Schiele, exaggerating narcissistically, presents himself as a weak man, stigmatized and dying. The issue at stake is not dialogue but domination and submission to rule.

The grim message of life and death, rule and submission, the magical power of the father figure and the fading strength of the other, is articulated in Schiele's use of colour. Dirty reds, browns and brownish blacks, with hints of blue, establish a kind of curtain of colour from which the two men's heads and hands emerge like the limbs of puppets. If we cover up the figural parts, it is easy to see the canvas as an abstract composition. The colours, confined to separate geometrical fields, still convey doomfulness. Schiele's contemporaries felt the picture was close in manner to Cubism, and saw this as a bad thing; but in fact we can now see this proximity, in retrospect, as a wholly positive attestation of Schiele's strength as a witness of his times. Art had moved on, from Impressionism and Art Nouveau through Cubism and Fauvism, and this modern evolu-

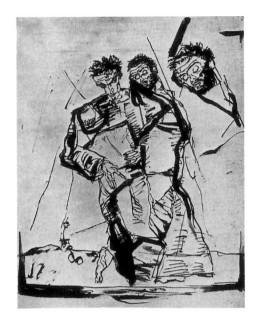

Self-Portrait with Gustav Klimt, 1912
Selbstporträt mit Gustav Klimt
(Study for *The Hermits*)
Indian ink, 24 x 19 cm
Private collection

Egon Schiele's study makes the underlying pyramidal structure of *The Hermits* evident, and shows how meticulously he worked out the positions of the heads and fingers.

PAGE 120:
The Hermits, 1912
Die Eremiten
Oil on canvas, 181 x 181 cm
Kallir P 229; Vienna, Sammlung Rudolf Leopold

"…the bodies of men tired of life, suicides, but the bodies of sensitive people. I see the two figures like a cloud of dust that resembles this world, gathering but doomed to collapse" wrote Schiele of *The Hermits*. It shows himself and Klimt. The wreaths of autumn fruits and thistle flowers, and the withered roses, are symbols of mortality.

tion was in his very blood, even if it led him to his own personal brand of Expressionism.

The main distinguishing features of the picture – its roughly square format, the two figures and their close, silent relation, and the autonomous, geometrical fields of colour – are in evidence in other pictures Schiele painted in 1911 and 1912.

One of his most important paintings is *The Hermits* (1912; p.120), a picture closely related in its motifs, showing the young Schiele and the elder Klimt in a pose of religious fraternity. The figure on the left and to the fore is Schiele, eyes wide open; behind him is Klimt, eyes closed, lips parted, garlanded with a wreath of symbolic autumn fruits. They are enveloped in large habits that take up the entire central portion of the composition, like a black rock full of mysterious inner power; the white highlighting that lends this dark area a little variety is barely visible. The hands, heads and one foot break free of this quasi-natural block like mythical creatures; we think of Atlas struggling with the forces of Nature. The wreath of thistle flowers on Schiele's head and the two withered roses behind him stand for pain and transience. Near the roses, the twenty-two-year-old Schiele signed his name three times, as if to tell the world that he existed and had no alternative but to do and paint as he did. In a letter to the collector Carl Reininghaus, Schiele offered this gloss on the painting: "In the big picture one cannot at first make out exactly how the two men are standing ... The lack of definition in the figures, which were in-

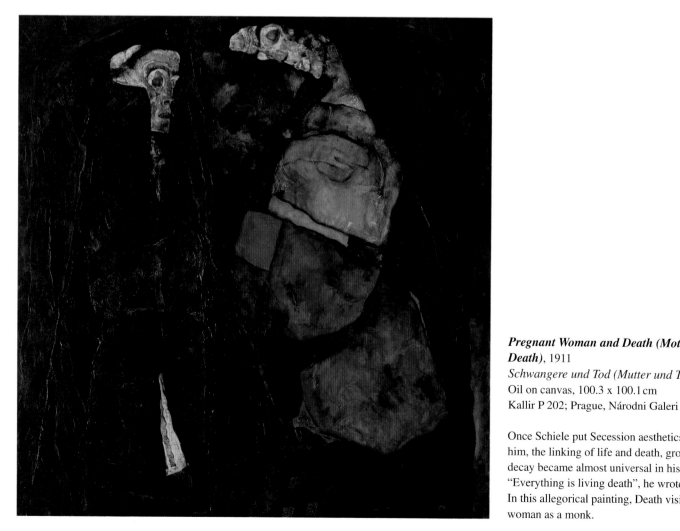

***Pregnant Woman and Death (Mother and Death)*, 1911**
Schwangere und Tod (Mutter und Tod)
Oil on canvas, 100.3 x 100.1 cm
Kallir P 202; Prague, Národni Galeri

Once Schiele put Secession aesthetics behind him, the linking of life and death, growth and decay became almost universal in his work. "Everything is living death", he wrote in a poem. In this allegorical painting, Death visits the woman as a monk.

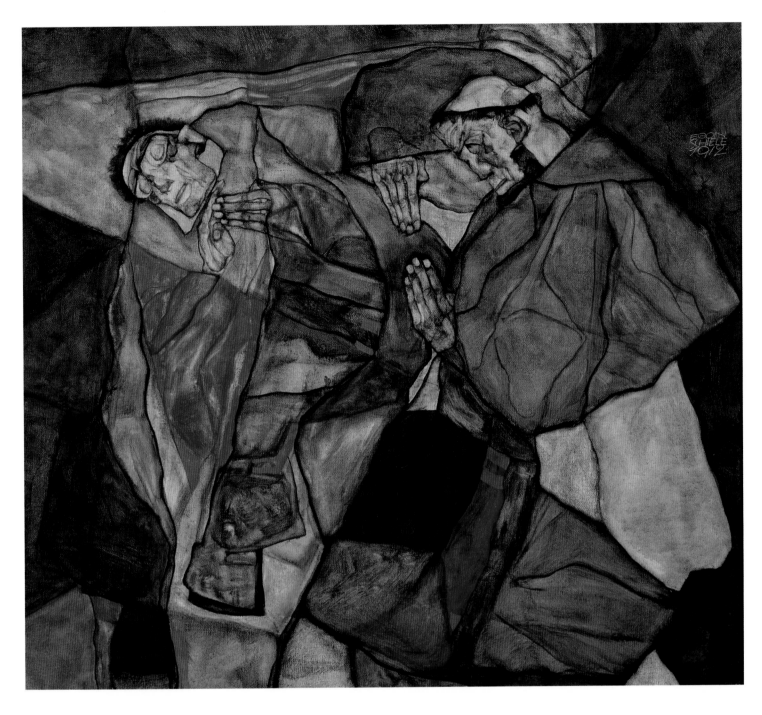

tended to be sagging … the bodies of men tired of life, suicides, but the bodies of sensitive people. I see the two figures like a cloud of dust that resembles this world, gathering but doomed to collapse."[7]

Schiele's reference to "the bodies of sensitive people" points to an important principle in Expressionist art. The figures in his portraits and allegories are always vehicles for expressive values, personifying basic attitudes, moods and emotions.

In *Pregnant Woman and Death (Mother and Death)* (1911; p. 122) Schiele turns to the dramatic cycle of growth and decay, birth and death. Death as a tonsured man in a habit recalls an actor in the *Everyman* morality play in Salzburg, as he emerges from a backdrop of dark colours marked out into abstract areas by strong lines. The face of the pregnant woman is spotlit like that of an iconic Virgin. The same subject matter of motherhood confronted with Death occurs with variations in *Dead Mother I* (1910; p. 126) and *Blind Mother* (1914; p. 124).

Agony, 1912
Agonie
Oil on canvas, 70 x 80 cm
Kallir P 230; Munich, Neue Pinakothek

An allegorical work again featuring a tonsured monk in his habit. His massive figure indicates Gustav Klimt, who appears here not as a friend but as a threat, against which the figure on the left, Schiele, seems to be raising his hands defensively. The painting is tantamount to a programmatic farewell to Secession aesthetics.

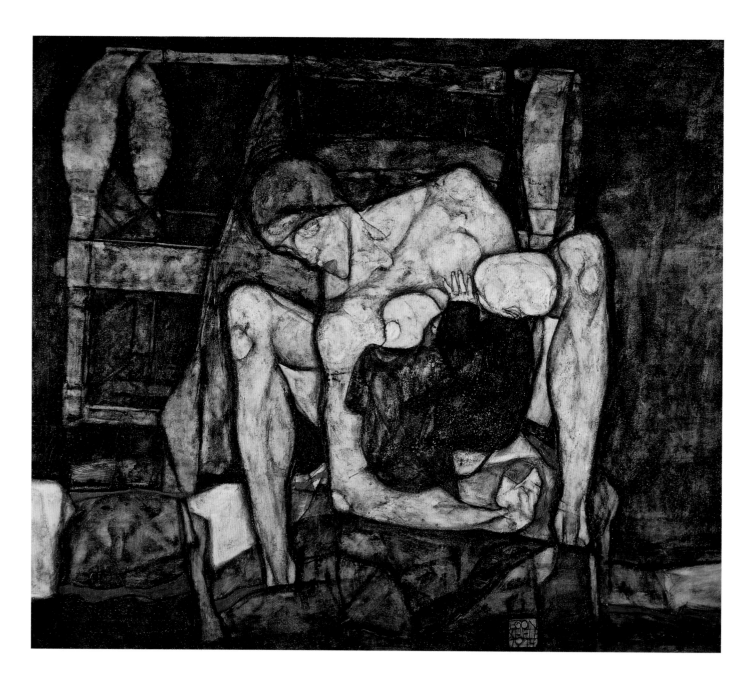

Blind Mother, 1914
Blinde Mutter
Oil on canvas, 99.5 x 120.4 cm
Kallir P 272; Vienna, Sammlung Rudolf Leopold

Schiele's pictures of the mother and child theme tend to have a monumental
quality, as in this work, where the body of the mother looks hewn from stone.
The heads of the two children are like balls of stone or ivory. This painting
marks a peak in the grand, monumental manner Schiele was capable of in his
figural work.

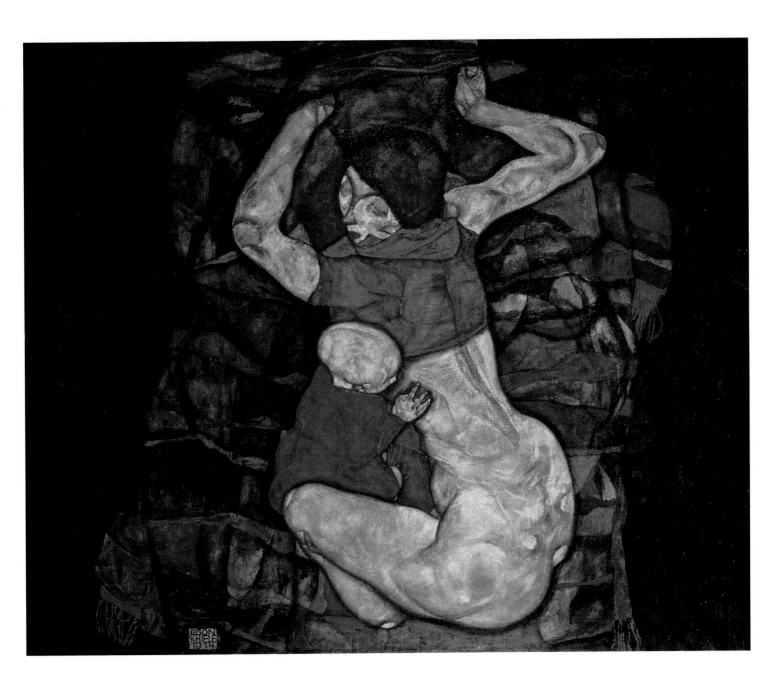

Young Mother, 1914
Junge Mutter
Oil on canvas, 100 x 110 cm
Kallir P 273; private collection, courtesy Galerie St. Etienne, New York

This young mother too has been seen with the eye of a sculptor. The twist of
the woman's body, counter to that of the child, and the uplifted arms, establish
a three-dimensional spatiality. The limbs are partially cropped to emphasize
the torso, and the eyes seem blind in order to eliminate personality.

Dead Mother I, 1910
Tote Mutter
Oil and pencil on wood, 32.4 x 25.8cm
Kallir P 177; Vienna, Sammlung Rudolf Leopold

Egon Schiele symbolizes the proximity of life
and death once more in this work. The child at
the centre looks as if it is in an amniotic sac, but
the black around it is like a shroud, while the mother's bony face and hands look deathly.

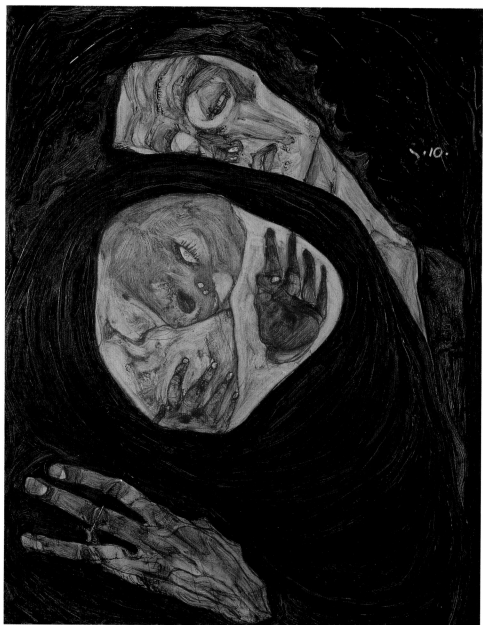

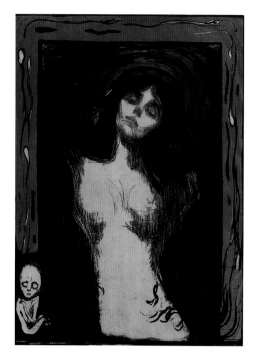

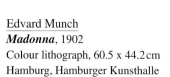

Edvard Munch
Madonna, 1902
Colour lithograph, 60.5 x 44.2cm
Hamburg, Hamburger Kunsthalle

These sombre paintings seem lit solely from within, by a light that emphasizes the polarity of life and death. In a letter of 1912, Schiele himself wrote: "The picture must give off its own light, bodies have light
of their own, which they use in the course of living; they burn up, they
are unlit."[8] In another letter he observed: "I paint the light that comes
from every body."[9]

It is surely correct to say that Schiele was influenced in this pessimistic
choice of subject by his difficult relations with his own mother. The careworn widow, left with three children and a small pension following the
early death of Schiele's father, never forgave her son for the aggressive
egocentricity with which he pursued his life in art. The worst of all was
that her hope that one day her son would be able and willing to support
her financially was never met.

While Schiele's treatment of motherhood can be seen as a way of ad-
dressing his own mother, there are other works that stress positive feelings about life. *Young Mother* (1914; p. 125) takes its subject as an occasion to lend a sculpturally plastic emphasis to the woman's body and

Holy Family, 1913
Heilige Familie
Gouache and pencil on parchment-like paper,
47 x 36.5 cm
Kallir P 248; private collection, courtesy Galerie
St. Etienne, New York

In this gouache, Schiele portrayed himself and
his then partner Wally. The child has the quality
of an apparition. About the woman's head there
is a yellow halo, and the hands seem to be making ritual gestures.

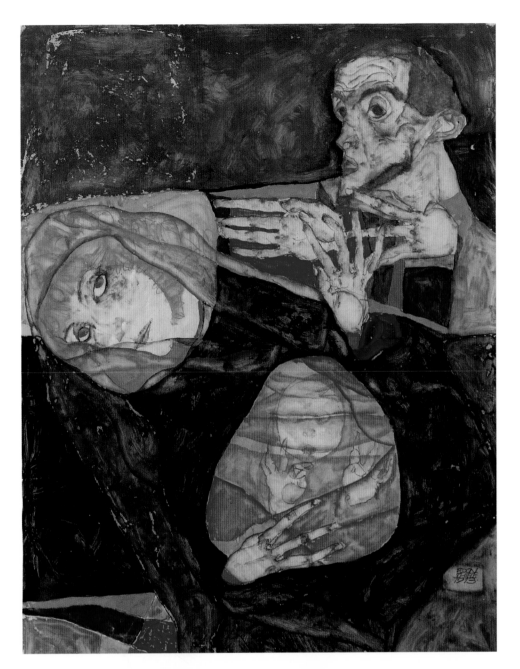

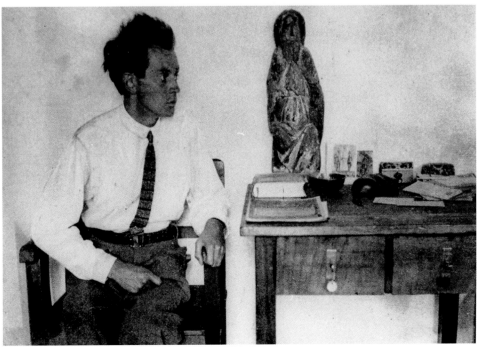

Egon Schiele in his studio in Hietzinger Hauptstrasse in 1915. At that date the wooden statuette
of a saint belonged to Arthur Roessler, but in
1917 he gave it to Schiele.

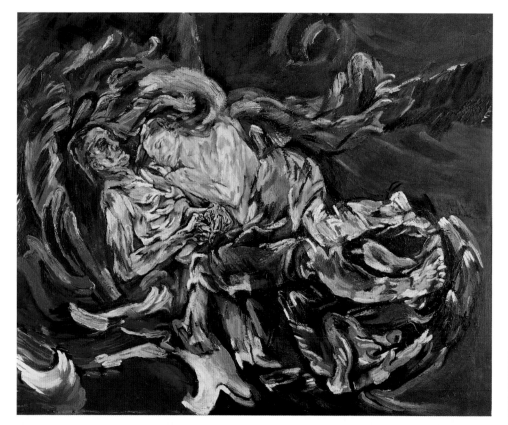

Oskar Kokoschka
The Tempest, 1914
Die Windsbraut
Oil on canvas, 181 x 220cm
Basle, Öffentliche Kunstsammlung,
Kunstmuseum

This painting was Oskar Kokoschka's way of
portraying his problematic relations with Alma
Mahler, the young widow of Gustav Mahler.

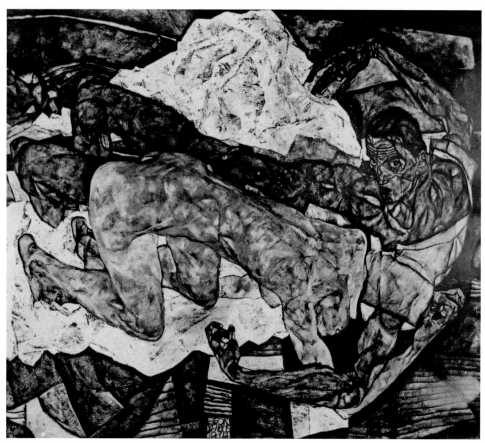

In the first, unsigned version of *Death and
Maiden* (p. 129), the girl's buttocks are exposed.

Man and Woman I (Lovers I), 1914
Mann und Mädchen (Liebespaar I)
Oil on canvas, 119 x 138cm
Kallir P 275; whereabouts unknown

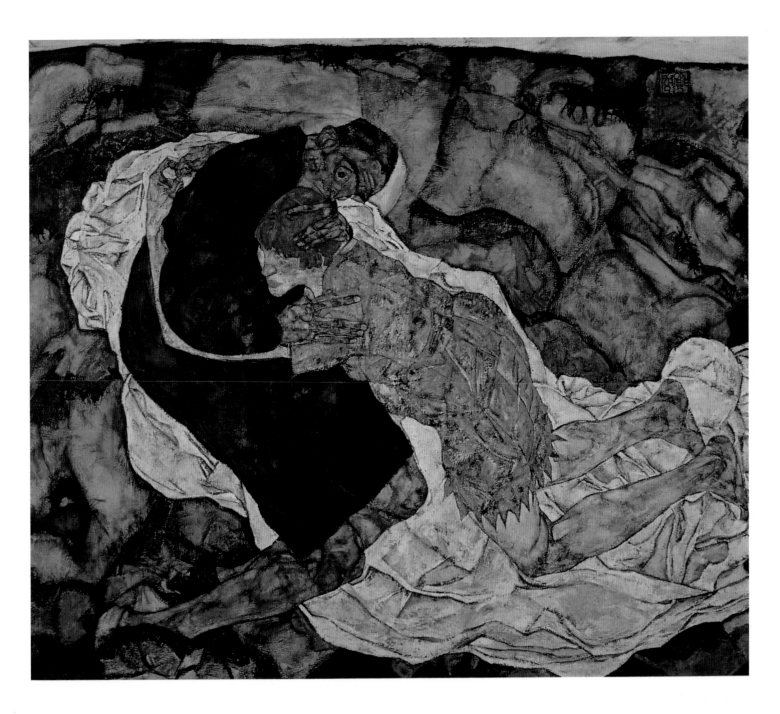

Death and Maiden (Man and Girl), 1915–16
Tod und Mädchen (Mann und Mädchen)
Oil on canvas, 150 x 180 cm
Kallir P 289; Vienna, Österreichische Galerie. Belvedere

The painting can be read, among other things, as Schiele's farewell to Wally
after their years together. Though the lovers are clinging to each other, in their
faces there is pain and the certainty that they must part. The man is wearing a
penitential robe. The unrelieved karst landscape behind them only confirms
the grim, despairing mood and the fearful foreknowledge of loneliness.

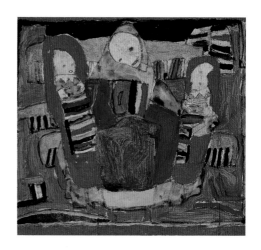

***Mother with Children, Flanked by Toys and
Ornaments (detail)***, 1915
*Mutter mit Kindern, in den seitlichen Feldern
Spielzeug und Ornamente*
Gouache and pencil, 17.5 x 43.5 cm
Kallir D 1799; Linz, Neue Galerie der Stadt Linz

On the back of the sheet Schiele has noted:
"Design for a handbag for Edith." The drawing
points to Schiele's predilection for folk art and
its colourfulness.

the child's head; their individual features interest the artist less. The
child's head is simply an oval, the woman's with its high eyebrows an
excuse for heavily stylized facial presentation. The exaggerated curves
of the woman's pelvis are echoed in the position of her arms, clutching
a pillow, upraised like the arms of a caryatid. Her left thigh leads our
gaze towards the centre of the composition, and has the effect of establishing spatial dimension. The two figures seem almost sculpted as we
see them in the light against the dark background of a patterned blanket.
This is no portrait account of individual people; it is a symbolic image
of Motherhood.

By contrast, the treatment in *Mother with Two Children III* (1917;
p. 131) seems as naive as the illustrations in children's books. Plasticity
has been forgone in favour of decorative values. The threesome draw
their life from the colourfulness of the children's striped clothes in contrast with the ashen pallor of the mother's nun-like garment. The two
children resting against their orange cushions have a puppet-like quality.
As for the mother, she looks troubled at heart; it is her sunken-cheeked
face that occupies the centre axis of the composition, as if Schiele had in
fact intended any positive statement on the matter of motherhood to be
weakened.

Schiele also amplified the subject of mother and child into the traditional group including the father. His renderings of this theme range from
the conventionally Christian, as in *Holy Family* (1913; p. 127), to more
subjective, secular allegorical work such as *The Family (Squatting
Couple)* (1918; p. 132). In the former picture, Schiele himself is seen in
the role of Joseph, while Mary bears the features of Wally. In the 1918
painting, Schiele again appears in the role of the father; the seated
woman, however, is not Edith, a circumstance that has prompted an
amount of speculation among the critics. But this is of little importance.
The women in Schiele's pictures – whether lover, wife, or model – were
essentially extras in the grand drama of Schiele's ego, a drama fought out
between manic self-doubt and manic self-infatuation. It is a drama that
Schiele repeatedly put before us, casting himself in the role of Death, as a
lover in *Man and Woman I (Lovers I)* (1914), as St. Joseph, or as a kind
of Adam in *The Family (Squatting Couple)*.

Alongside and in contrast to such allegorical images of humanity,
Schiele's œuvre contains works of parodic tendency in which his aim is
to unmask. In a manner quite opposed to tradition, for instance, he paints
the newborn and "innocent" child as an ugly creature in a crinkled bag of
skin too large for it. Conventionally, children in art were putti, angelic
little cherubs, the adorable infant Jesus; and Schiele parodied this convention with his hyper-realistic pictures of infants. He saw children as a critical eye might see them in a maternity ward. He painted and drew them as
if determined to show that his task as an artist was not to show the splendour of humanity but its pitiful wretchedness.

In 1910 a gynaecologist friend, Erwin von Graff, secured Schiele access to the university gynaecological clinic, and there he found his material for a realistic unmasking of the traditional iconography of children.
Newborn Baby (1910; p. 134) was one of the drawings Schiele did at this
time. The baby's head is outsize, the body rickety, the movements of the

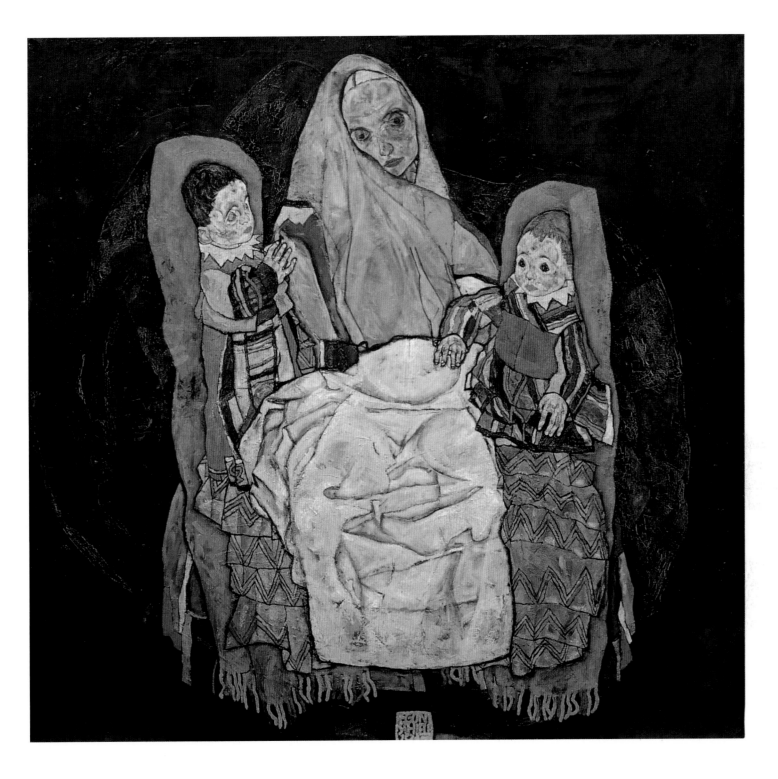

Mother with Two Children III, 1917
Mutter mit zwei Kindern III
Oil on canvas, 150 x 158.7 cm
Kallir P 303; Vienna, Österreichische Galerie. Belvedere

Elements of folk art can be seen here too. The colourful materials recall the
peasant costumes of Moravia, where Schiele's mother grew up. Schiele's
nephew, Anton Peschka jr., born in 1914, was the model for the children.
Though the colours are bright, the painting is tragic; the features of the
woman in habit-like garb are careworn, and Schiele may well have been
thinking of his own mother, by whom he never felt understood.

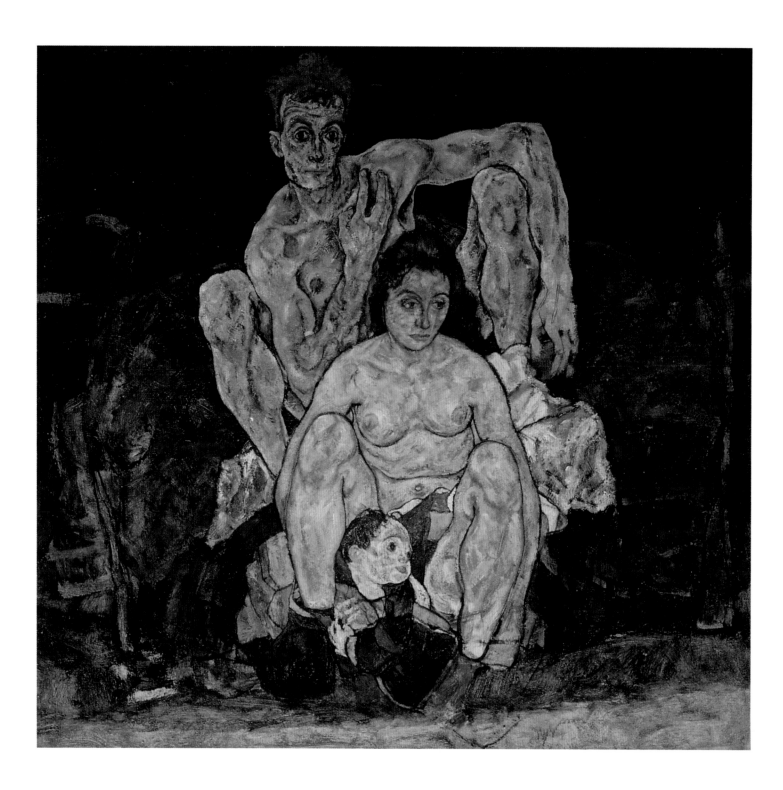

The Family (Squatting Couple), 1918
Die Familie (Kauerndes Menschenpaar)
Oil on canvas, 152.5 x 162.5 cm
Kallir P 326; Vienna, Österreichische Galerie. Belvedere

Egon Schiele painted this picture, plainly unfinished, in the year of his death.
The man is clearly the artist himself; the woman is not Edith, though. The
child was added later, probably when Schiele learnt that his wife was
pregnant. The picture moves us by its hopefulness and sense of a future,
unusual in Schiele. It appeared in the 1918 Secession catalogue as *Squatting
Couple,* but after the death of Schiele and his wife it was retitled *The Family.*

hands and legs as yet uncoordinated. Schiele drew the baby's hair standing on end, its facial features distorted and its half-closed eyes fixed in an expression that seems one of horror and suffering. Its belly is like a limp, leathery bag, and its navel is like a wound, a hole in its body. The red scrotum looks ulcerous between the spread, bluish legs, and the thin, purpled arms reaching up to the shoulders look cramped. This is the human child as homunculus. Schiele saw newborn infants as shrivelled ancients with grief in their eyes, as if they were afraid of beginning their journey through the worldly vale of tears.

That same year, Schiele did a number of sketches of youths, working-class children and urchins, and here too it is striking – for instance, in *Two Guttersnipes* (1910; p.136) – that his unsmiling subjects betray no *joie de vivre* and evince no youthful beauty. Their clothes are shabby, their expressions unfriendly and wary. The artist emphasizes their hands and heads, stressing what is rough and unattractive in them and anticipating the hardships of life that will sooner or later bow and ruin their bodies.

Cardinal and Nun (Caress) (1912; p.164) shows Schiele's parodic unmasking at its consummate height. The two figures in their kneeling embrace are positioned in the centre of a rigorous triangular composition established with substantial blocks of colour. The man, in the red robes of a cardinal, is caressing the woman, in the purple-black habit of a nun. The nun is gazing out at us fearfully, while the cardinal, in determined profile, is concentrating on the object of his desire.

This painting is without doubt a restatement and parody of Klimt's *The Kiss* (1907/08; p.164). Klimt's Olympian field of flowers has been replaced by the gloom of a convent cell. The vine-wreathed head of the pagan lover appears in Schiele as a bony profile topped with the red cardinal's biretta. In Klimt, the rapture of the lovers is a thing beyond ideas of sin; in Schiele, the dismal Christian and Catholic aversion to the flesh is seen being overcome by the force of natural impulse.

Like anti-clerical art through the ages, Schiele's painting had a revolutionary thrust, questioning the established order. The picture targets several taboos at once: taboos on sexual passion and sexual need as experienced by those who have opted for celibacy; the taboo on seeing lust and fear, instincts and the darker side of life, the preservation of social norms and the breaching of barriers, not as exceptional things in the human condition but as norms laid down by Fate. The subtitle, *Caress*, seems a harmless and idyllic way of describing palpably sinful lust; but it has its place with other taboo-breaking titles in Schiele's work, such as *The Red Host* (1911; p.68). *Cardinal and Nun (Caress)* can be read as both a parody of conventional spiritual allegories and as a secular allegory of revolution and anarchy.

Alongside his representations of unmasked and allegorical humanity, Schiele also brought a scrupulous eye and a deep capacity for fellow-feeling to his portrait work. Beyond the family circle – his sisters Gerti and Melanie, his mother and Uncle Leopold, whom he mainly portrayed in drawings and watercolours – Schiele would initially look to his fellow artists, critics and early collectors when he needed models. The portraits that resulted have left us an impressive gallery of Schie-

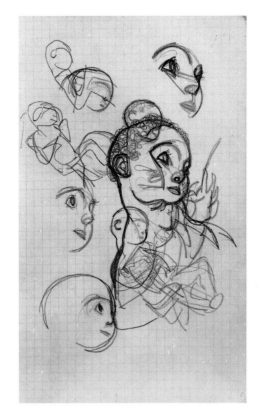

Sketch for **The Family**, 1918

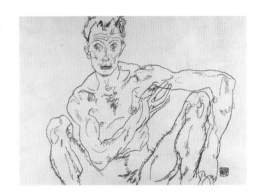

Crouching Male Nude (Self-Portrait), 1918
Kauernder Männerakt (Selbstbildnis)
Black crayon, 30.1 x 47.1 cm
Kallir D 2480; Vienna, Graphische Sammlung Albertina

Newborn Baby, 1910
Neugeborener
Watercolour and charcoal, 46 x 32 cm
Kallir D 382; private collection, courtesy Galerie
St. Etienne, New York

When Schiele turned his back on Viennese Art
Nouveau, with its celebration of the traditional,
stylish and costly, he set about dismantling conventional idealized images. Society ladies were
replaced by working-class girls and, similarly,
the traditional image of the child in art came
under Schiele's scrutiny. In 1910 he drew newborn babies in a gynaecological clinic, manikins
striking for their ugliness.

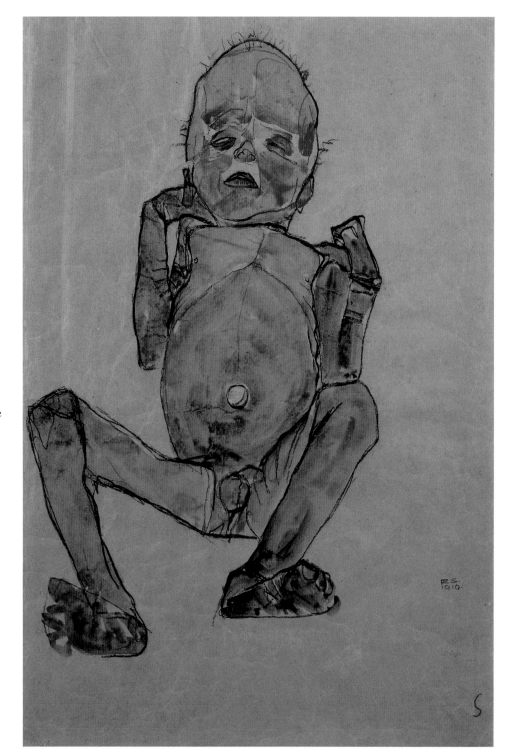

le's circle, even though they failed to serve their primary purpose of
earning him some money. The pillars of society and the élite of the art
world were prepared to negotiate the price of a portrait with Klimt, a
generation older, but not with Schiele, an unknown artist aged twenty.
The famous architect Otto Wagner urged Schiele to do a series of life-
size portraits of leading Viennese personalities, and would doubtless
have acted the go-between; but the project came to nothing. Even the
portrait of Wagner himself remained unfinished. Nonetheless, Schiele
would not be deterred from painting pictures of his friends in which a
fidelity to the real went hand in hand with his new, ecstatic experiments with style.

In 1910 he painted the *Portrait of Arthur Roessler* (p. 138). He had met the critic the previous year at the exhibition of the New Art Group. Roessler proved one of Schiele's most loyal and most important advocates, not only as critic but also as collector, agent, and author of the earliest studies of Schiele. The portrait is distinctive in composition and in its novel treatment of detail. The composition is based upon the contrast between movement and counter-movement. Roessler's left turn of the head and right arm are opposed by the right turn of his left arm and right leg. The sense of movement and tension that this produces gives both dynamism and coherence to the picture. The sitter's elongated, skeletal hands, crossed over, heighten an impression of asceticism.

The *Portrait of the Publisher Eduard Kosmack* (1910; p. 140) has a hypnotic presence created first and foremost by the fixed gaze of the subject. Seen frontally, Kosmack is holding his arms in front of him, hands clasped between his legs in a contemplative manner. The pantomime interplay of movements in the portrait of Roessler is absent here; this pic-

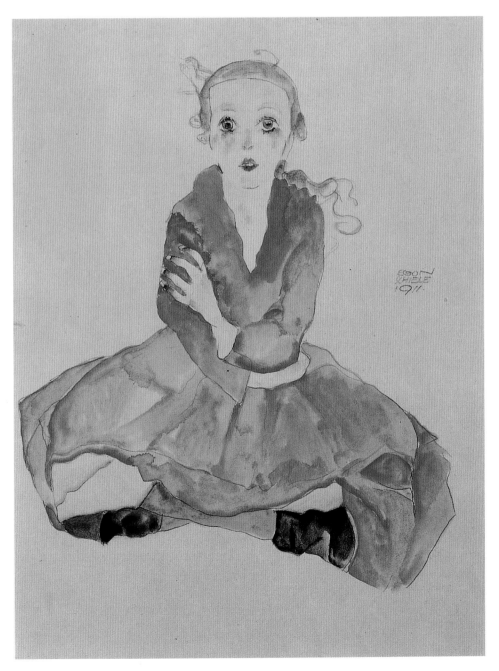

Seated Girl Facing Front, 1911
Sitzendes Mädchen, en face
Watercolour and pencil, 46.5 x 31.8 cm
Kallir D 789; Munich, Bayerische Staatsgemäldesammlungen

"Some of Schiele's portraits showed that he could turn humanity inside out, and one was horrified to see what had been so carefully concealed, stinking and mite-ridden and rotten … He saw and painted eyes as cold as gems in people's faces that were pale with the colours of decay, with death beneath the skin."
Arthur Roessler (1912)

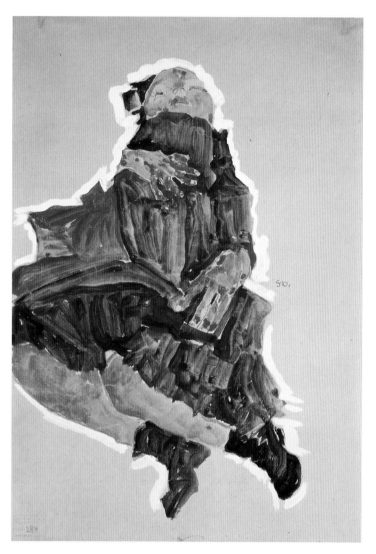

Sleeping Child, 1910
Schlafendes Kind
Gouache and pencil with white highlighting, 45.1 x 31.5 cm
Kallir D 421; Berlin, Galerie Pels-Leusden

Two Guttersnipes, 1910
Zwei Gassenbuben
Gouache, watercolour and pencil, 39.1 x 32.1 cm
Kallir D 445; private collection

PAGE 137:
Girl with Hood, 1910
Mädchen mit Haube
Gouache, watercolour and pencil, 43.5 x 30 cm
Kallir D 414; private collection

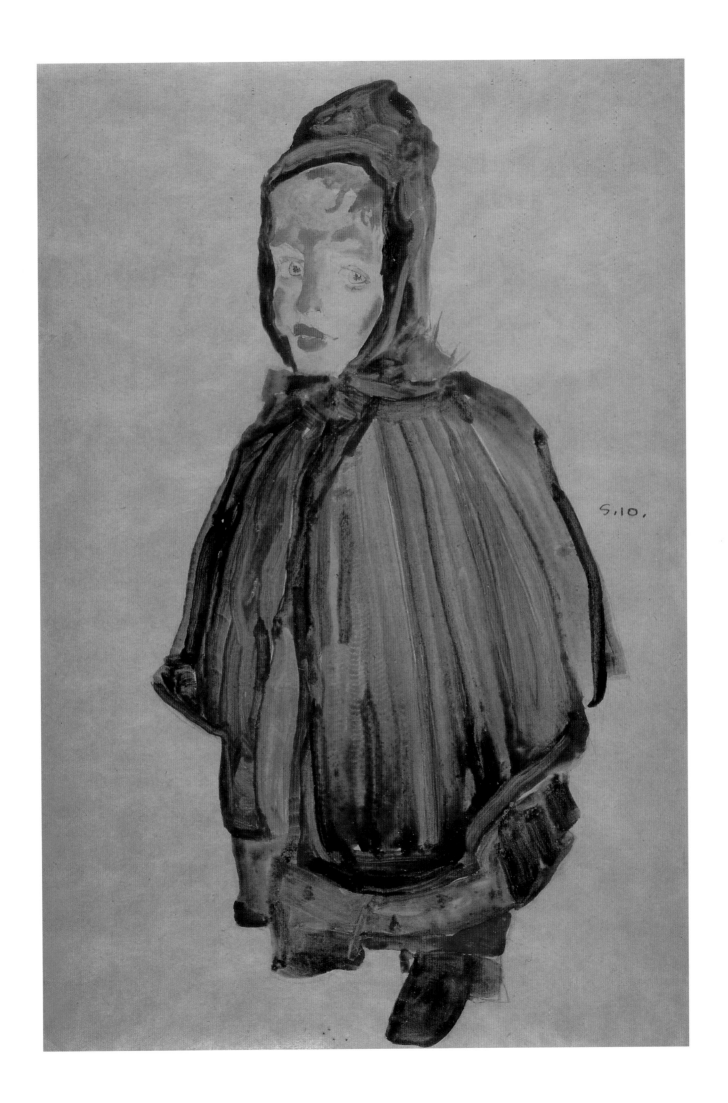

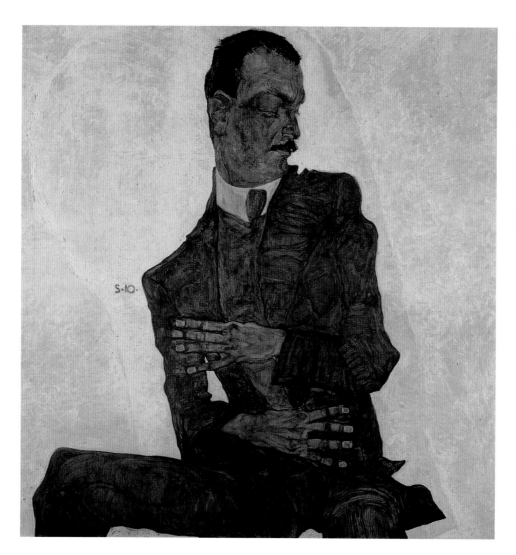

Portrait of Arthur Roessler, 1910
Bildnis Arthur Roessler
Oil on canvas, 99.6 x 99.8 cm
Kallir P 163; Vienna, Historisches Museum der
Stadt Wien

The Vienna architect Otto Wagner suggested that
Schiele paint well-known Viennese personalities.
One of the artist's models was the critic Arthur
Roessler, one of his earliest supporters. In the
portrait, Roessler's body is tensed in movements
and counter-movements that seem to express the
conflict of forces within.

ture draws its commanding life from the imperative gaze of the publisher,
which exerts a hypnotic compulsion over us. Slender and tight though his
body is, it seems to tower into space. His air of concentration suggests
great tensions kept in check. The portrait includes a withered sunflower
as a symbolic attribute.

In the *Double Portrait (Chief Inspector Heinrich Benesch and His Son
Otto)* (1913; p. 141) Schiele achieved a fine orchestration of gestures and
movements and penetrating eye contact. Heinrich Benesch was one of
Schiele's first and most faithful collectors. His son Otto, aged seventeen
when the double portrait was painted, was later an art historian and director of Vienna's Albertina museum from 1947 to 1962, and it was thanks
to him that the Albertina acquired its superlative Schiele holdings. The
striking gesture of the father's left arm, outstretched to and across his
son, is a token both of conjunction and of distance. In formal terms, this
horizontal links the two figures; but it serves as a barrier too. Was Schiele
symbolizing the authority of the father in that gesture, or his protective
care?

The son makes a dreamy and introverted impression, with the quiet re-
ticence of a monk, while his father is a determined and strong presence.
The seemingly abrupt turn of the father's head gives a certain dynamism
to his figure, whereas the son, seen frontally, is static. The red in Heinrich
Benesch's face also conveys energy; the son's narrow face, by contrast, is

pale. Lighting effects such as the white highlighting around the heads and the extended left hand of the father, and above all the contrast between the undefined background and the clearly outlined figures, give the double portrait a magical aura.

In some of his portraits, Schiele, without abandoning his core artistic principles, was willing to compromise with the representational wishes of his sitters. The *Portrait of Erich Lederer* (1912; p. 142) is a case in point. This stylish young man, the son of one of Schiele's collectors and patrons, is seen in riding attire. Elsewhere, though, Schiele would suffuse his paintings with magic, as in the *Portrait of the Painter Paris von Gütersloh* (1918; p. 143), one of his last works. This picture of his young artist friend, with arms upraised as if casting a spell, places the sitter amidst vibrant colour that flickers like tongues of fire.

Schiele's portrait work is characteristically tensed by the polarity between an Expressionist use of gesture and the representational fidelity to given reality. He had the ability to convey the states of mind, spirit and relations of his sitters in a very few eloquent touches, and furthermore could deploy a subjective symbolism in such a way as to make them the very embodiment of the Expressionist image of humanity.

Schiele usually penned his letters in an elaborate painterly script. In this one (below left) he is suggesting a time when Roessler can collect his portrait (p. 138):

"Beneath the white sky.
Now I see the city once again, which has remained the same as it always was, in it the paltry humdrum people are walking as they always did – the poor – so poor, the heady red autumn leaves smell like them. Yet how welcome autumn is in this windwinterland!
Your
Egon Schiele
On Friday at about 12, please, your portrait will be ready for collection – does that suit?"

In summer 1913 Arthur Roessler was at Altmünster near Salzburg, and Schiele visited him there with Wally. A number of photographs recorded their time together.

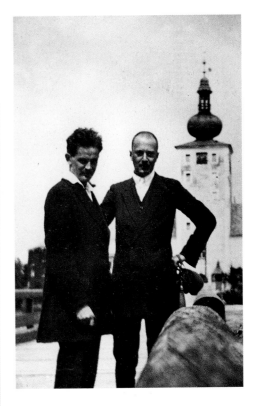

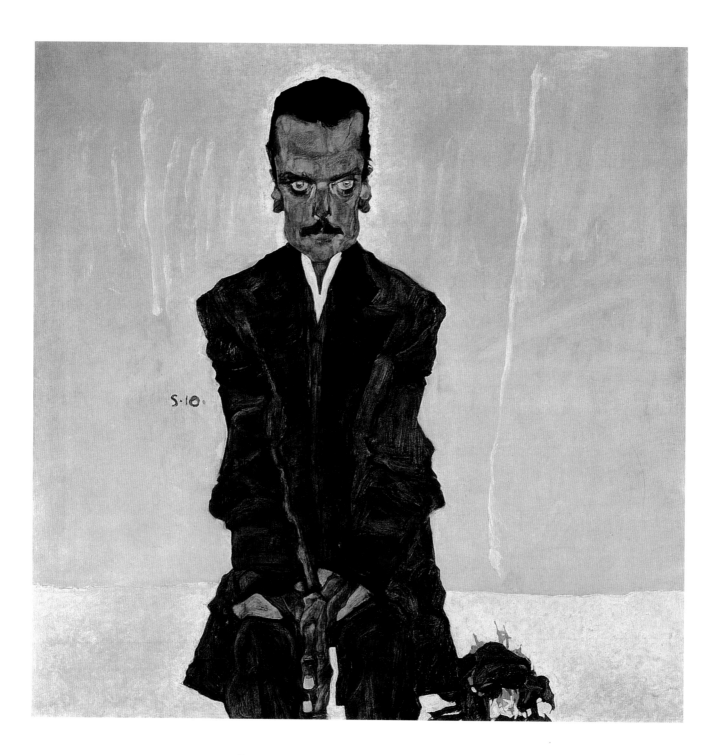

Portrait of the Publisher Eduard Kosmack, 1910
Bildnis des Verlegers Eduard Kosmack
Oil on canvas, 100 x 100cm
Kallir P 165; Vienna, Österreichische Galerie. Belvedere

In Egon Schiele's work, the human body was the vehicle for expression.
Every gesture and movement meant something. The portrait of Viennese
publisher Eduard Kosmack looks subdued and static on the surface, but
the considerable inner tension is apparent in the sitter's eyes and the restless
zigzag outline. His hypnotic gaze is compelling – and in point of fact
Kosmack was genuinely able to hypnotize, though Schiele supposedly did
not know this. The withered sunflower is meant symbolically.

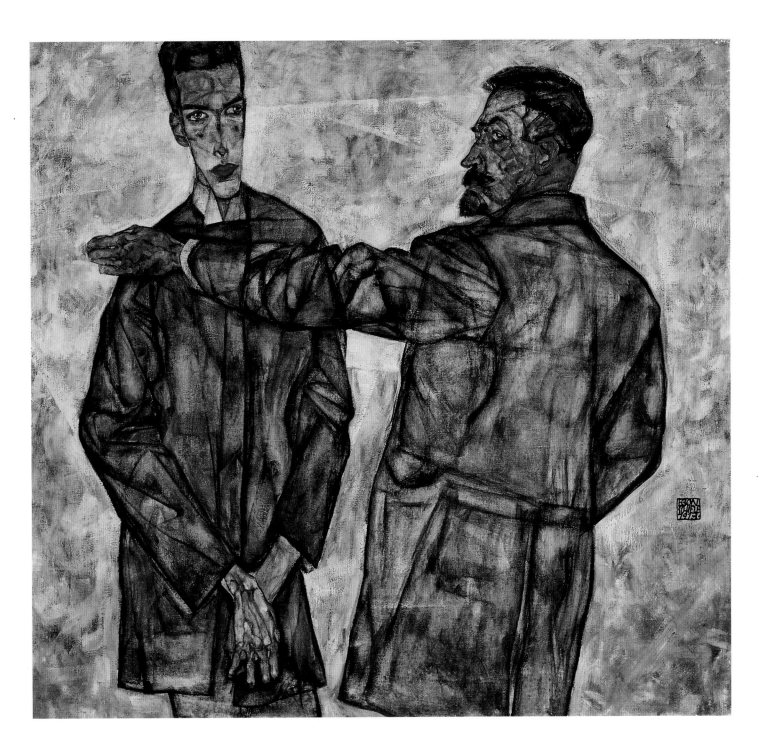

**Double Portrait (Chief Inspector Heinrich Benesch
and His Son Otto)**, 1913
*Doppelbildnis (Zentralinspektor Heinrich Benesch
und sein Sohn Otto)*
Oil on canvas, 121 x 131 cm; Kallir P 250
Linz, Wolfgang-Gurlitt-Sammlung in der Neuen Galerie der Stadt Linz

This double portrait is characterized by counter-movement and polarity.
Heinrich Benesch was one of the earliest and most loyal collectors of
Schiele's work. His son Otto, seventeen when this picture was painted, later
became director of the Albertina in Vienna. The contrast between the energetic
father and the introverted son is palpable in Schiele's account.

Portrait of Erich Lederer, 1912
Bildnis Erich Lederer
Oil and gouache, 139 x 55 cm
Kallir P 235; Basle, Öffentliche Kunstsammlung,
Kunstmuseum

At the invitation of the industrialist August
Lederer, Schiele spent Christmas and New Year
1912/13 at Györ in Hungary. There he did a number of sketches and the portrait of Lederer's son
Erich. As so often in Schiele, the background is
undefined, merely parcelled into juxtaposed
patches of colour.

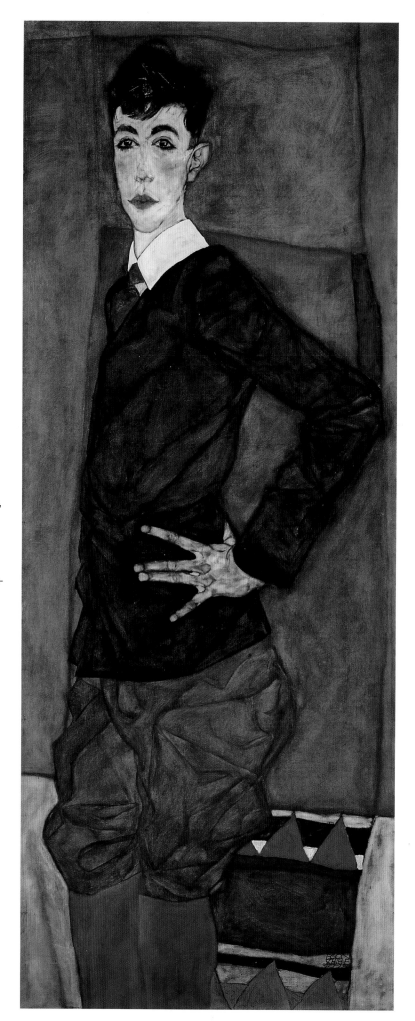

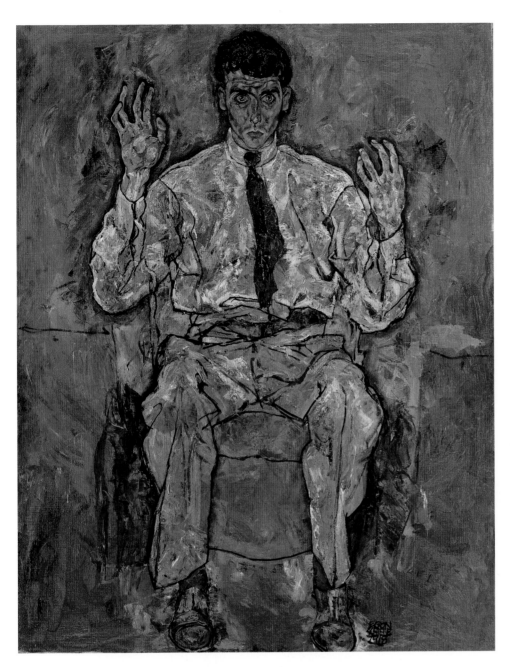

Portrait of the Painter Paris von Gütersloh,
1918
Bildnis des Malers Paris von Gütersloh
Oil on canvas, 140.3 x 109.9 cm
Kallir P 322; Minneapolis, The Minneapolis
Institute of Art

This vibrant portrait of a fellow artist is dynamic
in the extreme. Schiele has created his electric
effect not only through the pose of the sitter but
also by means of the flickering tongues of fire in
his brushwork. If this was to have been yet another new departure in Schiele's art, his early
death prevented him from pursuing it.

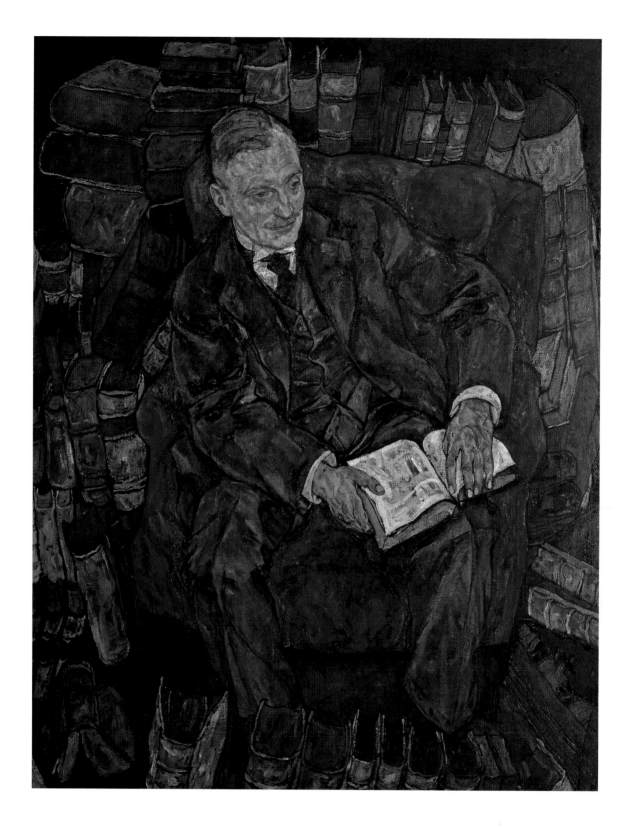

Portrait of Dr. Hugo Koller, 1918
Bildnis Dr. Hugo Koller
Oil on canvas, 140.3 x 109.6 cm
Kallir P 320; Vienna, Österreichische Galerie. Belvedere

In the last two years of his life, Egon Schiele became a sought-after portrait
artist in Vienna. The more classical style he was establishing doubtless
favoured this. Hugo Koller (1867–1942), a doctor of both medicine and
philosophy, was a highly-regarded Vienna industrialist and art lover. He
possessed an extensive library: hence the setting Schiele has placed him in.

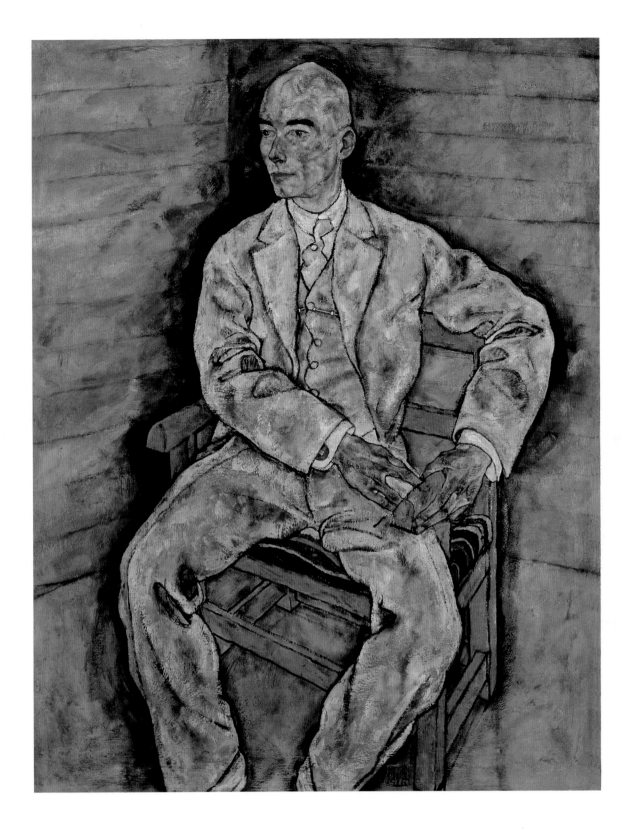

Portrait of Victor Ritter von Bauer, 1918
Bildnis Victor Ritter von Bauer
Oil on canvas, 140.6 x 109.8cm
Kallir P 317; Vienna, Österreichische Galerie. Belvedere

The sitter in this portrait, done in the last year of Schiele's life, is relaxed. The
realistically painted chair is at an angle that establishes spatial depth. The
picture contains no attributes to indicate the sitter's profession, tastes, or state
of mind. By cropping the feet, Schiele has left his subject in a curious state
of suspension.

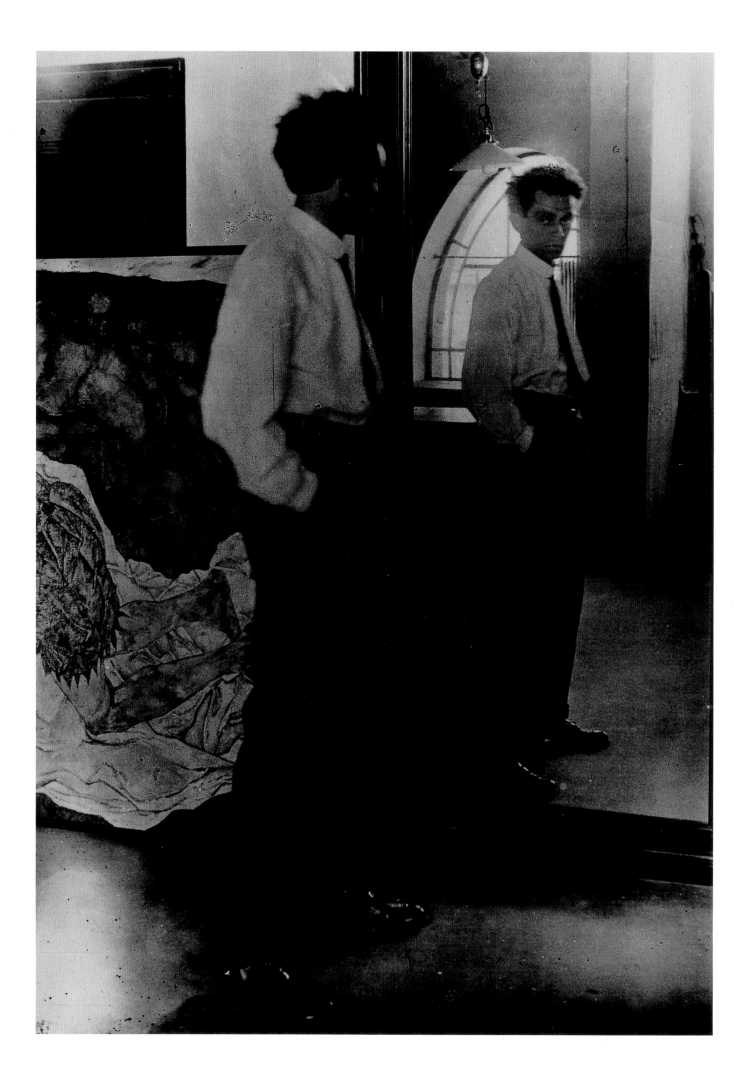

The Theatre of the Self

Allegory, unmasking, the presentation of a personable image, and close scrutiny of body language as influenced by the psyche, all met most palpably where Schiele's eye looked most searchingly – in his self-portraits, his odyssey through the vast lands of the self. His reflections on and of himself filled a great hall of mirrors where he performed a pantomime of the self unparalleled in twentieth-century art. No other artist but Rembrandt was so much under the spell, physically and psychologically, of his own image. He comes before us as doer and observer, *doppelgänger* and loner, saint and masturbator, hermit and dandy, prisoner and Death. The dual role of model and painter, actor and director, was clearly one that Schiele relished. In short, his innumerable visions of self, staged by himself, make his self-portraits the most absorbing part of his work. By his twenty-eighth year he had done about a hundred self-portraits; by the same age, Rembrandt had done no more than fifty.

A meticulous chronological description and assessment of Schiele's self-portraits would only account for a part of the fascination and unique power of Schiele's narcissistic, grimacing ego-trip, his dance to the choreography of genius. Ideally, Schiele's self-portraits would be viewed in a continuous sequence, like a film.

The long series of self-portraits exemplifies Schiele's development too – from his academic beginnings in a mood of Art Nouveau via the Expressionist peak in the years 1911 to 1915 to a calmer sense of form in the last years of his life, 1916 to 1918. But the force of his visual soliloquy, which is at once a dialogue with an alter ego, lies beyond the customary scope of academic discussions of form and content, contemporary style and individual talent. That force draws on the mysterious creative power that informs the work of every great artist.

As a sixteen-year-old Schiele was already creating an image of himself and then subjecting it to critical scrutiny in the mirror. In *Self-Portrait with Broad-Brimmed Hat* (1906; p. 147) he is Schiele the dandy, with an artist's hat, high collars, striped tie and buttoned waistcoat. His mouth is set in a somewhat fractious pout, as if he were wondering whether anything of significance would become of him. This charcoal drawing is academic in style and, despite the facial expression, suggests little of the artist's later contempt for the world.

Three years later, in the crayon drawing *Man with Blue Headband and Hand on Cheek (Self-Portrait)* (1909; p. 149), he was in the role of the Art Nouveau artist à la Gustav Klimt or Hermann Bahr. Klimt's circle

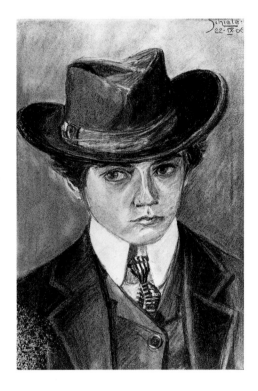

Self-Portrait with Broad-Brimmed Hat, 1906
Selbstbildnis mit breitem Hut
Charcoal, 38 x 26.7 cm
Kallir D 28; private collection

Egon Schiele was sixteen when he drew this self-portrait as a young gentleman, still highly conventional in style.

PAGE 146:
Egon Schiele in front of the mirror, 1915
Egon Schiele vor dem Spiegel stehend
Photograph
Vienna, Graphische Sammlung Albertina

This photograph was one of a series taken in 1915 by Johannes Fischer in Schiele's studio in Hietzinger Hauptstrasse. On the left we can make out *Death and Maiden (Man and Girl)* (p. 129), painted that year. Schiele had been given the large upright mirror by his mother.

147

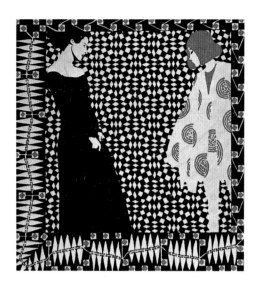 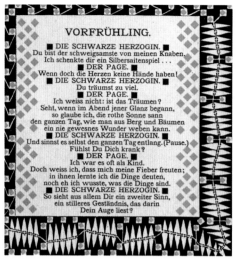

Koloman Moser
Early Spring, 1901
Vorfrühling
Drawing
Vienna, Galerie Pabst

Artist and architect Josef Hoffmann developed an idiosyncratic system of geometrical decorative features that became characteristic of Viennese Art Nouveau. Other designers such as Koloman Moser adopted and extended the repertoire, as in this book design.

and the Wiener Werkstätte favoured the artist's smock and affected a prophetic or priestly manner, the more to mark their difference from the middle classes in waistcoats with watch-fobs dangling.

The chessboard pattern of the headband was originally designed by Josef Hoffmann and was the Wiener Werkstätte's best-loved ornamentation. Schiele's line is as gentle, indeed transparent, as Klimt's; the blue areas are done in an Impressionist manner, while the unnatural rose colouring and the lines of the hair transform this area into a decorative feature. The hand pulling down the lower lid of the right eye seems to be making a sign in some secret ritual. This self-portrait marked Schiele's departure from academic aesthetics, and signalled allegiance to Klimt.

From an early date, Schiele's theatre of self was enacted before an enormous mirror that he had pestered his mother into giving him for his first studio (cf. p. 146). In the mirror he was his own model and had to obey the master's directions – a Narcissus in various forms and garbs. The photographs his friend Anton Josef Trčka took in 1913 and 1914 (cf. pp. 150/151) show how seriously Schiele took the staging of his own portraits. In them we see Schiele practising poses that he was later to adopt in paintings, or which he assumed purely for their expressiveness, as a ballet dancer might. In one of these photographs, *Egon Schiele full-length with arms upraised* (1914; p. 150), the artist's hands are entwined over his profiled head and he has adopted a striding stance. Schiele framed the plate and signed and dated it twice over, thus hallmarking it as a work of art in its own right and conferring on his pantomimic exercises a value of their own, beyond that of preliminary studies. In other photographs, such as *Egon Schiele (making a hand gesture)* (1914; p. 151), we see Schiele toying with the evocative power of hand gestures, with fingers spread or curled; or again he clenches and entwines his fingers, and raises them to his face. This use of the fingers has a decorative effect.

This theatre of the self before the mirror or the camera's lens could take complex forms, as in the drawing *Schiele, Drawing a Nude Model before a Mirror* (1910; p. 152). In the act of sketching the model from the rear, Schiele also includes himself in his picture, complete with pad, and the frontal view of the model. We have three visual levels to contend with: the rear view of the model on the "real" level, the mirrored frontal

PAGE 149:
Man with Blue Headband and Hand on Cheek (Self-Portrait), 1909
Mann mit blauem Stirnband, die Hand an die Wange gelegt (Selbstbildnis)
Coloured crayon and charcoal, 40.2 x 29.7 cm
Kallir D 344; Vienna, Graphische Sammlung Albertina

At the age of nineteen, in a chequered headband rather than hat and waistcoat, Schiele here declares his allegiance to Klimt and the Secession.

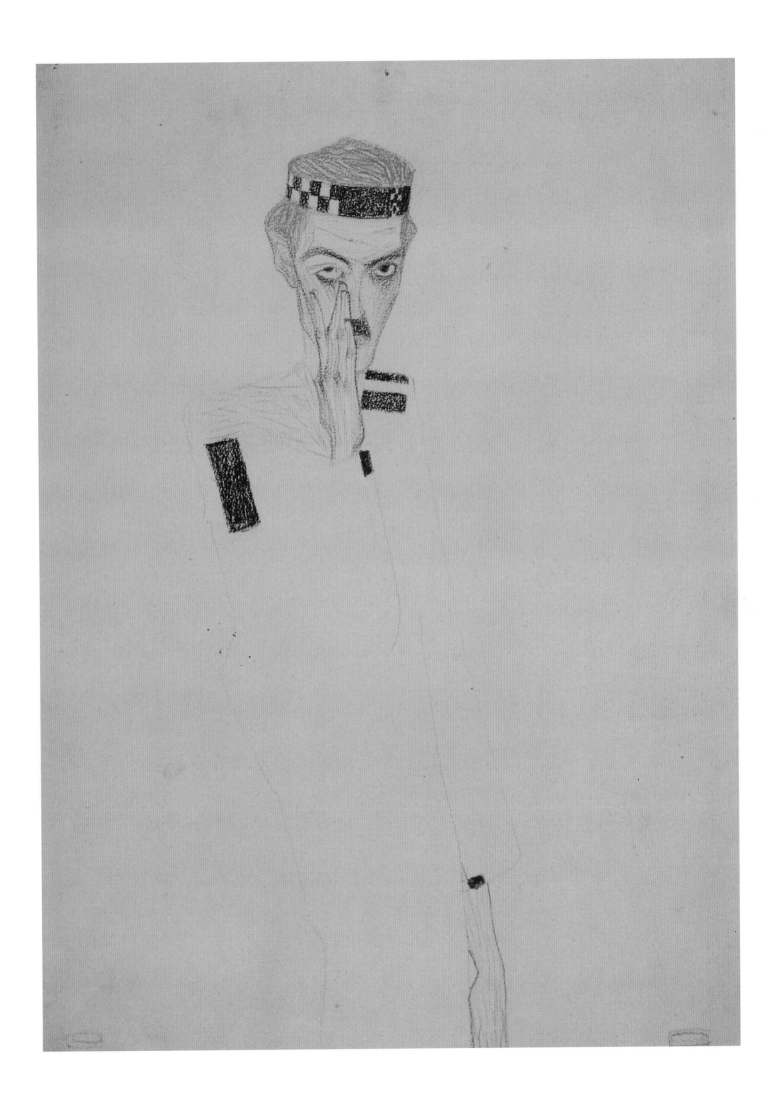

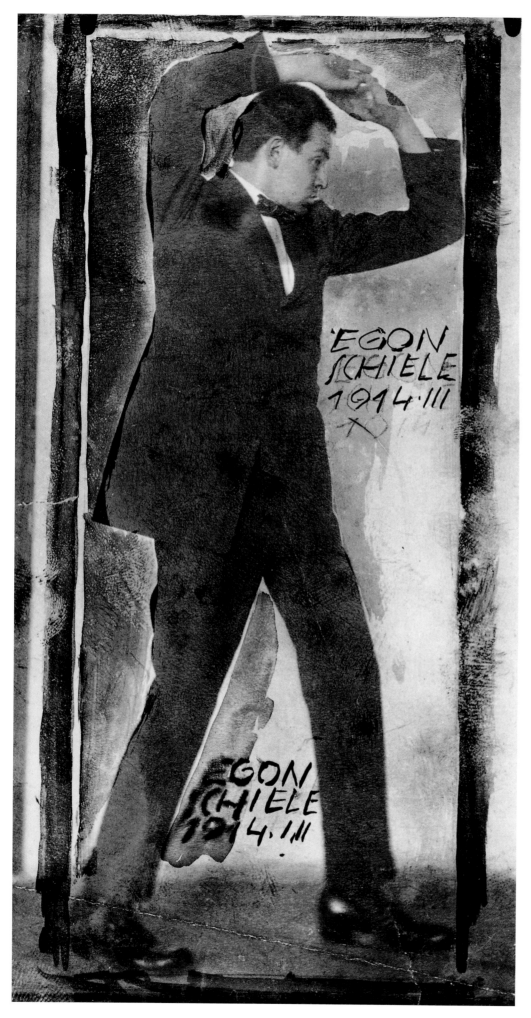

PAGE 151:
Anton Josef Trčka
Egon Schiele (making a hand gesture),
1914
Egon Schiele (mit posierender Handhaltung)
Photograph
Vienna, Graphische Sammlung Albertina

Anton Josef Trčka
Egon Schiele full-length with arms upraised, 1914
Egon Schiele in ganzer Figur mit erhobenen Armen
Photograph
Vienna, Graphische Sammlung Albertina

Photographer Anton Josef Trčka and
Schiele saw the pictures that Trčka took in
Schiele's studio in 1914 as their joint work,
and both men signed them. The photograph
on the left was watercoloured by the artist,
and signed and dated twice.

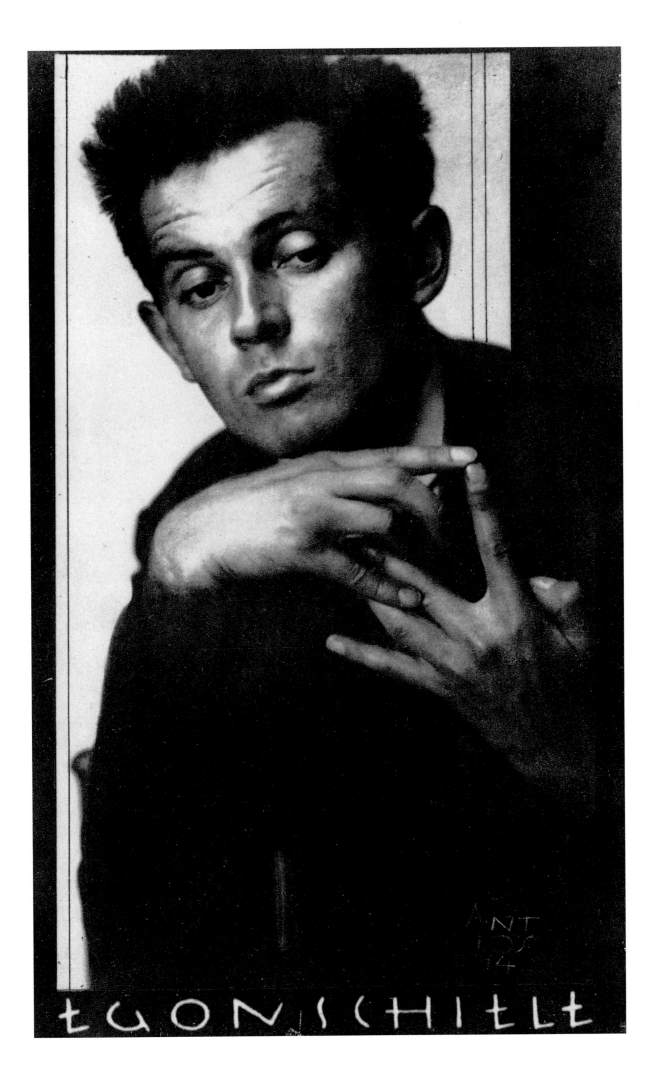

EGON SCHIELE

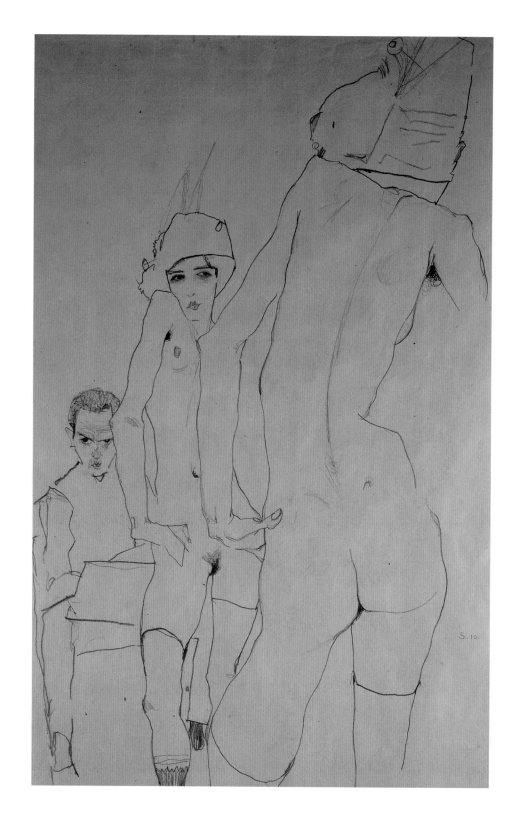

Schiele, Drawing a Nude Model before a Mirror, 1910
Schiele, ein Aktmodell vor dem Spiegel zeichnend
Pencil, 55.2 x 35.3 cm
Kallir D 737; Vienna, Graphische Sammlung Albertina

Schiele liked experimenting with different planes of reality and perception.
Here he sees himself in the mirror and his nude model (probably the dancer,
Moa) simultaneously from the front and the rear, the frontal view being the
mirror reflection.

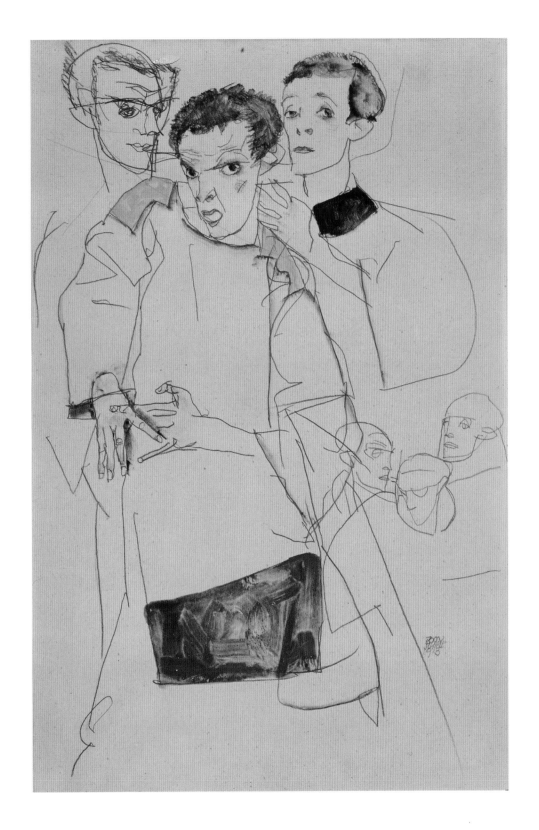

Triple Self-Portrait, 1913
Dreifaches Selbstportrait
Gouache, watercolour and pencil, 48.4 x 32 cm
Kallir D 1425; private collection

Schiele in artist's smock, multiplied without mirrors. The three self-portraits
record three moods, features distorted, aloof, and friendly and expectant. The
triple image is repeated at the right.

view, and Schiele's self-portrait. The multi-levelled mirroring reflects the fractured relations between artist and model, between palpable reality and mirror image. And the *doppelgänger* motif was of course to be one of Schiele's major self-portrait themes.

In the oil *The Self-Seers II (Death and Man)* (1911; p. 155) there is a pale, hazy phantom image – as at a seance – behind the darker portrait in the foreground, and it is as if this phantom had been called up by the hand that rises from the depths. The portrait sitter's eyes are wide in alarm, his eyebrows raised, as he sees his second image as Death behind him. The *doppelgänger* as mask and death mask; the opposition of the present and a menacing, fateful future. The recurring death motif in his work prompted Schiele to offer a written comment. For him, life and death were co-present, as the *doppelgänger* images imply. In a poem of 1910 or 1911 he wrote: "I am a man, I love death and love life."[10]

The split self appears again in *Prophets (Double Self-Portrait)* (1911; p. 156), in two figures, one light and one dark. The two are linked like Siamese twins. The dark foreground may be read as a curtain from behind which the two prophetic figures confront us, one covered and the other naked; or it may be a habit worn by the figure on the right, the prophet with the hollow staring eyes. This intentional ambiguity is present not only in the setting and costumes but also in the contrast between realistic portions, such as the light-coloured nude self-portrait, and the mask-like head at the top right. Not that the "realism" is complete: the nude is a cropped torso, the arm amputated below the shoulder. Where are the boundaries of reality and the imaginary dream world? Are we to think of these as two figures, or as one with a second, "astral" body? The *doppelgänger* motif is the perfect way of articulating a split self. The familiar repertoire of Freudian psychology, with its ego and super-ego, conscious and unconscious realms, might equally be applied to these dual self-portraits.

But there are dualist images that dispense with mythology or seance imagery, such as the gouache *Double Self-Portrait* (1915), the interest of which derives from the twofold gaze and the tender nestling of the two heads. The two Schieles are looking in different directions; variations on a theme, wholly realistic and clear, without any further levels of meaning. It is as if Schiele could not get enough of the variety possible in his own features. He wanted to see himself not just once but twice or even three times, all at once – as in the *Triple Self-Portrait* (1913; p. 153), where he appears in three-quarter and half length and as a head. There are also three more heads on the right of the drawing, so that perhaps we ought to see this gouache as a sixfold self-portrait.

For an artist to give such preferential treatment to his own body and face, to use his available person so insistently, to look so addictively into the studio mirror, is inconceivable if the artist is not also narcissistic beyond the usual.

Schiele's work in self-portraits is copious and diverse; but certain basic types of self-interpretation can be identified. Foremost is his recurrent self-presentation as monk, hermit or saint, as in the gouache *Self-Portrait as St. Sebastian* (1914/15; p. 167), which he used as a poster for an exhibition in the Galerie Arnot. The artist, wearing a red habit, his arms upraised, is pierced by arrows like the saint of the title.

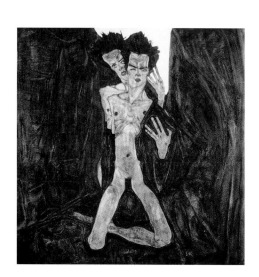

***The Self-Seers I**, 1910*
Die Selbstseher
Oil on canvas, 80 x 79.7 cm
Kallir P 174; whereabouts unknown

The self-seer pictures are records of Schiele's duality too. In this first, the two selves are still almost identical: one Schiele is looking over the other's shoulder. It is unclear exactly to whom the hand reaching out in front belongs.

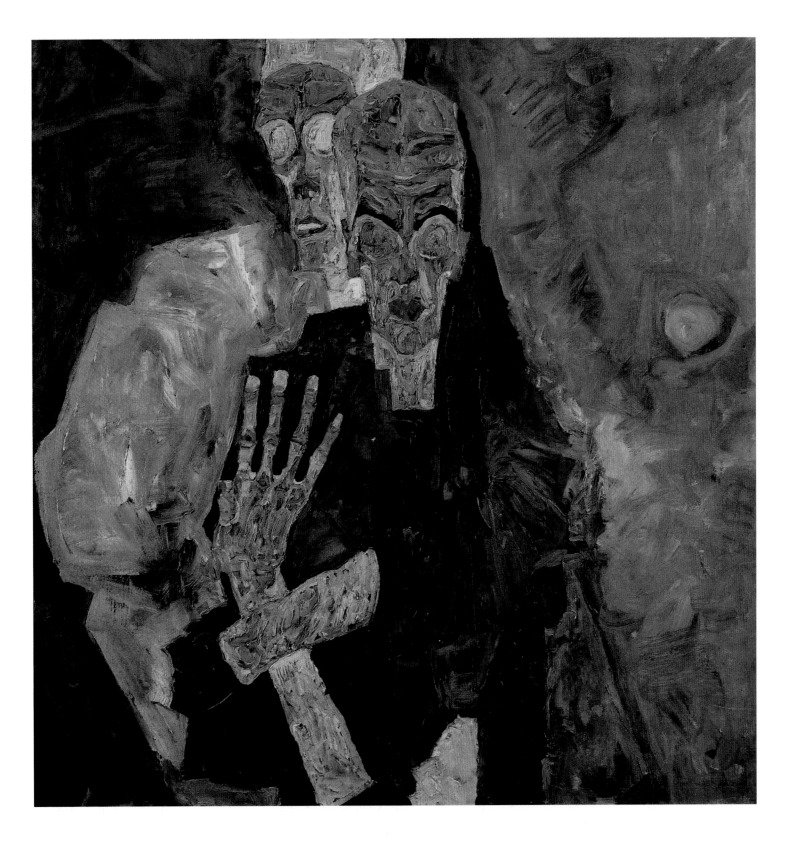

The Self-Seers II (Death and Man), 1911
Die Selbstseher II (Tod und Mann)
Oil on canvas, 80.3 x 80cm
Kallir P 193; Vienna, Sammlung Rudolf Leopold

An eerie picture. The man staring into the mirror, eyes wide open, sees a
shimmering phantom behind him – himself as Death. The picture is painted in a
manner that recalls visions of Hell, and this gives it a force almost transcendent.

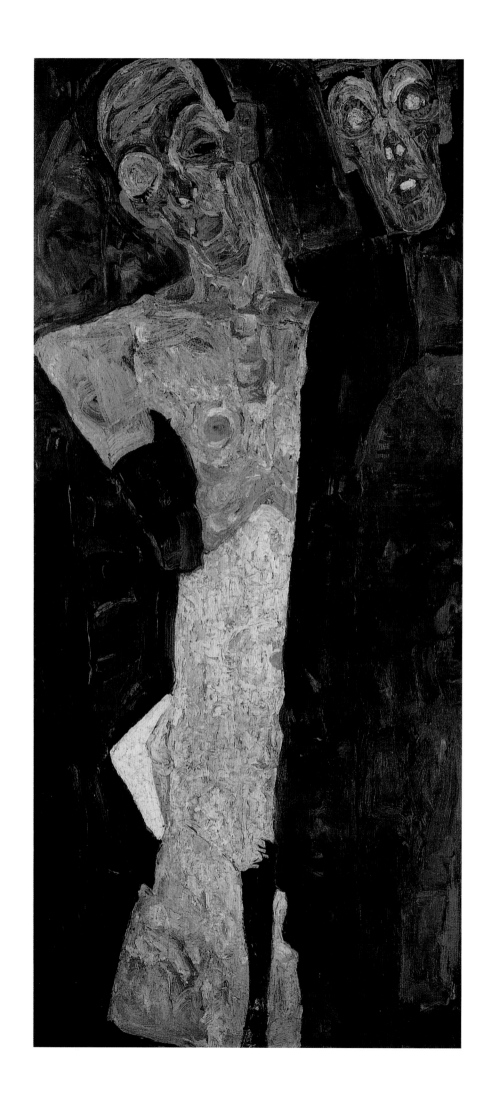

There is a 1913 photograph showing Schiele with the now lost painting *Encounter (Self-Portrait with Saint)* (the title is variously given); in the painting, Schiele, wearing a thigh-length habit, is turning toward us even as he follows an elder man with a monk's cap and halo. The double portrait with Klimt, *The Hermits* (1912; p. 120), likewise presents Schiele in the role of disciple, with a wreath of thistle flowers symbolically on his brow. When Schiele commented on the role of the artist as saint, he did so in the tones of the preacher: "My being, my decaying, translated into abiding values, must have a compelling power over other well or better educated beings, like a religion that appears credible."[11]

A saint bows to force, in a sense, since he must submit to the dictates of God; and similarly the artist seems to do violence to his body by showing it as a mutilated torso. In *Self-Portrait with Bare Stomach* (1911; p. 157) the body, with no arms and crowned with a shock of tangled hair, looks like the very stake to which martyrs were bound, and the facial expression is one of alarm.

Seated Male Nude (Self-Portrait) (1910; p. 165), done in yellow and brown oil and gouache, has mutilated legs, lopped off above the ankles. The figure looks as if it has been taken down from a Gothic crucifix: it is angular, and looks carved. Schiele was seeing himself as Christ without a loin-cloth. The red highlights of the eyes, nipples, navel and genitals make the body look as if it were glowing from within. This martyred, ascetic body is the very image of suffering.

But Schiele did not only see himself as a suffering saint in his self-portraits. In his prison pictures and elsewhere he saw himself as the victim and accuser of society. As we have seen, Schiele was arrested on 13 April 1912 on a charge of seducing a minor, and in due course sentenced to three days' imprisonment for disseminating immoral drawings, the original charge being dropped. He was released on 8 May. The judge who symbolically set fire to one of Schiele's drawings helped provide the artist with an excuse to cast himself as a victim; and, indeed, the fortnight that Schiele spent in custody seems to have shaken him badly. The self-portraits he did in prison have accusing titles; they are also, incidentally, the only ones he did from memory, without a mirror.

Hindering the Artist Is a Crime, It Is Murdering Life in the Bud! (1912; p. 29) shows Schiele as a broken prisoner on his cell bed, huddled under his coat. His hollow eyes are staring out in accusation, his unshaven face is pale and drawn. In the two other prison self-portraits, Schiele again appears as the despairing accuser of society. In *Prisoner!* (1912; p. 31) his head is bowed as if beneath a heavy weight and his mouth is open as if to groan. And in *For Art and for My Loved Ones I Will Gladly Endure to the End!* (1912; p. 31) his clawed hands are reaching desperately into the empty air.

There is a substantial group of self-portraits that draw a special expressive power from their use of compositional pairings of opposites. In the *Self-Portrait with Black Clay Vase and Spread Fingers* (1911; p. 160) the expressive body language – the angled stance, the splayed fingers – is countered by the subdued sadness in the dark eyes. The colouring is dramatic: the black of the shirt and the clay vase (shaped like a head) is offset by the glowing colours of the fabrics. The artist's pale face and the

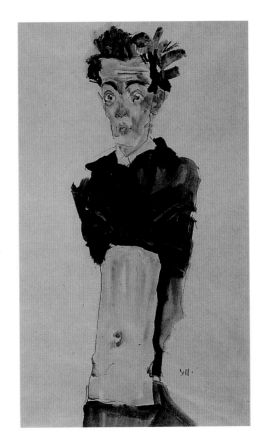

Self-Portrait with Bare Stomach, 1911
Selbstbildnis mit entblößtem Bauch
Watercolour and pencil, 55.2 x 36.4cm
Kallir D 946; Vienna, Graphische Sammlung Albertina

In this self-portrait the artist looks terrified. His eyes are wide open, his brow furrowed, his hair on end. He seems to see something we cannot.

PAGE 156:
Prophets (Double Self-Portrait), 1911
Propheten (Doppelselbstbildnis)
Oil on canvas, 110.3 x 50.3cm
Kallir P 191; Stuttgart, Staatsgalerie Stuttgart

Schiele offers us a similar vision here. One figure is naked and vulnerable, the other cloaked in dark garb. "I am all things at once, but never shall I do all things at one and the same time", Schiele wrote in a poem.

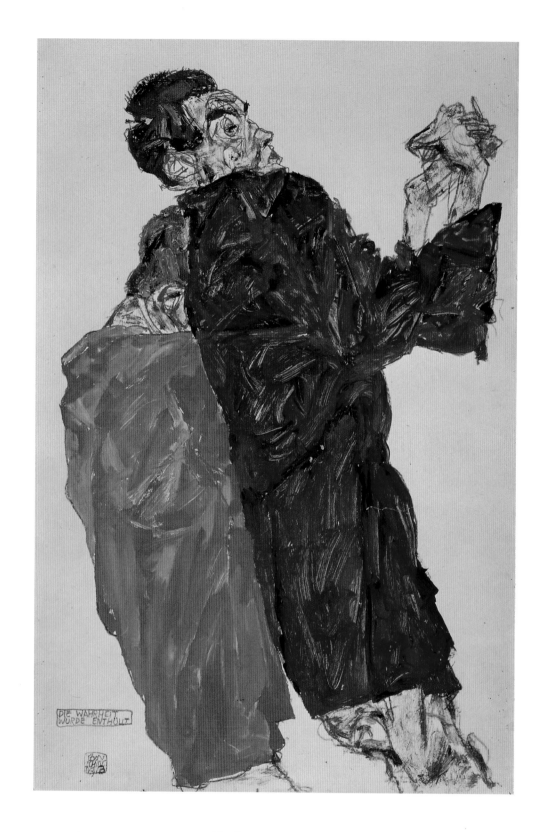

The Truth Unveiled, 1913
Die Wahrheit wurde enthüllt
Gouache, watercolour and pencil, 48.3 x 32.1 cm
Kallir D 1443; private collection

Another double self-portrait, or two different figures? The title is not
informative in this respect. The artist, fingers entwined, is wearing a tunic;
a second figure is concealed behind him.

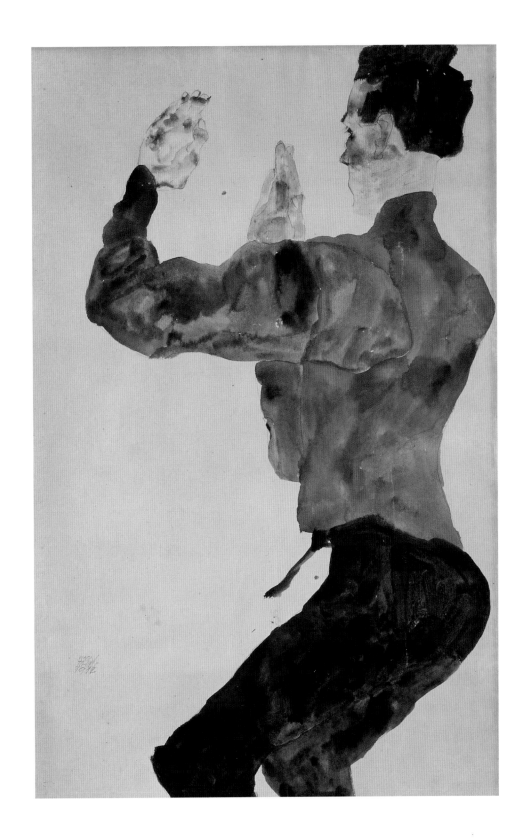

Self-Portrait with Raised Arms, Back View, 1912
Selbstbildnis mit erhobenen Armen, Rückenansicht
Gouache and pencil, 52 x 33 cm
Kallir D 1164; private collection, courtesy Fischer Fine Art, London

Posed much like a dancer, as in the photographs taken by Anton Josef Trčka,
Schiele looks intent, as if in some rite of conjuration. The stance has a
choreographed quality.

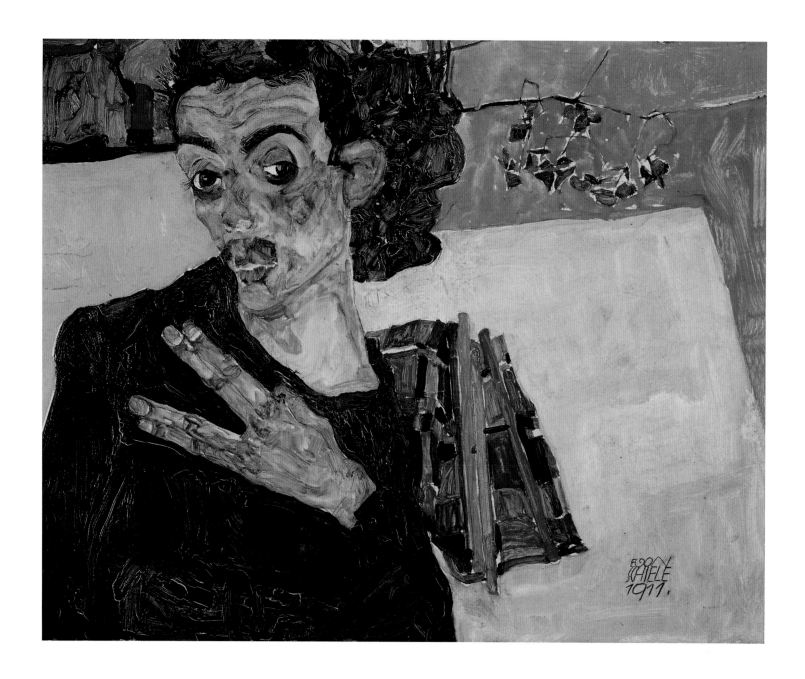

black clay face behind him, both facing in opposite directions, together
add up to a kind of Janus face.

In *Male Nude in Profile Facing Left (Self-Portrait)* (1910) there is a
white silhouette frame behind the actual outline of the body – an "astral"
body. The real body, with its hair at the belly and pubic region, has a *doppelgänger* in this insubstantial white ghost. "I see myself evaporate,"
wrote Schiele, "breathing out more and more vehemently, the vibrations
of my astral light become faster, abrupter, simpler, and resemble a great
recognition of the world…"[12]

In *Nude Self-Portrait, Grimacing* (1910) the body is grotesquely muscular and the arms over-long and disjointed. The grimace on Schiele's
face seems one of disgust at his own physical self. The double self-portrait *The Truth Unveiled* (1913; p.158) shows a foreground figure
robed in purple partly concealing another in red. Schiele's hands are
lifted in appeal or defence. The truth, he seems to be saying, lies in perceiving one's own dual image. (There are, however, critics who feel the
second figure is female, perhaps Wally.)

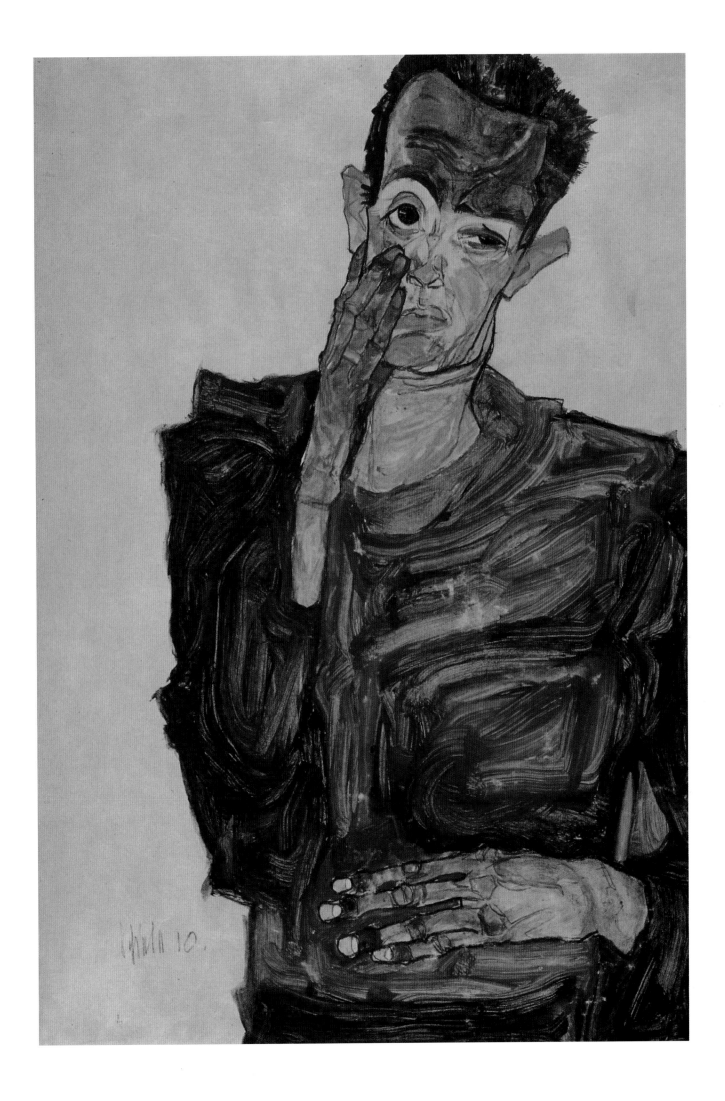

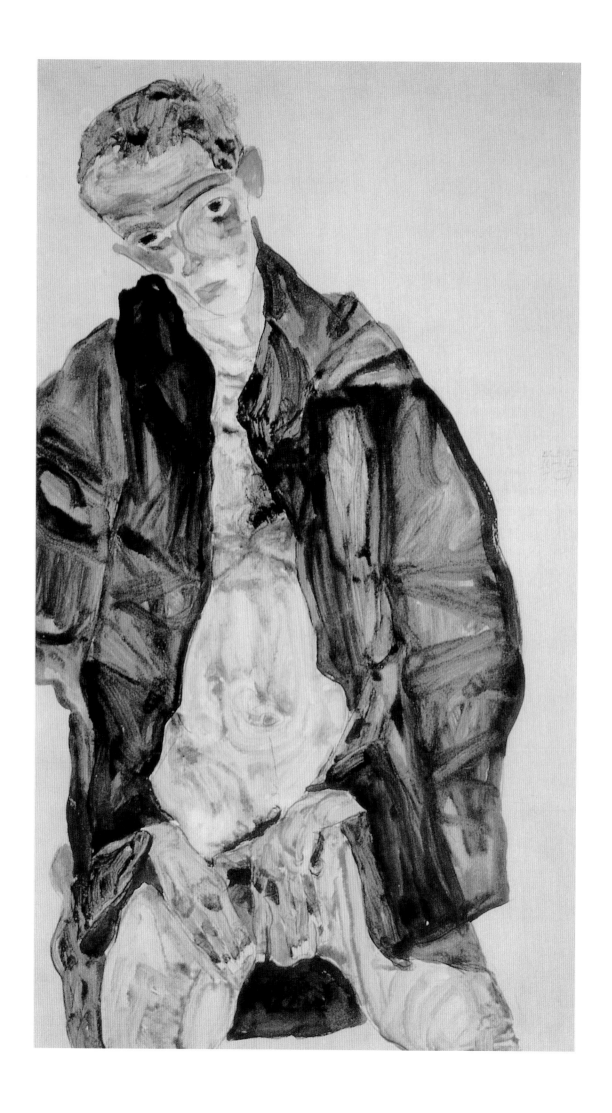

There is a further set of self-portraits in which Schiele uses his body as a vehicle of expression, a means of presenting feeling. His person becomes a resonant vessel; once a note is struck, it vibrates long and with increasing intensity. In *Self-Portrait with Hand to Cheek* (1910; p. 161) the artist is making a gesture of palpable depression, drawing down the flesh beneath his eye with a couple of fingers; the scale of emotion is reduced to melancholy. In *Self-Portrait in Black Cloak, Masturbating* (1911; p. 162), on the other hand, he is concentrating entirely on sensual lust, which in this case also implies the narcissistic exclusion of any exchange, physical or spiritual, with a second person. In the *Self-Portrait with Orange Cloak* (1913) a mood of contemplative quiet is emphasized by the posture of the head and hand.

Schiele did not only leave self-portraits in muted, minor keys. The *Self-Portrait with Checked Shirt* (1917), for instance, shows a cheerful and youthfully relaxed Schiele, striking an inviting attitude with his hand and head. He seems to want us to share his pleasure; and, indeed, it is infectious, as if magically transmitted. Again the gestures are powerfully expressive; Schiele's head is bowed so far over that it is almost parallel to his outstretched hand.

The broad spectrum of Schiele's self-portrait work ranges from academic, conventional pictures to provocative pieces that challenge convention, from private mythologies to pictures in which existence seems distilled to a single gesture or emotion, from *doppelgänger* images to cropped torsos. What links them all is their expressive gestures, their pantomime quality, lending expression to a dramatic range of emotions and attitudes.

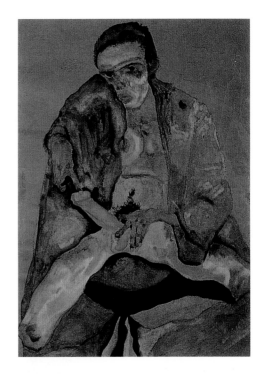

Eros, 1911
Gouache, watercolour and black crayon,
55.9 x 45.7 cm
Kallir D 948; private collection

As in *The Red Host* (p. 68) or the self-portrait opposite, Schiele is exploring instinctual drives in this work. His interest is less in provoking the public than in understanding his own nature. Just as he confronted his feelings in the mirror, here he is confronting his sexuality.

PAGE 162:
Self-Portrait in Black Cloak, Masturbating,
1911
Selbstbildnis masturbierend von schwarzer Draperie umhüllt
Gouache, watercolour and pencil, 48 x 32.1 cm
Kallir D 947; Vienna, Graphische Sammlung Albertina

Schiele used the self-portrait for unflinching scrutiny of his own emotions and instincts. This self-portrait shows him driven by solitary desire. His facial expression is difficult to describe; but it seems clouded by emptiness and sadness.

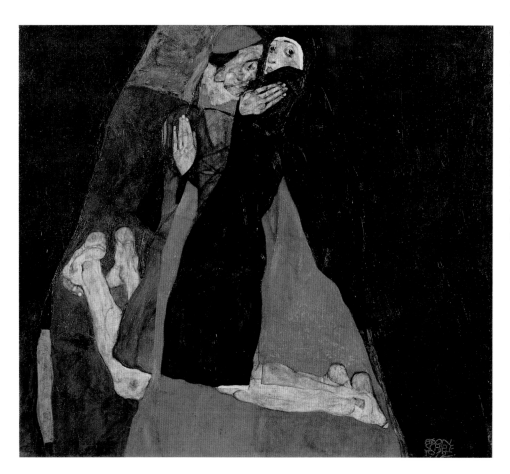

Cardinal and Nun (Caress), 1912
Kardinal und Nonne (Liebkosung)
Oil on canvas, 69.8 x 80.1 cm
Kallir P 232; Vienna, Sammlung Rudolf Leopold

This Expressionist paraphrase of Klimt's *The Kiss* was meant both as an anti-clerical provocation and an allegory of sexuality. Klimt had given an ecstatic, paradisiacal account of love, but Schiele's couple are in the toils of a darker, more imperative passion inseparable from guilt. The power of the priesthood and the conventional God-fearing chastity of nuns are emphatically challenged in Schiele's picture.

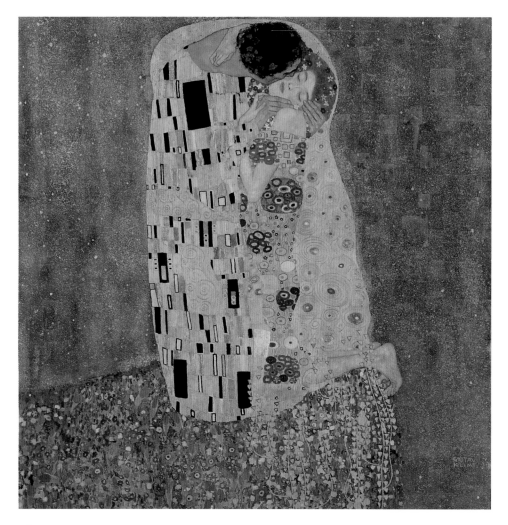

Gustav Klimt
The Kiss, 1907/08
Der Kuß
Oil and gold on canvas, 180 x 180 cm
Vienna, Österreichische Galerie. Belvedere

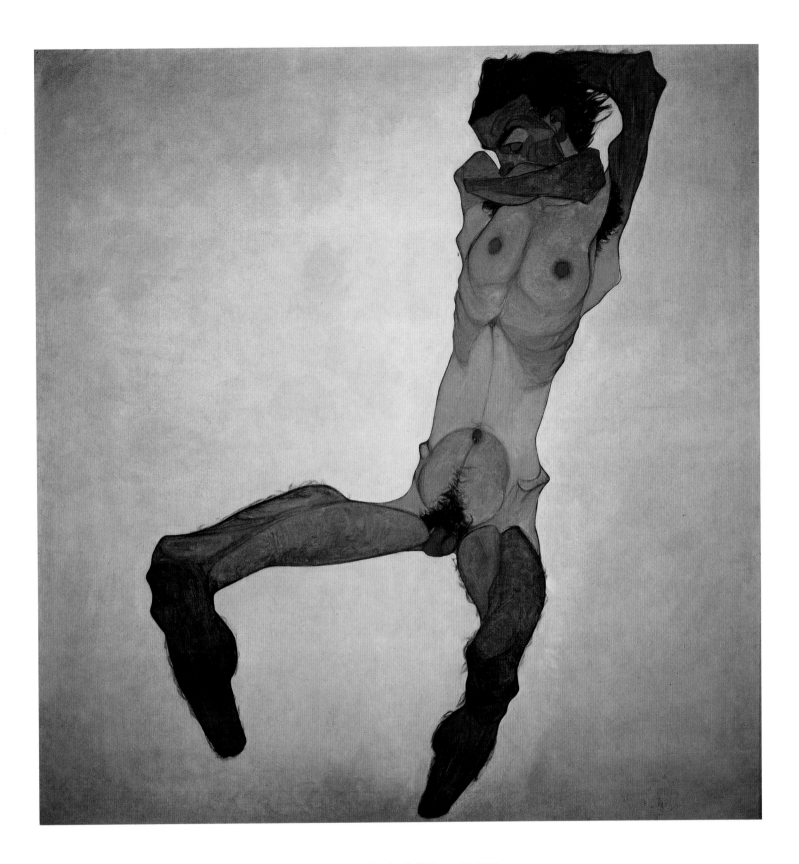

Seated Male Nude (Self-Portrait), 1910
Sitzender männlicher Akt (Selbstbildnis)
Oil and gouache, 152.5 x 150cm
Kallir P 172; Vienna, Sammlung Rudolf Leopold

Egon Schiele's merciless scrutiny of his own body came close to vivisection.
This figure, all the more naked against its bare white background, strongly
recalls both the skeletal figures of the Dance of Death and the crucified
Christ of traditional iconography. The body hair, genitals, ribs and bony joints
are soberly set down, as if Schiele, far from being interested in beauty,
were insisting on ugliness.

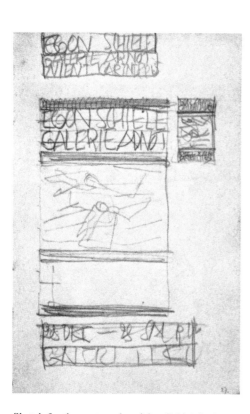

Sketch for the poster advertising Schiele's show at the Galerie Arnot, 1914

Portrait of Guido Arnot, 1918
Bildnis Guido Arnot
Charcoal, 47.2 x 30.2cm
Kallir D 2456; Zurich, Kunsthaus Zürich,
Graphische Sammlung

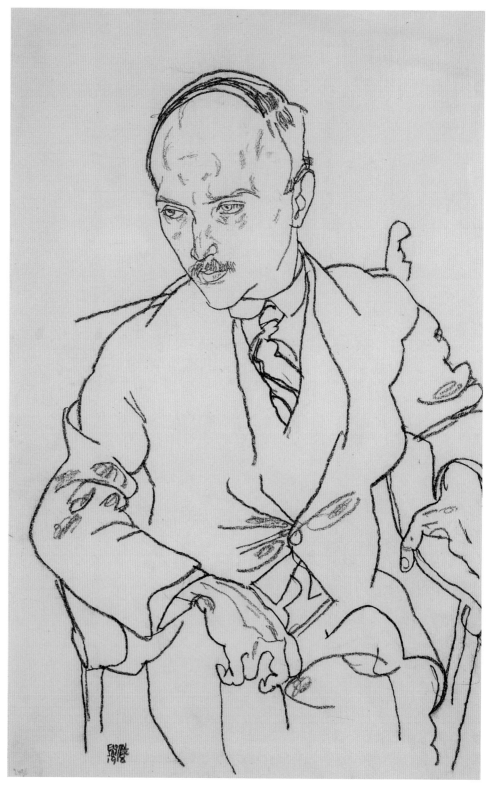

PAGE 167:
Self-Portrait as St. Sebastian (Poster),
1914/15
Selbtporträt als heiliger Sebastian
Gouache, black crayon and ink on cardboard,
67 x 50cm
Kallir D 1659; Vienna, Historisches Museum der
Stadt Wien

Schiele was not averse to portraying the artist as a suffering martyr. We can trace the motif from the drawings he did in his Neulengbach cell through *The Hermits* (p. 121) to this self-portrait as St. Sebastian pierced by arrows. Schiele designed the poster for his exhibition at the Galerie Arnot from a 1914 drawing. The show ran from 31 December 1914 to 31 January 1915.

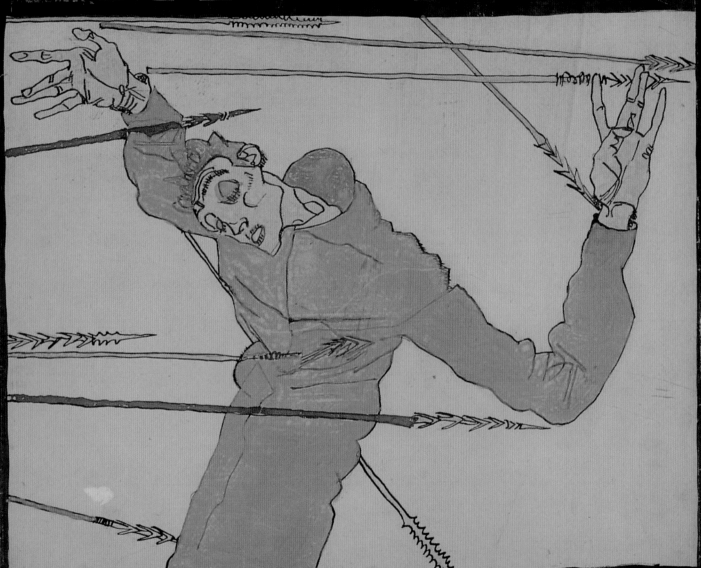

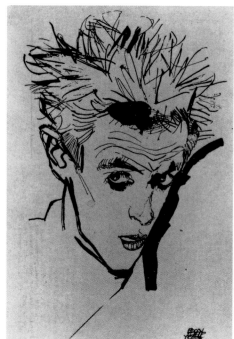

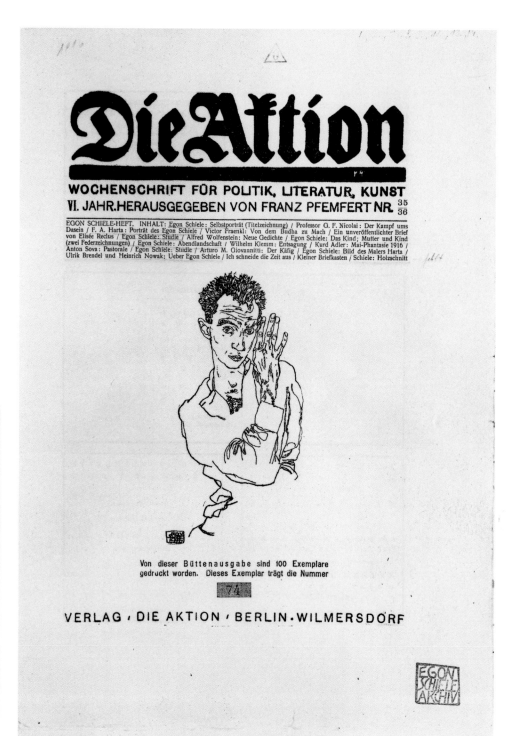

Self-Portrait, 1913
Selbstporträt
Pencil and ink
Kallir D 1434; whereabouts unknown

Not all Schiele's self-portraits showed him tortur-
ously or coolly scrutinizing himself. Contemporaries found him charming – and there are pictures that amply confirm this impression. This
1913 ink drawing was done for a postcard published by the Berlin weekly *Die Aktion* and dis-
tributed in Berlin and Vienna.

Cover of the Egon Schiele issue of *Die Aktion,*
1916
Vienna, Graphische Sammlung Albertina

The Egon Schiele issue (no. 35/36, vol. VI) of
Die Aktion featured a self-portrait of the artist
on the cover and five more drawings within, as
well as his woodcut *Men Bathing*. In issue
39/40 the woodcut *Male Head* was published.

VISIONEN·

ALLES WAR MIR LIEB, ICH WOLLTE DIE
ZORNIGEN MENSCHEN LIEB ANSEHN DAMIT
IHRE AVGEN GEGENTVN MVSSEN VND
DIE NEIDIGEN WOLLT' ICH BESCHENKEN
VND IHNEN SAGEN DASS ICH WERTLOS BIN·
– ICH HÖRTE WEICHE WVLSTWINDE
DVRCH LINIEN VON LVFTEN STREICHEN; –
VND DAS MADCHEN DAS MIT KLAGENDER
STIMME VORLAS, VND DIE KINDER DIE
MICH GROSS ANSCHAVTEN VND MEINEN
GEGENBLICK DVRCH KOSEN ENTGEGNETEN,
VND DIE FERNEN WOLKEN SCHAVTEN MIT
GVTEN FALTENAVGEN AVF MICH· —
DIE WEISSEN BLEICHEN MADCHEN ZEIGTEN MIR
IHREN SCHWARZEN FVSS VND DAS ROTE
STRVMPFBAND VND SPRACHEN MIT DEN
SCHWARZEN FINGERN· — ICH ABER DACHTE
AN DIE WEITEN WELTEN, AN FINGERBLVMEN
VND NASSE MORGEN· OB ICH SELBST DA BIN
HATT' ICH KAVM GEWVSST· — ICH SAH DEN
PARK GELBGRVN, BLAVGRVN, ROTGRVN,
ZITTERGRVN, SONNIGGRVN, VIOLETTGRVN
VND HORCHTE DER BLVHENDEN
ORANGEBLVMEN· — DANN BAND ICH MICH
AN DIE OVALE PARKMAVER VND HORCHTE
DER DVNNFVSSIGEN KINDER, DIE BLAVGETVPFT

Visions (poem), 1914

The poems that Schiele wrote, particularly in his
early rebellious phase, were long neglected. Published in various periodicals, among them *Die
Aktion,* they afford eloquent insight into his
inner state. This poem "Visions" was printed in
issue 11 of *Die Aktion* in 1914.

Visions

All things I loved, I tried to look
at angry people with the eyes of love
so their eyes would have to respond,
to give to the envious and
to tell them I am worthless.
– I heard soft thick winds
brushing amid lines of air; –
and the girl, reading out
in a plaintive voice, and the children
looking at me wide-eyed, answering
my gaze with their caresses;
and the far-off clouds looked down
at me, their eyes goodly and wrinkly.
The white pale girls showed me
their black foot and the red
garter belt and talked with their
black fingers. – But I was thinking
of the wide worlds, of finger flowers
and wet mornings. I hardly knew
if I was there myself. – I saw the
park yellowy green, blue green, reddish green
quavery green, sunshot green, violet green
and listened to the flowering
orange blossoms. – Then I tied myself
to the oval park wall and listened
to the slender-footed children, who …

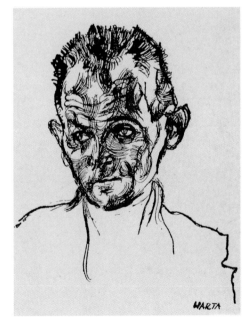

Felix Albrecht Harta
The Painter Egon Schiele, 1916
Der Maler Egon Schiele

One of the few portraits done of Schiele by other
artists, this study by Felix Albrecht Harta was
published in the Schiele issue of *Die Aktion.*

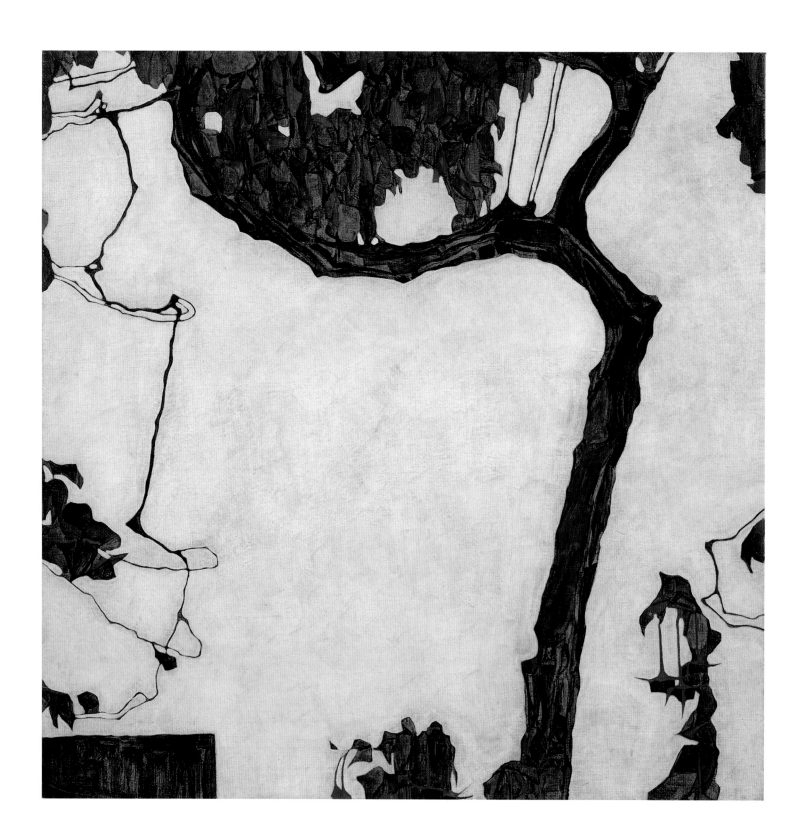

Withered Flowers and Dead Cities: Autumn Landscapes of the Soul

Schiele's visions of animate Nature and his dream pictures of dead cities marked a high achievement in landscape art not only in his own œuvre but in the painting of Expressionism as a whole. But Schiele began by painting landscapes in a variety of available styles.

In 1907, at the age of seventeen, he travelled to the Adriatic city of Trieste, then in the Austro-Hungarian empire, with his sister Gerti. He was particularly excited by the shapes and reflections of boats in the harbour and recorded his impressions in a manner that owed much to the style of late Impressionism. His treatment of rippling waves in *Harbour of Trieste* (1907; p. 9) nonetheless bears the seed of an Expressionist idiom in it.

Impressionism had also schooled the eye with which he saw the houses in his neighbourhood in *Study of Houses (Hofkirchnergasse, Klosterneuburg)* (1908), and the reflections of architecture in an early painting of *Stein on the Danube* (1908). These small oil sketches were merely records of light and colour in a manner taken from the late 19th century, no more than an emerging talent trying his hand.

In *Autumn Tree with Fuchsias* (1909; p. 170) Schiele employed the decorative idiom of Art Nouveau. He was inspired by Klimt's *Golden Apple Tree* (1903; p. 171). The treatment is two-dimensional and decorative, and, as with most Secessionist paintings, it is square in format. The sharp contrast of dark tree and flower silhouettes against the plain chalk-white background owes its inspiration, as did the entire Art Nouveau movement, to Japanese woodcuts. Yet here too we can see Schiele's departure from decorative line and his adoption of a more dramatic approach anticipated in the angular shape of the tree trunk, for instance, or the wiry fuchsia stems.

Schiele went beyond merely faithful accounts of appearances and the presentation of decorative patterns, and his evolution can be strikingly traced in his sunflower pictures. The earliest, *Sunflower I* (1908; p. 173), still owes much to the decorative style of the Secession as seen above in *Autumn Tree with Fuchsias*. The blown head of the big flower, with its fullness of black seeds, has been placed at the very top of the picture, most of which is occupied by leaves in silhouette, looking as if they had been cut out of paper and stuck on – or, in negative, as if they had been sawn out of the pale background. The leaf pattern stresses horizontals while the flower stalk provides a sturdy vertical. The overall pattern lacks a sense of space, like a poster.

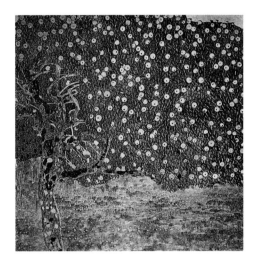

Gustav Klimt
Golden Apple Tree, 1903
Goldener Apfelbaum
Oil on canvas, 100 x 100 cm
Sammlung August Lederer, Vienna; destroyed by fire in 1945 at Immendorf Palace

In his landscapes as in his portraits, Klimt stripped natural and spatial realities down to ornamental patterns – "painted mosaics", as they were known. The colours blend into a great tapestry. In pictures such as this, Nature seems immune to change, growth and decay.

PAGE 170:
Autumn Tree with Fuchsias, 1909
Herbstbaum mit Fuchsien
Oil on canvas, 88.5 x 88.5 cm
Kallir P 158; Darmstadt, Hessisches Landesmuseum

Schiele's early landscapes and Nature pictures still owed everything to Viennese Art Nouveau. Here, the twists of the tree and fuchsias extend decoratively against the pale background. Klimt was the godfather of such art, but Schiele's own distinctive idiom is apparent in the nervous, angular lines.

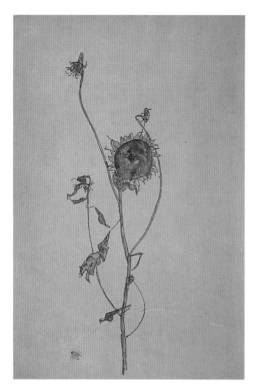

Wilted Sunflower, 1912
Welke Sonnenblume
Gouache and pencil, 45 x 30cm
Kallir D 1212; private collection, courtesy
Galerie St. Etienne, New York

Schiele's landscapes betray a fascination with autumn, decay and death. In his pictures of sunflowers, the blooms are past their best, their leaves dead and dry, playthings of the wind.

PAGE 173:
Sunflower I, 1908
Sonnenblume I
Oil on card, 44 x 33cm
Kallir P 144; Vienna, Niederösterreichisches Landesmuseum

The sunflower, occupying the entire pictorial plane, is firm and upright but already fading. The main head of the flower is at the very top of the picture, and the cropping confers a monumental grandeur on the dying flower.

In *Sunflower II* (1909; p. 177) the formal idiom is a symbolic idiom too. The dark head of the flower, turned to the fore, betokens autumn, transience, and death. The dead leaves are hanging limp from the stalk. The high, narrow format emphasizes the vertical values and the elongated shapes. The flower has the same spatial function as a pillar in a Gothic church: it leads the eye up, to heights where the weight of gravity can be forgotten. In this sense, we might well call this sunflower Gothic. The subject of the picture has become entirely symbolic, standing for decay and death – the farewell of a rueful autumn flower-spirit.

Two years later we see Schiele combining the decorative and the symbolic in two more sunflower pictures, the oil *Sunflowers* (1911; p. 175) and a watercolour of the same title (p. 176). The leaves and flowers are at once decorative, arranged in such a way as to fill the space, and symbolic, representing the traditional autumn complex of transience and death. The movement of the plant in a breeze serves to underline its symbolic power, suggesting as it does the yearly cycle of growth, ripeness and decay.

Vincent van Gogh took sunflowers as a symbol too; but his blooms were bright, hot, yellow suns bodying forth energy and ripeness, warmth and the full feeling of life. Van Gogh's sunflowers might burn up in their own heat, but they would never simply wither away. They stand for the southern sun of Provence as seen in a blue and cloudless sky, climbing to its zenith and still giving life and warmth as it sets.

Schiele's sunflowers, recorded in the sparing light of a more northerly autumn, with blackened heads and leaves browned by the season, are not symbols of life, as in van Gogh, but of death. The Austrian poet Georg Trakl (1887–1914), a contemporary of Schiele, matches the mood of Schiele's pictures in his poem "The Sunflowers":
"You golden sunflowers, ardently bowed to die,
you humble sisters,
in such silence Helian's year of mountain cool ends.
His drunken brow pales with kisses,
amidst those golden blooms of melancholy
the unspeaking darkness governs his spirit."

As in Trakl, the true landscape of the spirit is, for Schiele, an autumn one. He does not celebrate the springtime beginning of life, or the ripeness of summer. His attention is on the passing and ending of things. Nature is always experienced in an elegiac mode in Schiele: the flowers and trees are autumnal, the cities are dead. But Nature is not merely appropriated to illustrate moods; its very form and content are identical with states of mind. Schiele shows us not simply melancholy flowers, but flower beings in the process of dying; so too with his trees and cities – they are quintessential creatures, defined by doom and death. It is an anthropomorphic way of seeing, and only if we grasp this will we understand the full profundity of Schiele's landscape art. The artist is virtually saying: I am this flower and I feel rueful, I am this tree and feel a naked, transient thing, I am this city and feel as if I were dead. In this sense, metaphorically speaking, Schiele's flowers, landscapes and cities are also self-portraits.

In a letter to the collector Franz Hauer, Schiele described this view of landscape and cities as a vehicle of emotion in his own words:

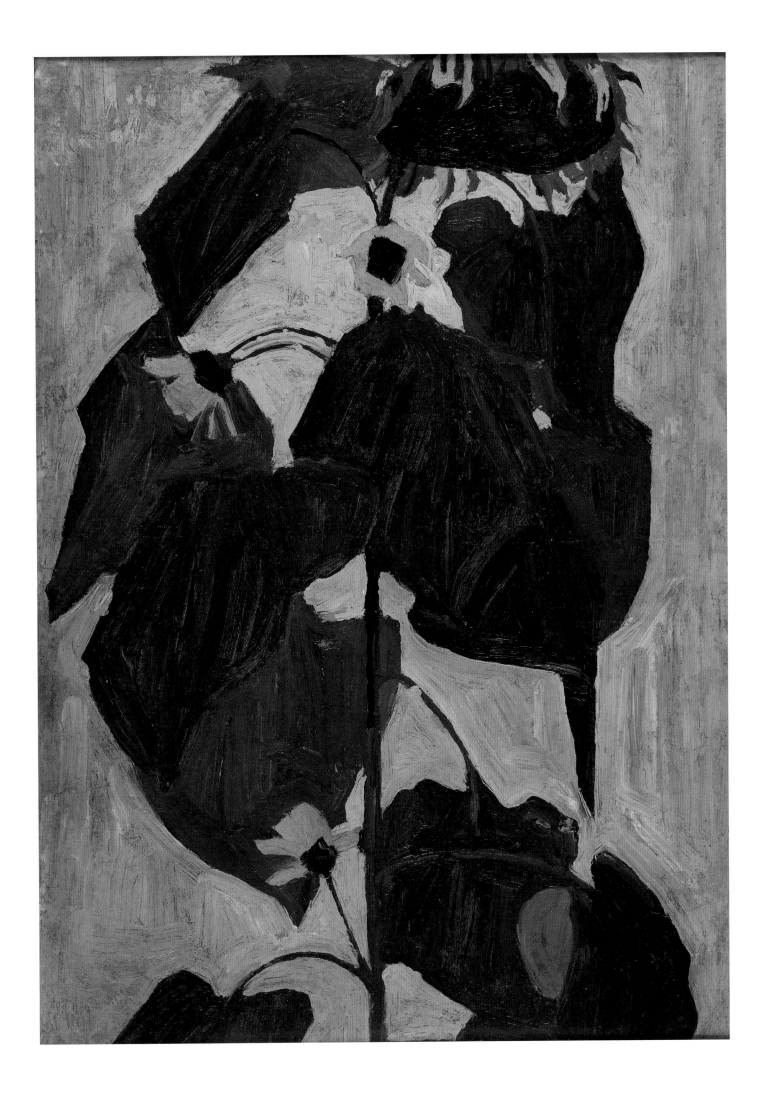

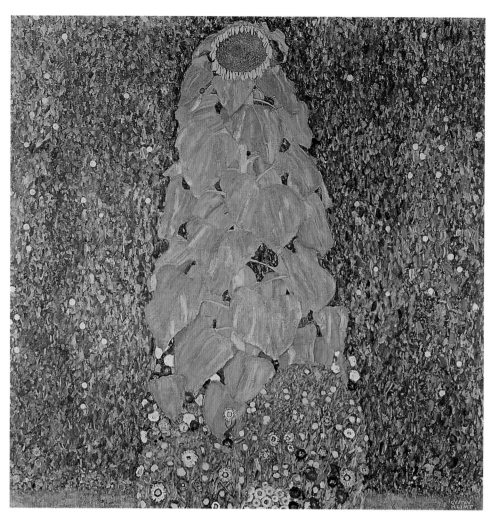

PAGE 175:
Sunflowers, 1911
Sonnenblumen
Oil on canvas, 90.4 x 80.5cm
Kallir P 221; Vienna, Österreichische Galerie.
Belvedere

Autumn colours, the hues of fading and decay,
were what engaged Schiele's eye for sunflowers
in this oil, even if some of the blooms are still in
their full finery.

BELOW:
Vincent van Gogh
Fourteen Sunflowers in a Vase, 1889
Oil on canvas, 100.5 x 76.5cm
Tokyo, Yasuda Fire & Marine Insurance
Company

For Vincent van Gogh, sunflowers embodied the
power of the southern sun. Here it is as if fourteen hot suns were vying in luminous splendour.

ABOVE:
Gustav Klimt
The Sunflower, 1906/07
Die Sonnenblume
Oil on canvas, 110 x 110cm
Private collection

Klimt celebrated the full glorious majesty of the sunflower, enthroning
it like a queen amidst dazzling flowers and plants.

PAGE 176:
Sunflowers, 1911
Sonnenblumen
Watercolour and pencil, 43.5 x 29.3cm
Kallir D 985; Vienna, Graphische Sammlung Albertina

PAGE 177:
Sunflower II, 1909
Sonnenblume II
Oil on canvas, 150 x 29.8cm
Kallir P 159; Vienna, Historisches Museum der Stadt Wien

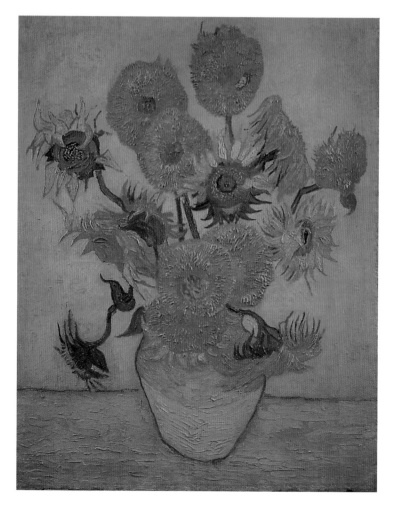

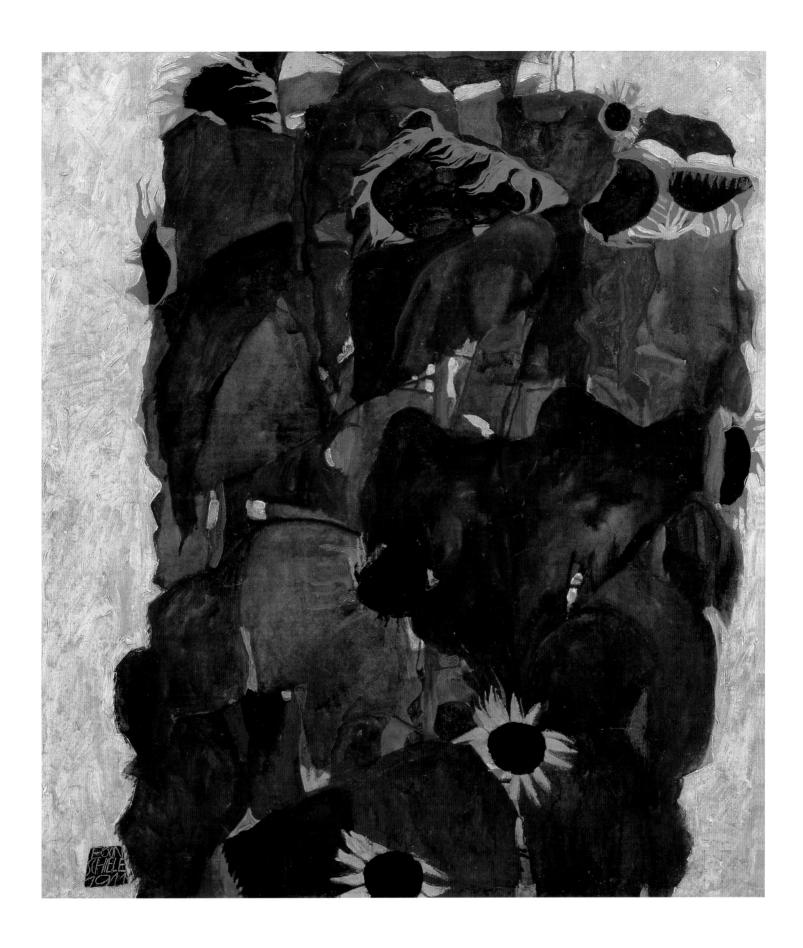

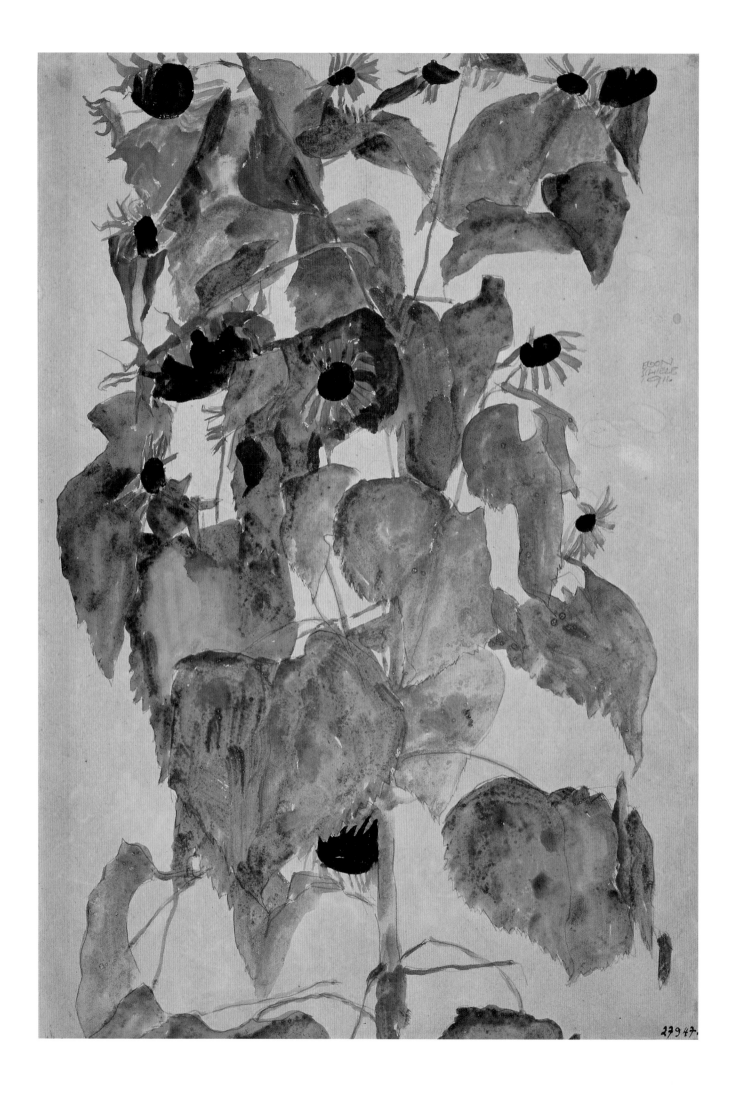

"I also do studies, but I feel and know that drawing from Nature means nothing to me, because I am better at painting pictures from memory, as a vision of landscape. Then, what I chiefly pay attention to is the physical dynamics of mountains, water, trees and flowers. Everywhere one is reminded of similar movements made by human bodies, similar movements of joy or suffering in plants.

Painting is not enough for me; I know that one can use colours to establish qualities. – One is profoundly affected, in one's heart and being, to see an autumnal tree in summer and it is that sad wistfulness that I should like to paint."[13]

Taken in series, Schiele's pictures of sunflowers most impressively exemplify, now more and now less intensely, the connection between observation of Nature and symbolism. In like fashion, his autumn landscapes can be seen as a group with its own unity, documenting his development in form and technique from 1911 to 1917.

In *Autumn Trees* (1911; p. 180) we see three young trees still tied to sapling posts. There are brown leaves and red fruit on the thin branches. The three trees are on a triangular patch of earth that is not clearly defined: it may be a field, or a corner of a garden, or it may, in symbolic vein, be an allusion to Calvary. The background bears horizontal lines of red and blue, suggesting landscape but also decorative in effect. The grid of branches and leaves is enmeshed in a second network of dry black lines that define the foreground space around the trees. Together, the horizontal landscape lines in the background and the verticals of the grid to the fore have the effect of making the picture look as if the entire surface were a vibrant circuitry of electrical wiring. Even more fancifully, we might read the horizontals as lines in a musical score, on which the autumn trees provide the notation. The formal deliberation is palpable in every detail, and the picture marks the divide, as do comparable drawings of trees by the Dutch artist Piet Mondrian, between a representation of Nature and abstraction.

In the small picture *Autumn Tree in Turbulent Air (Winter Tree)* (1912; cf. the photograph on p. 178), the step into abstract composition has almost been taken. The bare branches of the small tree are as intimately bound up with the patchy white of the background (the rapidly changing cloud patterns of an autumn sky) as the outlines of a prehistoric cave drawing are with the curvatures and depressions of the rock. Even so, all is dynamic in this picture, from the sweep of the trunk to the curling branches, from the last yellow leaves highlighted with white contouring and the pitch-black line of the horizon to the lights and shadows in the background. The icy cold of a windy day in late autumn is a metaphor of death and loss in this work.

In *Autumn Sun I (Sunrise)* (1912; p. 181), rays emanate from the pale, white autumn sun, breaking the horizontals of the mountains in the background. The two brown hillocks in the foreground are in marked contrast. On each of them is a windblown tree; for purely painterly reasons, Schiele made one of the support posts dark blue and the other bottle green, and garlanded the brow of the hillocks with flowers and leaves in red, yellow, blue and white, to stand out against the greyish-white sky. The foreground is occupied by a Fauvist abstraction of colour, the back-

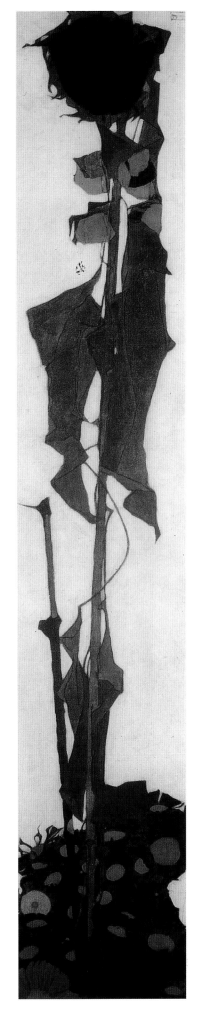

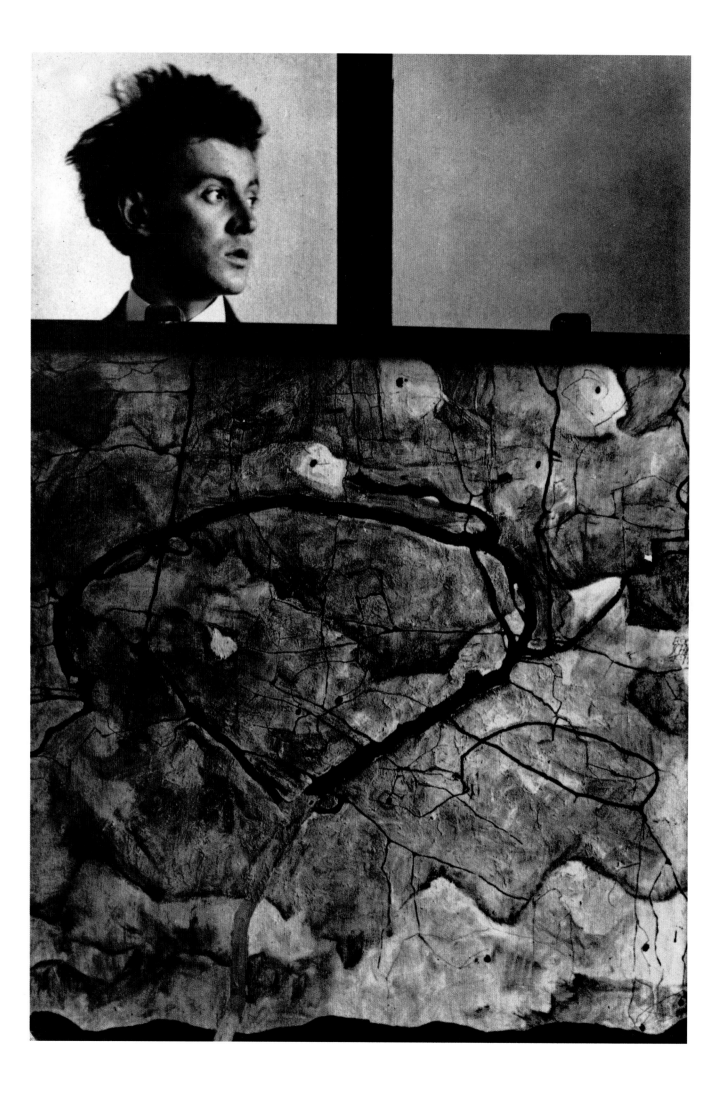

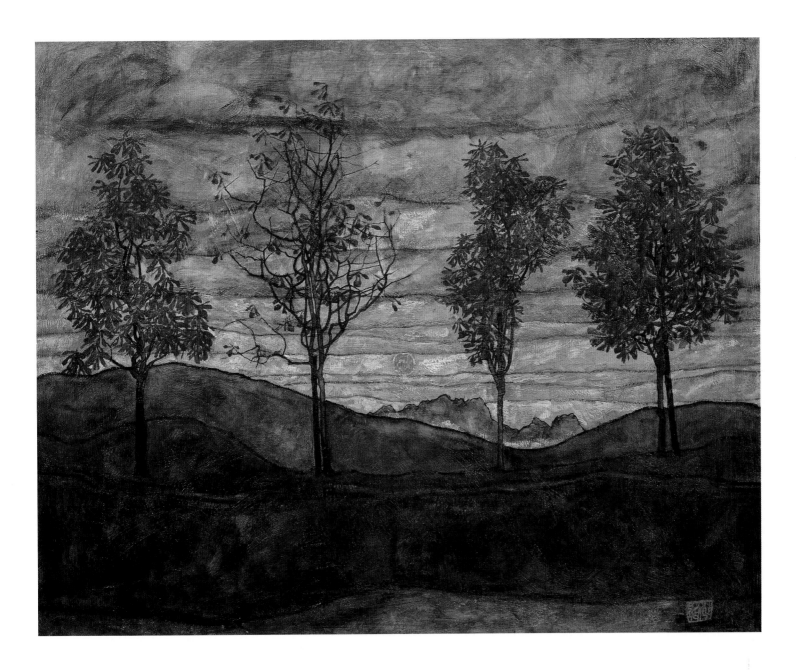

ground by formal abstraction, as if Schiele had been determined to keep his interest in abstraction and his inclination toward the decorative strictly separate.

In later works, Schiele no longer distinguished so stringently between colour symbolism and formal symbolism, and his style achieved a greater painterly harmony. *Four Trees* (1917; p. 179) is once again steeped in farewell. It shows four chestnut trees against a dark green line of hills, three of them with rust-red foliage and the fourth almost bare of leaves. The sun, a small red disc, is setting over the blue tops of the mountains in the distance. Though the sky is banded with horizontal strips, as in the earlier landscapes, the colours are gently, somewhat hazily defined. In this, Schiele is closer to an Emil Nolde than a Mondrian. What was strident and sharp and angular in Schiele's early work has now become muted in a manner almost academic.

In his townscapes, as in his Nature and landscape studies, Schiele ran the gamut of symbolic content and formal composition. The notion of the dead city prompted him to the most magnificent metaphoric work in his urban pictures. His subject was almost invariably Krumau, the roofs and

Four Trees, 1917
Vier Bäume
Oil on canvas, 110.5 x 141 cm
Kallir P 310; Vienna, Österreichische Galerie. Belvedere

PAGE 178:
Egon Schiele in Neulengbach, 1912
Photograph
Vienna, Historisches Museum der Stadt Wien

Vegetation, like the human body, was a vehicle to express emotion for Schiele. Plants could embody feelings or symbolize the co-presence of life and death. *Autumn Tree in Turbulent Air (Winter Tree)* is one of the most affecting works of this kind; the tree seems dead, and yet it is as if life were only temporarily in abeyance. The photograph showing Schiele with the painting was taken in his Neulengbach studio.

179

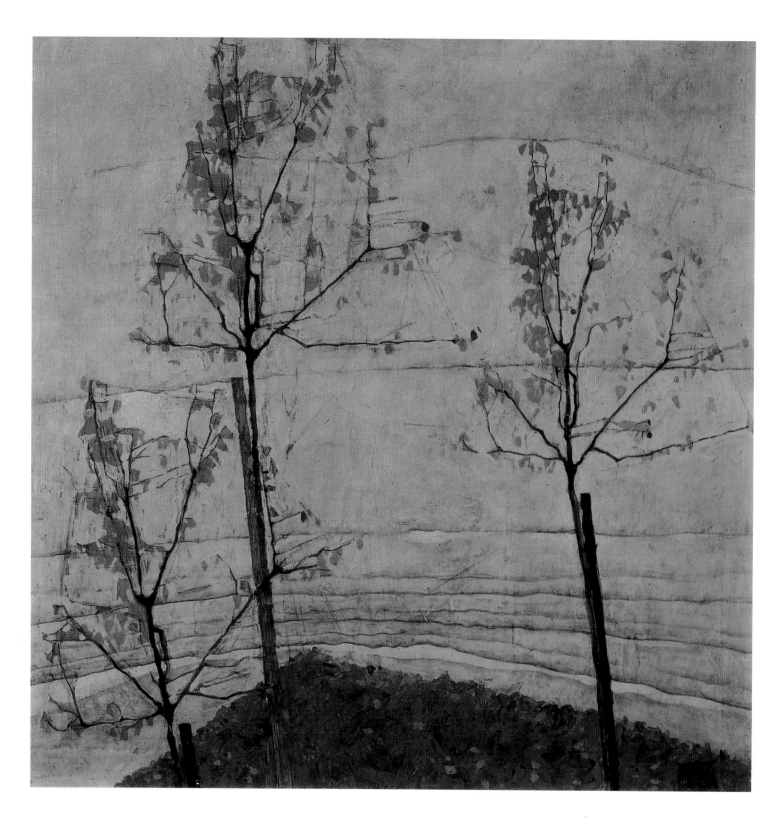

Autumn Trees, 1911
Herbstbäume
Oil on canvas, 79.5 x 80cm
Kallir P 218; private collection

"What I chiefly pay attention to", wrote Schiele, "is the physical dynamics of
mountains, water, trees and flowers. Everywhere one is reminded of similar
movements made by human bodies…" The three trees, almost bare, are
stylized into lamenting beings of Nature – perhaps on a Calvary? Frail and
alone, they proclaim the onset of winter with its icy rigour.

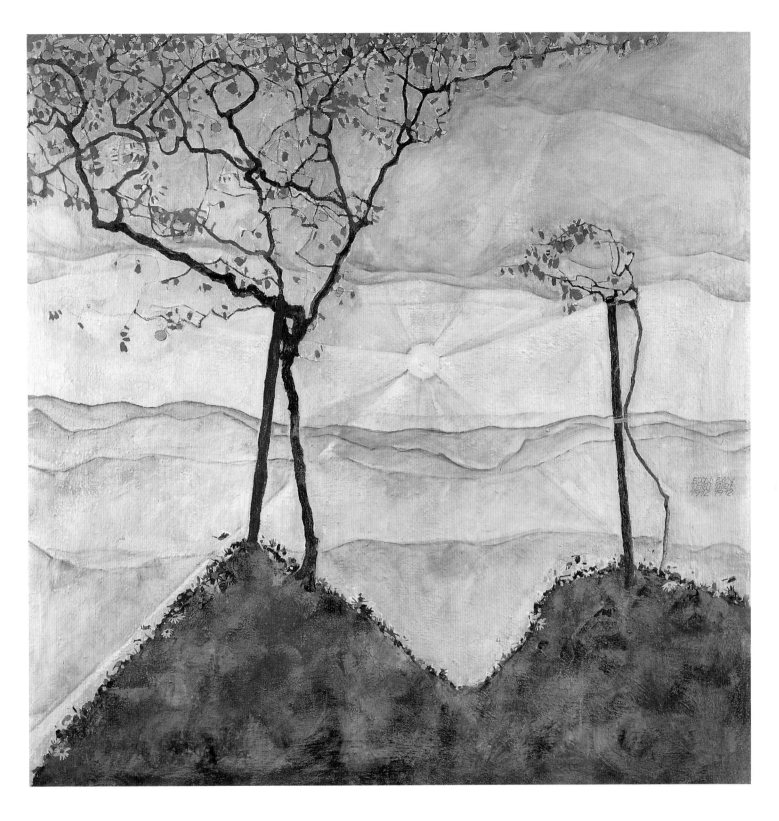

Autumn Sun I (Sunrise), 1912
Herbstsonne I (Sonnenaufgang)
Oil on canvas, 80.2 x 80.5 cm
Kallir P 236; private collection, courtesy Galerie St. Etienne, New York

Secessionist decorativeness and a tendency to abstraction meet in this oil. The
astringently structured landscape is somewhat relieved by the flowers on the
hillocks and the golden apples that hang upon the branches.

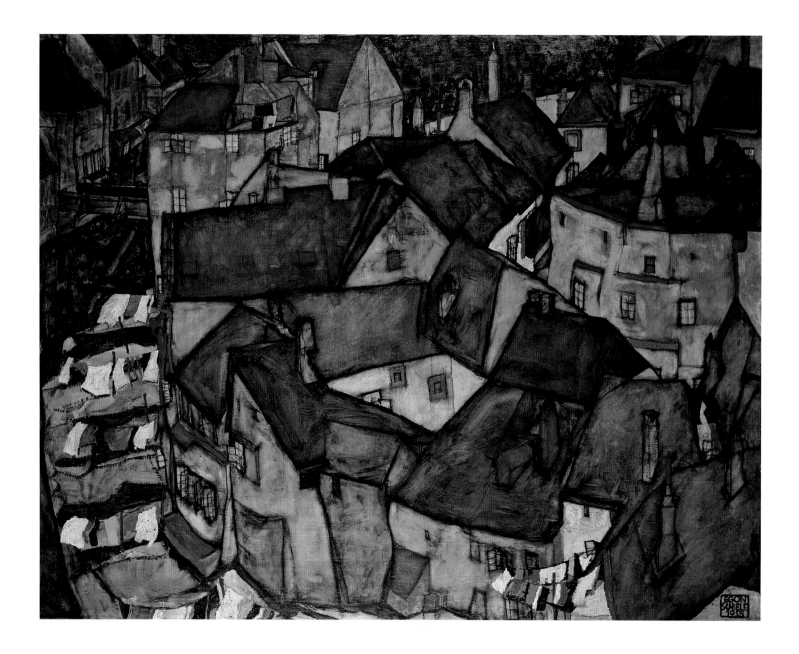

Krumau Town Crescent I (The Small City V), 1915/16
Krumau Häuserbogen (Die kleine Stadt V)
Oil on canvas, 109.7 x 140cm
Kallir P 291; Jerusalem, The Israel Museum

For Schiele, towns, like flowers and trees, were focal points where associations clustered. He deliberately avoided the motif of the Metropolis, the symbol of Modernism, and painted small old towns with weatherworn walls. The colours here are lurid. The laundry flapping in the wind seems to have a life of its own, independent of people.

walls of which he transformed into a townscape that seemed alive, a creature that knew of birth and death, could speak and fall silent, wake and sleep. Describing old cities such as Venice, Toledo, Prague or Bruges as dead or dying was a core motif in the literature and music of the Modernist period; we need only think of Georges Rodenbach's novel *Bruges-la-Morte* (Dead Bruges) (1892), Gabriele D'Annunzio's play *La Città Morta* (The Dead City) (1898) or Erich Wolfgang Korngold's opera *Die tote Stadt* (The Dead City) (1920).

We have already discussed Schiele's gloom-laden urban visions such as *City on the Blue River II* (1911; p.62) and *Dead City III (City on the Blue River III)* (1911; p.63). Apart from those grim nightmares there are also brighter, more colourful townscapes which can be seen as metaphors of a revival of spirits. In *Krumau Town Crescent I (The Small City V)* (1915/16; p.182) the colours are as luminous as Bengal lights, although we are perhaps put in mind of fire or wartime danger rather than rejoicing. The bright red roofs and drainpipes that mark the verticals in *Yellow City* (1914; p.183) are more like signals – to spark a rebellion, say.

Schiele's townscapes were not only images of doom or imminent danger. He also did purely graphic townscapes, as if seeing with an architect's or technician's eye. In the large version of *Stein on the Danube (Seen from the South)* (1913) the town is seen with a puritanical precision, as if on the drawing-board. With no sense of depth, the various horizontals of the river at the bottom, the roofs in the middle and the vineyards above are interlinked through the verticals of the two church towers.

This townscape derives its true appeal from its proportions. With its square to the left, its façades and the two church towers, it is a toytown, a Lilliputian town. The small wine-growing town on the Danube, gave Schiele his occasion to create a seemingly idyllic, unspoilt world, as if with building blocks; the industrial age, with its factory chimneys and its iron and steel constructions, has not yet made any impact on this place.

This kind of painting – related works include *Façade of a House (Windows)* (1914; p. 67) and *House with Drying Laundry* (1917; p. 185) – should be seen as a graphic, decorative exercise, in which the artist was taking sheer pleasure in impressions of form and colour. In the 1914 painting, Schiele introduces – by his use of colour and form alone – a distinct dynamic into a white house front with two horizontal strips of tiling and four rows of windows; and similarly the 1917 picture seems done for the sheer visual charm of the subject.

Schiele's eye was heavily dependent on colour and light; for him, indeed, colour and light were the same thing, as we can see in a small drawing done in 1912 in his Neulengbach prison cell, *The Single Orange Was the Only Light* (p. 30). In his gloomy cell, on his bunk bed, the artist sees an orange which his partner Wally has brought him. It is as if a transcendent transformation were taking place of the fruit into light; in this trans-

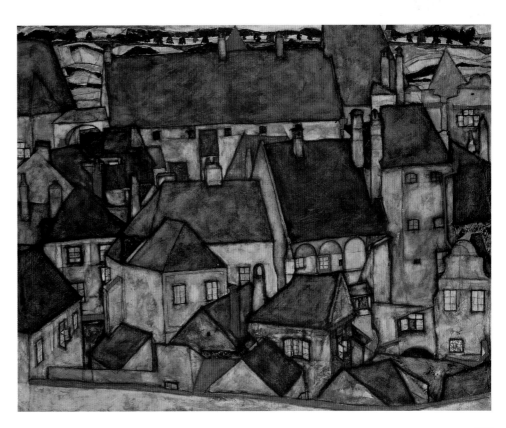

Yellow City, 1914
Gelbe Stadt
Oil on canvas, 110 x 140 cm
Kallir P 286; private collection

Again the colours are lively, but here Schiele's angle of vision is lower. The red chimneys and drainpipes are like signals. The buildings jostle and crowd, but there is order in their array. At the furthermost horizon a strip of natural landscape forms a distant backdrop to this man-made but deserted townscape.

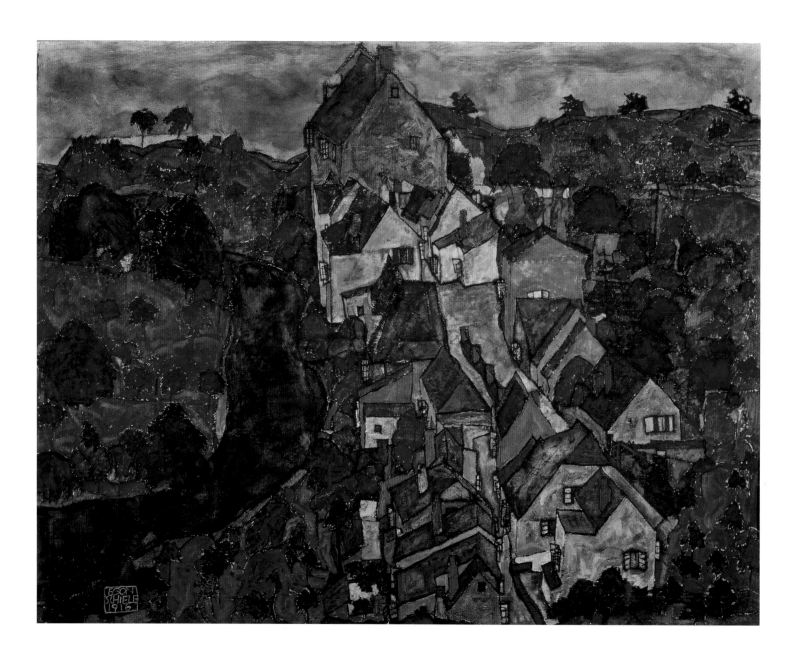

Krumau Landscape (Town and River), 1915/16
Krumauer Landschaft (Stadt und Fluß)
Oil on canvas, 110.5 x 141 cm
Kallir P 298; Linz, Wolfgang-Gurlitt-Sammlung in der
Neuen Galerie der Stadt Linz

Schiele's townscapes are compositionally poised between a symbolic treatment and the more formal contrast of the cubic, geometrical architecture and
the colourful, organic shapes of the natural surroundings. This oil tends
strongly toward the latter approach.

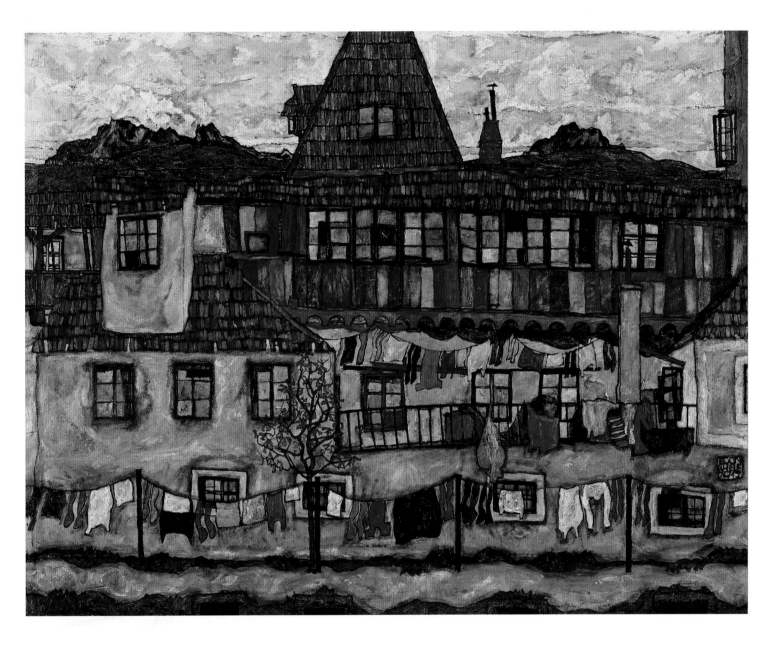

House with Drying Laundry, 1917
Haus mit trocknender Wäsche
Oil on canvas, 110 x 140.4 cm
Kallir P 311; Los Angeles, Nathan and Marion Smooke Collection

The visual appeal of the engaging façades and the colourful laundry doubtless
prompted this unusually cheerful picture. Again no people are to be seen, but
this time we do not feel that the town is dead.

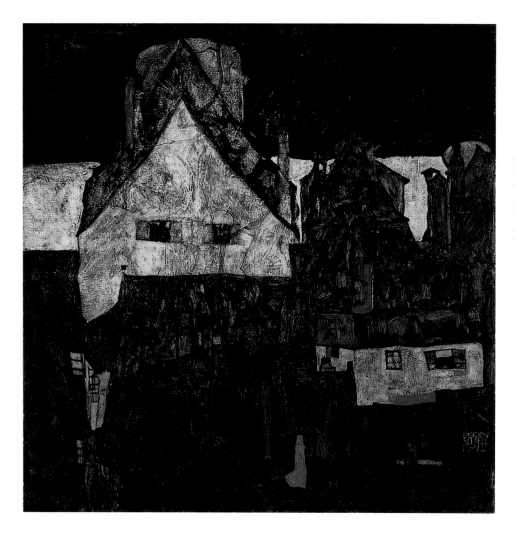

formation Schiele articulates the profoundly religious sub-current of Expressionism in a visual idiom. This orange is light, is a symbol of hope.
Its glowing disc is close kin to the red disc of the sun in *Four Trees*
(p. 179). Just as, in the Catholic mass, the bread and wine become the
body and blood of Christ, so too, by the artist's transforming power, a
sunflower becomes autumn, a tree winter, or an orange light.

Egon Schiele died in Vienna on 31 October 1918 of Spanish influenza.
His wife Edith, in the six month of pregnancy, had died before him, on
28 October, of the same illness. We can speculate that if Schiele had sur-
vived that year of 1918 and the First World War, he would have gone on
to enjoy wider recognition than ever before. His last words have been
variously reported. According to his sister-in-law Adele Harms, they
were: "The war is over – and I must go. Let them exhibit my paintings in
all the museums of the world!"[14] Edith and Egon Schiele were buried at
the cemetry at Ober St. Veit in Vienna.

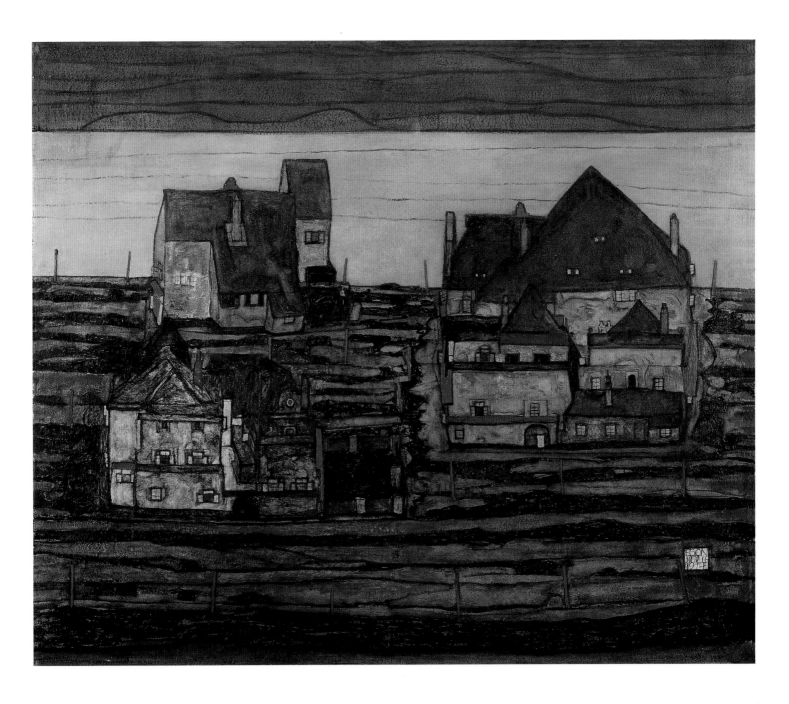

Suburb I, 1914
Vorstadt I
Canvas mounted on pressed wood,
101 x 120.5 cm
Kallir P 282; Stuttgart, Staatsgalerie Stuttgart

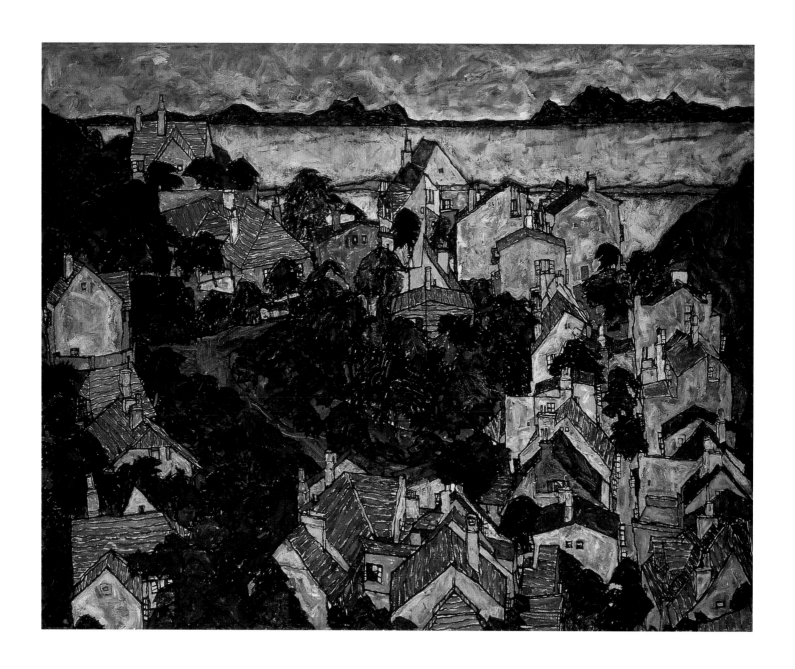

Summer Landscape, 1917
Sommerlandschaft
Oil on canvas, 110.3 x 138.9 cm
Kallir P 312; private collection

Schiele's later landscapes, too, evinced classical harmonies and lighter moods.
Though he kept the bird's-eye view, this summer landscape has an almost
southerly feel as it extends to a horizon marked by mountains.

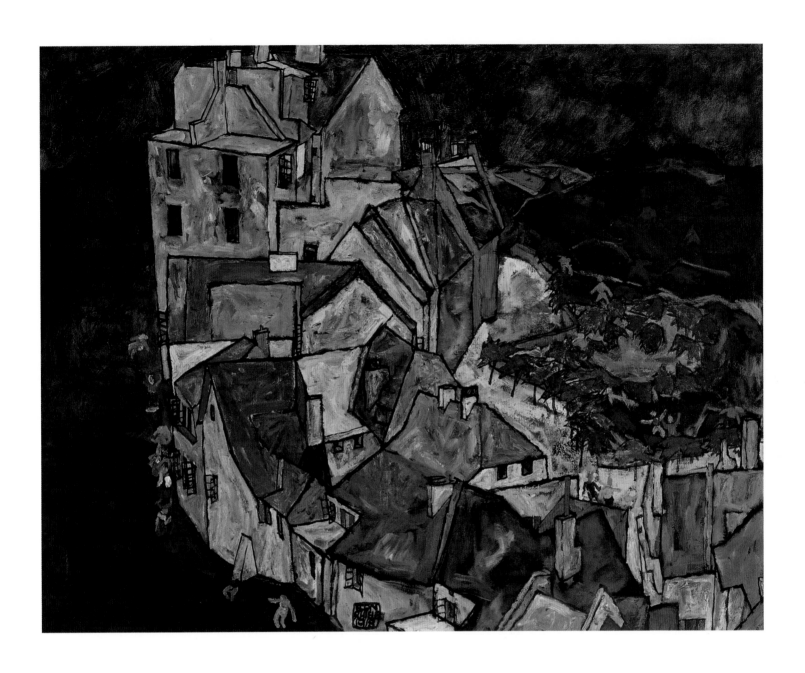

Edge of Town (Krumau Town Crescent III), 1918
Stadtende (Krumau Häuserbogen III)
Oil on canvas, 109.5 x 139.5 cm
Kallir P 331; Graz, Neue Galerie am Landesmuseum Joanneum

In this picture life has returned to the town. There are people in the streets
who even seem to be waving to the painter at his lofty vantage point. The
buildings, so pale in earlier pictures, are now painted in bright colours: it is as
if, as the horrors of the war years drew to a close, Schiele's view of the world,
and of this town, had taken a turn for the better.

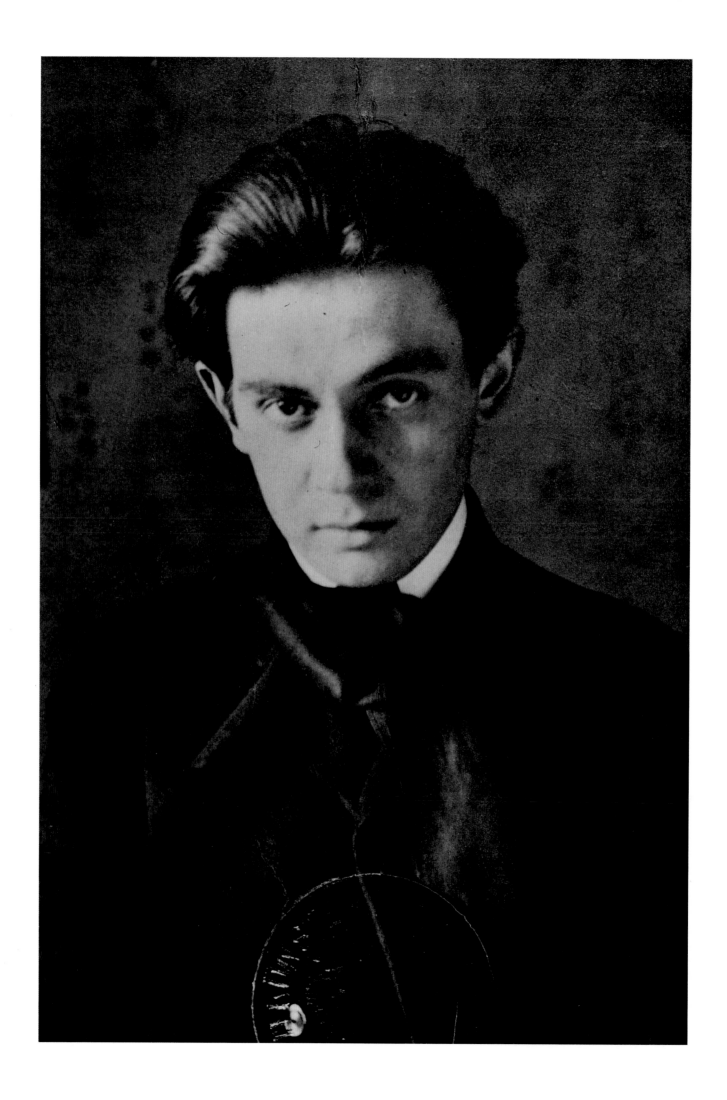

Egon Schiele – A Chronology

1890   Egon Schiele is born in Tulln on 12 June, the son of Adolf Eugen Schiele (1851–1905), a stationmaster with the Imperial Austrian Railways, and Marie Schiele, née Soukoup (1862–1935). He has three sisters: Elvira (1883–1893), Melanie (1886–1974) and Gerti (1894–1981).

1896   Goes to school in Tulln, and later to grammar school in Krems.

1902   Moves to Klosterneuburg, and goes to grammar school there. Does his first drawings of the station at Tulln.

1905   Schiele's father, who was pensioned off in 1902 because of mental instability, dies on 1 January. Schiele does a large number of paintings, including several self-portraits. His uncle Leopold Czihaczek, a railway official, becomes his guardian.

1906   Against his guardian's wish, Schiele takes the Vienna Academy entrance exam and joins Christian Griepenkerl's painting class. His teacher's views are conservative and the tension between them grows; Griepenkerl hankers after the Austro-Hungarian golden age of the late 19th century, Schiele is more interested in contemporary art.

1907   Schiele meets Gustav Klimt and remains his friend till the elder artist's death. Moves to his own flat at 6, Kurzbauergasse in Vienna. Visit to Trieste with his sister Gerti.

1908   First showing in a public exhibition at Klosterneuburg.

1909   Schiele leaves the Academy. Founds the New Art Group (Neukunstgruppe) with his fellow artists Anton Peschka, Anton Faistauer, Franz Wiegele, Hans Massmann, Karl Zakovšek and others. They are subsequently joined by Paris von Gütersloh and Hans Böhler. In the winter the New Art Group exhibits at the Salon Pisko. Schiele does his first work for the Wiener Werkstätte and meets its director Josef Hoffmann.

1910   At the Pisko exhibition Schiele meets art critic Arthur Roessler, who introduces him to collectors Carl Reininghaus and Dr. Oskar Reichel and publisher Eduard Kosmack. Schiele paints large-format portraits of Roessler, Reichel, Kosmack and others, including the Viennese architect Otto Wagner. In the autumn he meets Heinrich Benesch, a railway official who is to be a constant supporter. Schiele exhibits a decorative mural with Klimt's group at the 1st International Hunting Exhibition.

1911   Schiele exhibits at the Galerie Miethke in Vienna. Roessler and Gütersloh

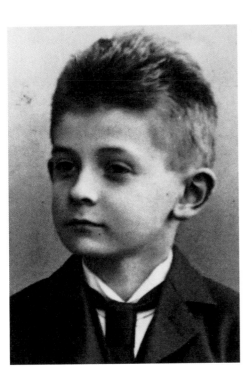

Egon Schiele as an eight-year-old schoolboy, 1898

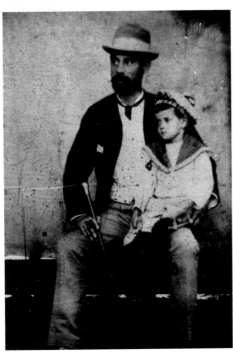

Egon Schiele with his father Adolf, 1892

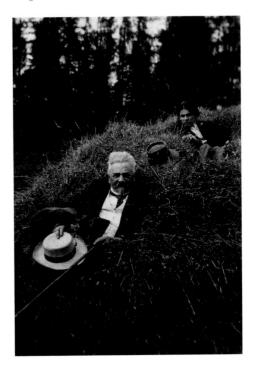

Egon and his uncle Leopold Czihaczek at Neulengbach, 1908

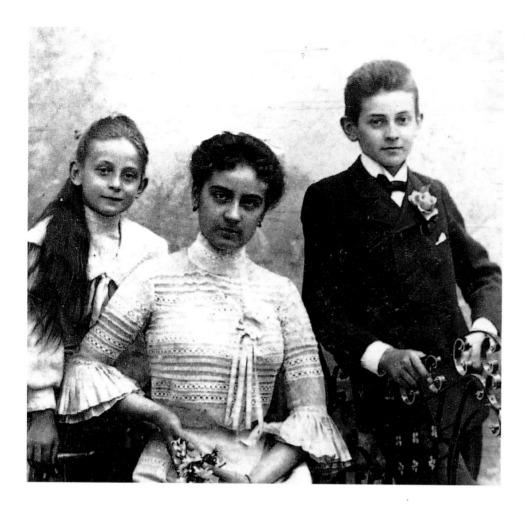

publish essays on his art. In mid-May Schiele rents a garden house in Krumau, his mother's birthplace. However, his living together with his model Wally Neuzil offends small town morality and they are obliged to leave Krumau in early August.

1912 Schiele exhibits with the New Art Group in Budapest and shows at the Munich Secession exhibition. In March his first print, the lithograph *Nude*, is published. Schiele cannot remain in Neulengbach either; he is arrested on a charge of seducing a minor and put in gaol in St. Pölten. The charge is dropped but Schiele is given a three-day sentence for disseminating immoral drawings, since children had been exposed to nude drawings in his studio. On 8 May he is released. Travels to Carinthia and Trieste. Stays with his mother, then in Erwin Osen's Vienna studio from July. In July he shows in the Hagenbund exhibition and meets Franz Hauer. Exhibits at the Sonderbund show in Cologne. In August he

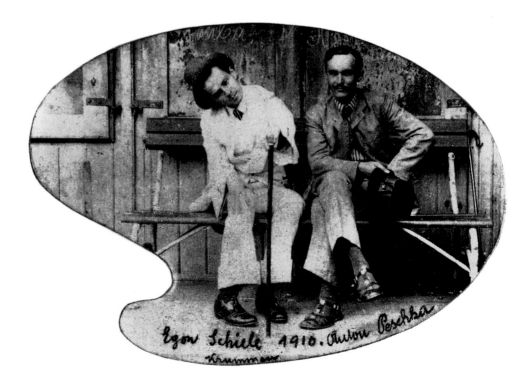

Egon Schiele and Anton Peschka in Krumau, 1910

The photograph was taken by Erwin Osen.

travels to Munich, Bregenz and Zurich. In November he moves into the studio at 101, Hietzinger Hauptstrasse and which he is to keep for several years. At Christmas and New Year he is the guest of industrialist August Lederer at Györ. Erich Lederer, a son of the family, becomes his pupil.

1913   Lives in Vienna but makes excursions to the Wachau district and to Krumau. In March he exhibits in a Federation of Austrian Artists show in Budapest, having joined the group recently. In July he travels to Munich for a show of his work at the Galerie Goltz. Visits Villach and Tarvis and then takes Wally and stays with Arthur Roessler near Salzburg. Shows at the International Black-and-White Exhibition in Vienna and the 43rd Secession exhibition. Principally through Roessler and Hans Goltz, Schiele exhibits widely in Germany, with the Munich Secession, at the Folk-

wang Museum in Essen, and at Hagen, Hamburg, Breslau, Stuttgart, Dresden and Berlin. Schiele contributes to the Berlin periodical *Die Aktion*.

1914   Meets Edith and Adele Harms, whose family live across from his studio at 114, Hietzinger Hauptstrasse. Learns etching and woodcut techniques from artist Robert Philippi. Exhibits with the International Secession in Rome, at the Werkbund show in Cologne, with the Munich Secession, and in Brussels and Paris. On 31 December a show of his works opens at the Galerie Arnot in Vienna and runs till the end of January.

1915   The Kunsthaus Zürich exhibits Schiele drawings and watercolours. On 17 June he marries Edith Harms, and reports for military duty in Prague four days after the wedding. His wife goes with him. After training at Neuhaus in Bohemia, Schiele re-

turns to Vienna in late July. He is assigned guard duties and clerical tasks near Vienna, and given permission to sleep at the Hietzing studio.

1916   Exhibits in a Viennese show in the Berlin Secession and also with the Munich Secession, at the Galerie Goltz, and in a graphics show in Dresden. The army assigns him to "unarmed duties": from May till late August he is in the food supplies section at the officers' POW camp at Mühling in Lower Austria, where he is able to draw and is even provided with a makeshift studio. From there, Schiele makes excursions to the Wachau region. In early September he returns to Vienna. *Die Aktion* runs a Schiele issue.

1917   With other leading artists, Schiele proposes to establish a "Kunsthalle" artists' cooperative. He is assigned to the supply

Egon Schiele, 1914
The photograph was taken by Anton Josef Trčka.
Vienna, Graphische Sammlung Albertina

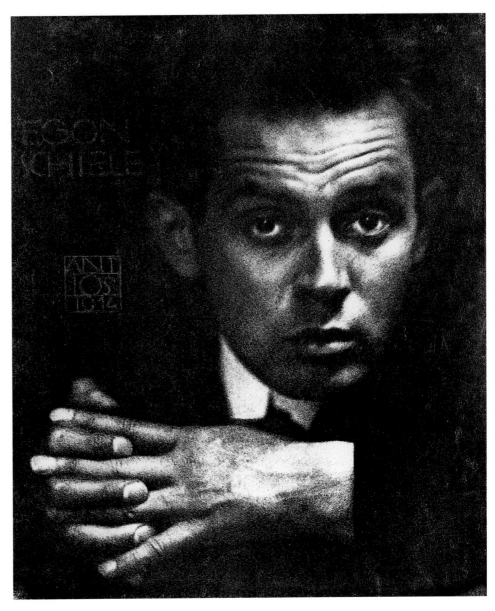

193

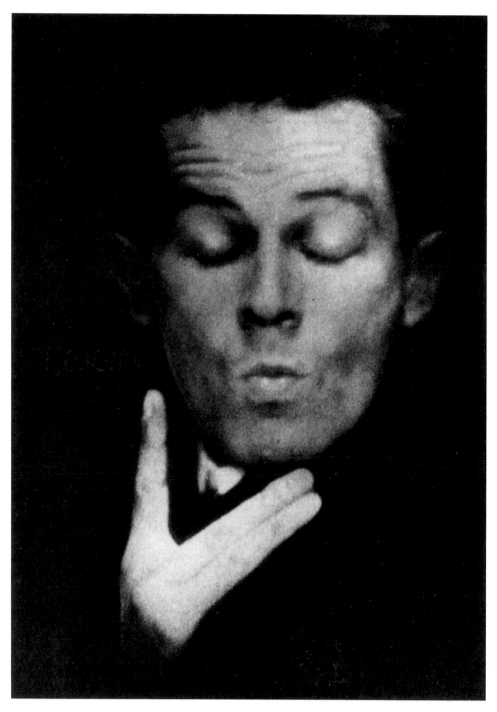

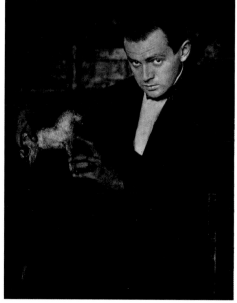

Egon Schiele with a toy horse, 1914
Photograph
Vienna, Graphische Sammlung Albertina

Egon Schiele, 1914

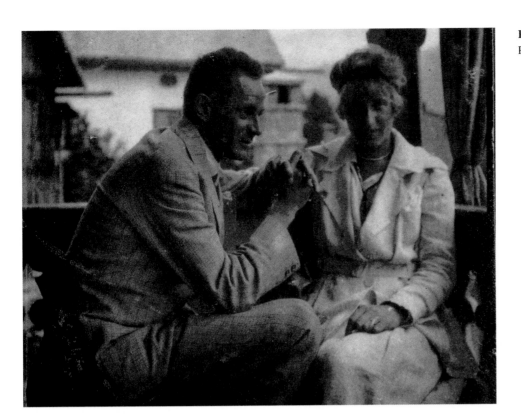

commissary in Mariahilfer Strasse. With the art dealer Karl Grünwald, an officer at the commissary, Schiele visits Tyrol in June and July. In late September he is in Munich, then in October begins duties in the Army Museum. He has work in the War Exhibition in Vienna's Kaisergarten, in a Munich Secession show, and in exhibitions of Austrian art in Amsterdam, Stockholm and Copenhagen in the autumn and winter. In October, Richard Lanyi publishes a portfolio of collotypes after Schiele drawings. In December he begins to contribute to a new Vienna periodical, *Der Anbruch*.

1918 The special show at the 49th Vienna Secession exhibition in March is an artistic and financial success for Schiele, and he receives numerous new commissions. He is unable to agree on terms with the Association for Art Reproduction, which wants to include a Schiele lithograph in its annual portfolio, but leading Viennese personalities are showing increased interest in having their portraits painted by him. In July Schiele moves into a new Hietzing studio at 6, Wattmanngasse. At the end of the month he visits Kovácspatak in Hungary. In the autumn his wife contracts Spanish influenza and dies on 28 October. Egon Schiele catches the same illness. He is cared for by his wife's family but dies on 31 October.

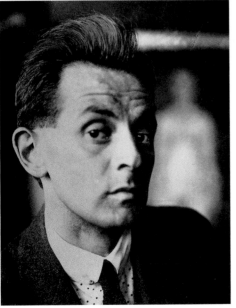

Egon Schiele, 1918
Photograph
Vienna, Graphische Sammlung Albertina

The grave of Egon and Edith Schiele
Photograph
Vienna, Graphische Sammlung Albertina

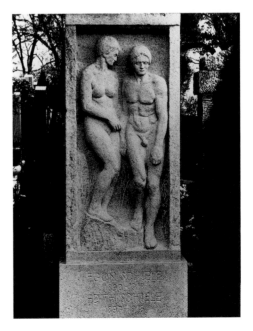

The Major Exhibitions

1908
Imperial Room at Klosterneuburg monastery (May–June): "I. Kunstausstellung".

1909
Kunstschau, Vienna (May–October): "Internationale Kunstschau Wien".
Salon Pisko, Vienna (December): "Neukunstgruppe".

1910
Prague: "Neukunstgruppe".

1911
Salon Miethke, Vienna (April–May): "Egon Schiele".
Ulrich Putze Bookseller and Gallery (formerly Hans Goltz), Munich (October): "Buch und Bild".

1912
Secession, Munich (spring): "Frühlingsausstellung".
Hagenbund, Vienna (spring): "Frühlingsausstellung".
Städtische Ausstellungshalle Cologne (May–September): "Internationale Kunst-Ausstellung des Sonderbundes westdeutscher Kunstfreunde und Künstler".

1913
Neue Kunst Hans Goltz, Munich (June–July): "IX. Kollektiv-Ausstellung: Egon Schiele, Wien".

1914
Kunstsalon G. Pisko, Vienna (January–February): "Ausstellung Preis-Konkurrenz Carl Reininghaus: Werke der Malerei".
Kunsthalle, Bremen (February–March): "Internationale Ausstellung".

1915
Galerie Arnot, Vienna (December–January): "Kollektiv-Ausstellung Egon Schiele, Wien".

1917
Liljevalche Konsthall, Stockholm (September): "Österrikiska Konstutställningen, Katalog 8".

1918
Secession, Munich (March): "XLIX. Ausstellung der Vereinigung bildender Künstler Österreichs".

1919
Gustav Nebehay Kunsthandlung (Gallery), Vienna (April): "Die Zeichnung: Egon Schiele".

1923
Neue Galerie, Vienna (November–December): "Egon Schiele".

1925/26
Kunsthandlung Würthle (Gallery), Vienna (December–January): "Egon Schiele".

1928
Hagenbund and Neue Galerie, Vienna (October–November): "Gedächtnisausstellung Egon Schiele" (memorial exhibition to mark the 10th anniversary of Schiele's death).

1939
Galerie St. Etienne, Paris (February–March): "L'Art Autrichien".
Galerie St. Etienne, New York (November–December): "Egon Schiele".

1945
Neue Galerie, Vienna (September–November): "Klimt, Schiele, Kokoschka".

1948
Austrian pavilion, 24th Venice Biennale (summer): "XXIV. Biennale di Venezia".
Graphische Sammlung Albertina, Vienna (autumn): "Egon Schiele: Gedächtnisausstellung".

Neue Galerie, Vienna (October–November): "Egon Schiele–Gedächtnisausstellung zum 30. Todestag" (exhibitions to mark the 30th anniversary of Schiele's death).

1956
Gutekunst und Klipstein, Berne (September–October): "Egon Schiele: Bilder, Aquarelle, Zeichnungen, Grafik".

1960
Institute of Contemporary Art, Boston (October–November): "Egon Schiele". This exhibition travelled to the Galerie St. Etienne, New York (November–December; the J.B. Speed Art Museum, Louisville, KY (January 1961); the Carnegie Institute, Pittsburgh (March–April 1961); and the Minneapolis Institute of Arts (April–May 1961).

1964
Marlborough Fine Art, London (October): "Egon Schiele: Paintings, Watercolours and Drawings".
Galerie St. Etienne, New York (October–November): "Twenty-Fifth Anniversary Exhibition, Part I".

1965
Solomon R. Guggenheim Museum, New York (February–April): "Gustav Klimt and Egon Schiele".

1967
Mathildenhöhe, Darmstadt (July–September): "2. Internationale der Zeichnung".

1968
Graphische Sammlung Albertina, Vienna (April–June): "Gustav Klimt–Egon Schiele: Zum Gedächtnis ihres Todes vor 50 Jahren".
Historisches Museum der Stadt Wien, Vienna (April–September): "Egon Schiele: Leben und Werk".
Österreichische Galerie, Vienna (April–September): "Egon Schiele: Gemälde".

Galerie St. Etienne, New York (October–December): "Egon Schiele (1890–1918): Watercolours and Drawings" (exhibitions to mark the 50th anniversary of Schiele's death).

1969
Marlborough Fine Art, London (February–March): "Egon Schiele: Drawings and Watercolours, 1909–1918".

1971
Des Moines Art Center, Iowa (September–October): "Egon Schiele and the Human Form: Drawings and Watercolours".

1972
Fischer Fine Art, London (November–December): "Egon Schiele: Oils, Watercolours and Graphic Work".

1975
Haus der Kunst, Munich (February–March): "Egon Schiele". Fischer Fine Art, London (June–July): "Schiele: Watercolours, Drawings, Graphics".

1978
Serge Sabarsky Gallery, New York (June–September): "Egon Schiele as He Saw Himself".

1981
Kunsthalle, Hamburg (April–May): "Experiment Weltuntergang: Wien um 1900".

Historisches Museum der Stadt Wien, Vienna (September–November): "Egon Schiele: Zeichnungen und Aquarelle". This exhibition of drawings and watercolours travelled to the Neue Galerie, Linz (November 1981–January 1982); the Museum Villa Stuck, Munich (spring 1982); and the Kestner Gesellschaft, Hanover (April–June 1982).

1985
Künstlerhaus, Vienna (March–October): "Traum und Wirklichkeit: Wien 1870–1930".

1986
Historisches Museum der Stadt Wien, Vienna (February–April): "Otto Kallir-Nirenstein: Ein Wegbereiter österreichischer Kunst".

1989
Kunsthaus, Zurich (November 1988–February 1989): "Egon Schiele und seine Zeit: Österreichische Malerei und Zeichnungen von 1900 bis 1930, aus der Sammlung Leopold". This exhibition travelled to the Kunstforum, Vienna (March–June) and the Kunsthalle der Hypo-Kulturstiftung, Munich (September–January).

1990
Nassau County Museum, USA (January–April): "Egon Schiele: A centennial retro-

spective". Historisches Museum der Stadt Wien, Vienna (May–September): "Egon Schiele: frühe Reife, ewige Kindheit". Albertina, Vienna (September–November): "Egon Schiele in der Albertina. Die Zeichnungen und Aquarelle aus eigenem Besitz". Retrospectives, like that in London (below, 1991), to mark the centenary of Schiele's birth.

1991
Royal Academy, London (March–April): "Egon Schiele: a centenary exhibition 1890–1918"

1995
Kunsthalle Tübingen (September–December): "Egon Schiele. Die Sammlung Leopold". This exhibition from the Leopold Collection will be on view at the Kunstsammlung Nordrhein-Westfalen, Düsseldorf (December 1995–March 1996); the Kunsthalle, Hamburg (March–June 1996); and the Musée National d'Art Moderne, Paris (summer 1996).

Bibliography

Arnold, Matthias: *Egon Schiele. Leben und Werk.* Belser Verlag, Stuttgart, 1984

Benesch, Heinrich: *Mein Weg mit Egon Schiele.* Johannespresse, New York, 1965

Clair, Jean: *Vienne 1880–1938: L'Apocalypse Joyeuse.* Centre Georges Pompidou, Paris, 1986

Comini, Alessandra: *Schiele in Prison.* New York Graphic Society, New York, 1973

Comini, Alessandra: *Egon Schiele's Portraits.* University of California Press, Berkeley, 1974

Comini, Alessandra: *Egon Schiele.* George Braziller, New York, 1976

Comini, Alessandra: *The Fantastic Art of Vienna.* Alfred A. Knopf, New York, 1978

Des Moines Art Center, Iowa: *Egon Schiele and the human form: Drawings and Watercolors.* Exhibition catalogue, 1971

Dichand, Hans: *Die Künstler der klassischen Moderne in Österreich.* Akademische Druck- und Verlagsanstalt, Graz, 1986

Fischer, Wolfgang G.: *Der Aufstieg Egon Schieles zu Weltruhm.* Publications of the Österreichische Galerie, Vienna, 1988–89

Friesenbiller, Elfriede (ed.): *Egon Schiele: Ich ewiges Kind: Gedichte.* Christian Brandstätter Verlag, Vienna, 1985

Graphische Sammlung Albertina: *Egon Schiele. Die Zeichnungen und Aquarelle aus eigenem Besitz.* Exhibition catalogue, Vienna, 1990

Historisches Museum der Stadt Wien: *Schiele, Egon: Frühe Reife, ewige Kindheit.* Exhibition catalogue, Vienna, 1990

Hofmann, Werner: *Egon Schiele: Die Familie.* Reclam Verlag, Stuttgart, 1968

Institute of Contemporary Art, Boston: *Egon Schiele.* Exhibition catalogue, 1960

Kallir, Jane: *Egon Schiele: The Complete Work, Including a Biography and a Catalogue Raisonné (with an Essay by W.G. Fischer on the Reception of Schiele).* Harry N. Abrams, New York, 1990

Kallir, Jane: *Egon Schiele. With an essay by Alessandra Comini.* Harry N. Abrams, New York, 1994

Kallir-Nirenstein, Otto: *Egon Schiele. Œuvre Catalogue of the Paintings.* Crown Publishers and Paul Zsolnay Verlag, New York and Vienna, 1966

Kallir-Nirenstein, Otto: *Egon Schiele. The Graphic Work.* Crown Publishers and Paul Zsolnay Verlag, New York and Vienna, 1970

Koschatzky, Walter (ed.): *Egon Schiele. Aquarelle und Zeichnungen.* Verlag Galerie Welz, Salzburg, 1968

Künstlerhaus, Vienna: *Traum und Wirklichkeit: Wien 1870–1930.* Exhibition catalogue, 1985

Leopold, Rudolf: *Egon Schiele: Gemälde, Aquarelle, Zeichnungen.* Residenz Verlag, Salzburg, 1972

Lindner, Bernd: *"Ich bin so reich, daß ich mich fortschenken muß": der Dichter Egon Schiele.* Bildende Kunst, 1990

Malafarina, Gianfranco: *L'Opere di Egon Schiele.* Rizzoli Editore, Milan, 1982

Marchetti, Maria (ed.): *Le Arti a Vienna.* Edizione La Biennale and Mazotta Editore, Venice and Milan, 1984

Mitsch, Erwin: *Egon Schiele: Zeichnungen und Aquarelle.* Verlag Galerie Welz, Salzburg, 1961

Mitsch, Erwin: *Egon Schiele, 1890–1918.* Residenz Verlag, Salzburg, 1974

Nebehay, Christian M.: *Egon Schiele: Leben und Werk.* Deutscher Taschenbuch Verlag, Munich, 1975

Nebehay, Christian. M. (ed.): *Egon Schiele (1890–1918): Die Gedichte.* Wiener Bibliophile Gesellschaft, Vienna, 1977

Nebehay, Christian M.: *Egon Schiele, 1890–1918: Leben, Briefe, Gedichte.* Residenz Verlag, Salzburg and Vienna, 1979

Nebehay, Christian M.: *Egon Schiele: Leben und Werk.* Residenz Verlag, Salzburg, 1980

Nebehay, Christian M.: *Gustav Klimt, Egon Schiele und die Familie Lederer.* Verlag Galerie Kornfeld, Berne, 1987

Nebehay, Christian M.: *Egon Schiele: Von der Skizze zum Bild.* Verlag Christian Brandstätter, Vienna and Munich, 1989

Powell, Nicolas: *The sacred spring: The arts in Vienna 1898–1918.* Greenwich (CT) New York Graphic Society, New York, 1974

Protzman, Ferdinand: "Leopold makes a deal (Austrian government has decided to acquire Rudolf Leopold's collection of Egon Schiele works)". *Art News*, 1994

Roessler, Arthur (ed.): *Briefe und Prosa von Egon Schiele.* Richard Lanyi, Vienna, 1921

Roessler, Arthur (ed.): *In Memoriam Egon Schiele.* Richard Lanyi, Vienna, 1921

Roessler, Arthur: *Erinnerungen an Egon Schiele: Marginalien zur Geschichte des Menschentums eines Künstlers.* Carl Konegen, Vienna, 1922 (Wiener Volksbuchverlag, Vienna, 1948)

Roessler, Arthur (ed.): *Egon Schiele im Gefängnis: Aufzeichnungen und Zeichnungen.* Carl Konegen, Vienna, 1922

Sabarsky, Serge: *Egon Schiele: Disegni Erotici.* Edizioni Gabriele Mazzotta, Milan, 1981

Sabarsky, Serge: *Egon Schiele: 100 Zeichnungen und Aquarelle.* Edition Cantz, Stuttgart, 1988

Sabarsky, Serge: *Egon Schiele. 1890–1918. A centennial retrospective.* Nassau County Museum of Art, 1990

Sabarsky, Serge: *Egon Schiele.* Schiele Centrum, Český-Krumlov-Krumau, 1993

Schroeder, Klaus Albrecht and Szeemann, Harald (eds.): *Egon Schiele und seine Zeit. Österreichische Malerei und Zeichnung von 1900 bis 1930 aus der Sammlung Leopold.* Prestel Verlag, Munich, 1988

Selz, Peter: *German Expressionist Painting.* University of California Press, Berkeley, 1957

Solomon R. Guggenheim Museum, New York: *Gustav Klimt and Egon Schiele.* Exhibition catalogue, New York, 1965

Steiner, Reinhard: *Egon Schiele. 1890–1918. The Midnight Soul of the Artist.* Benedikt Taschen Verlag, Cologne, 1993

Varnedoe, Kirk: *Vienna 1900: Art, Architecture & Design.* The Museum of Modern Art, New York, 1986

Vergo, Peter: *Art in Vienna 1898–1918.* Phaidon, London, 1975

Vogt, Paul: *Expressionism: German Painting 1905–1920.* Harry N. Abrams, New York, 1980

Waissenberger, Robert (ed.): *Wien 1870–1930: Traum und Wirklichkeit.* Residenz Verlag, Salzburg and Vienna, 1984

Whitford, Frank: *Egon Schiele.* Thames and Hudson, London, 1981

Notes

1 Christian M. Nebehay: *Egon Schiele.*
   Leben und Werk in Dokumenten
   und Bildern, Munich, 1983, pp. 23–24
2 ibid., p. 75
3 ibid., p. 38
4 ibid., p. 95
5 ibid., p. 185
6 ibid., pp. 102–103
7 Rudolf Leopold: *Egon Schiele. Gemälde,*
   Aquarelle, Zeichnungen, Salzburg, 1972,
   p. 212
8 Arthur Roessler: *Briefe und Prosa von*
   Egon Schiele, Vienna, 1921, p. 157
9 Nebehay, op. cit., pp. 102–103
10 ibid., pp. 79–81
11 ibid., p. 184
12 ibid., p. 184
13 ibid., p. 270
14 ibid., pp. 230 ff.

The publishers wish to thank the museums, archives and photographers for permission to reproduce illustrations and for their support in making this book possible. Particular thanks are due to the Graphische Sammlung Albertina and the Egon-Schiele-Archiv, Vienna; Jane Kallir, New York; and Fischer Fine Art, London. In addition to the collections and institutions identified in the picture credits, thanks are due to:

Archiv für Kunst und Geschichte, Berlin (Erich Lessing): 18, 26, 65, 66, 120, 124, 155, 165; Photograph © 1994, The Art Institute of Chicago. All Rights Reserved: 40;
Artothek, Peissenberg: 16, 17, 43 (Blauel/ Gnamm), 57 (Blauel/Gnamm), 114 (Joachim Blauel), 122 (Jochen Remmer), 123 (Blauel/Gnamm), 135 (Blauel/Gnamm), 185, 188, 189;
Bildarchiv Preußischer Kulturbesitz, Berlin: 184;
Bilderdienst Süddeutscher Verlag, Munich: 127;
Angela Bröhan, Munich: 15;
Martin Bühler, Basle: 98;
Galerie St. Etienne, New York: 8;
Christie's Colour Library, London: 11, 12, 13, 101, 137;
Wilhelm Elias, Vienna: 34;

Fischer Fine Art, London: 14, 37, 38, 50, 53, 54, 56, 58, 62, 63, 71, 72, 76, 77, 80, 82, 83, 84, 86, 88, 89, 91, 93, 100, 103, 107, 109, 111, 113, 115, 117, 126, 136, 147, 153, 158, 159, 164, 183;
Graphische Sammlung Albertina, Vienna: 2, 14, 18, 26, 28, 34, 35, 44, 45, 150, 151, 190;
Marianne Haller, Vienna: 24, 138;
Colorphoto Hans Hinz, Allschwil: 128;
Historisches Museum der Stadt Wien, Vienna: 18, 32, 139;
Christoph Hobi, Zurich: 47;
Studio Mayr, Vienna: 109;
Fotostudio Otto, Vienna: 10, 12, 23, 36, 67, 144, 145, 164, 173, 175, 179;
Elke Walford, Hamburg: 126;
Ingo F. Walther, Alling: 174